A Study of the
Toyota Production System
From an Industrial Engineering Viewpoint

Shigeo Shingo

A Study of the Toyota Production System From an Industrial Engineering Viewpoint

Revised Edition

SHIGEO SHINGO

Newly translated by
Andrew P. Dillon

With a Foreword by
Norman Bodek
President, Productivity, Inc.

Productivity Press
Cambridge, Massachusetts and Norwalk, Connecticut

Productivity Press
P.O. Box 3007
Cambridge, MA 02140   or
(617) 497-5146

Productivity, Inc.
101 Merritt 7 Corporate Park
Norwalk, CT 06851
(203) 846-3777

Library of Congress Catalog Card Number: 87-60544
ISBN: 0-915299-17-8

Cover design by Susan Cobb
Set in Galliard by Rudra Press, Cambridge, MA
Printed and bound by Arcata/Halliday
Printed in the United States of America

Library of Congress Cataloging-in-Publication Data

Shingō, Shigeo, 1909-
  Toyota seisan hōshiki no IE-teki kōsatsu.
  A study of the Toyota production system from an industrial engineering
    viewpoint/Shigeo Shingo; newly translated by Andrew P. Dillon — Rev. ed.
      p. cm.
  Translation of: Toyota seisan hōshiki no IE-teki kōsatsu.
  Includes index.
  ISBN 0-915299-17-8
  1. Production control.   2. Just-in-time systems.   3. Toyota Jidōsha Kōgyō
Kabushiki Kaisha.   I. Dillon, Andrew P.   II. Title.
TS157.S5513   1989
658.5 — dc20   89-60303
                                                                    CIP

Contents

List of Figures

List of Tables

Publisher's Foreword

The publication of our revised English edition of Shigeo Shingo's *A Study of the Toyota Production System from an Industrial Engineering Viewpoint* marks the completion of an important cycle of activity at Productivity, Inc.

The story begins with our second Study Mission to Japan in 1981. On a plant tour to Nippondenso, someone gave Jack Warne (then CEO of Omark Industries) and me a copy of the original English version of this book, entitled *Study of Toyota Production System from Industrial Engineering Viewpoint*, Dr. Shingo's first book translated into English. Jack and I read it and realized at once that it was a truly remarkable and powerful book. Jack immediately ordered five hundred copies for his managers. He encouraged everyone in his organization to read the book and discuss it a chapter at a time in small study group meetings. Jack believes that this initial effort paved the way for Omark to become one of the best JIT companies in the world.

For my part, I contacted the publisher, Japan Management Association, because I wanted to become U.S. distributor for the book. In addition, I worked hard to get back to Japan to meet Dr. Shingo personally and obtain English language rights to his other books. We have done many more Study Missions since then and have made some extraordinary contacts in Japan, but this meeting was the most momentous event for me personally.

On a subsequent trip, I met Mr. Taiichi Ohno. He and Dr. Shingo invented the Just-In-Time system — the backbone of the Toyota production system. The synergy between Dr. Shingo, the teacher, and Mr. Ohno, the manager, created this industrial revolution, the powerful effects of which have altered the international economic order. Productivity is proud to make the work of these two industrial giants available for the benefit of the English-reading world.

Dr. Shingo is an absolutely tireless worker. He works every day, 52 weeks a year. I've never heard of him taking a vacation. Even though he turned 80 last January, he still takes weekly trips to teach somewhere — inside Japan or overseas. Every night, he records his observations and reflections and has convinced many of his clients to write down improvement ideas for inclusion in his books. Weekends are also spent writing; he is working on his twenty-fourth book now.

Having solved many seemingly impossible problems, he is intolerant of excuses and does not accept statements like: "It can't be done," or "That's the way it is." He is never satisfied with an improvement, there must be a constant searching for *continuous* improvement.

His teaching methods are difficult for many Americans who are not accustomed to being told what to do. He might reproach someone by saying, "Don't give me any excuses. You know something has to be done, so go and do it!" and will not accept errors.

I watched him teach in many situations. His insight is always sharp and clear and he effectively communicates his powerful ideas. The following example comes to mind: While touring a plant, he stopped at a small stamping machine and watched a worker feed in some material. He turned to the group of engineers accompanying him and asked, "How much of the time is value being added?" Someone said, "100 percent of the time, because the man is always working." Someone else suggested, "80 percent of the time."

Dr. Shingo finally answered his own question: "17 percent of the time is adding value, 83 percent is waste. Only when the metal is bent is value being added; only when materials are being changed or assembled is value being added." This was a very important lesson for me, to learn what waste actually is.

Dr. Shingo is the same brilliant industrial engineer he was when he first developed the theories outlined in this book. But the world is listening to him more carefully now; readers are more willing to acknowledge his genius. There are many stories about companies successfully implementing his methods and increasing their competitive edge. Members of Utah State University's School of Management demonstrated their admiration by awarding him an honorary doctorate in business administration last year and instituting the Shingo Prize for Manufacturing Excellence in his honor. The first year's winners have been announced, and there is every indication that the competition for this prize will only get hotter in coming years.

Reframing the book for English-speaking readers was an effort Productivity, Inc., staff was happy to make because Dr. Shingo clearly contributed a great deal to the growth and development of this organization. The ideas presented are no different from those contained in the first English version; they are, however, expressed in much more accessible form. Readers no longer have to work hard to extract the teachings but can get right to work on studying methods and techniques. We hope that many people will take advantage of this opportunity.

Those who read the original "Janglish" version, a very complex translation prepared in Japan, should be very proud of their achievement. The more than 30,000 people who worked through it are testimony to the great value of the ideas presented and to the desire of American manufacturing companies to increase their productivity.

We decided to retranslate the book because the powerful principles and practices explained in it merit wider distribution. American manufacturers are demonstrating their commitment to provide training and make continuous improvements, and we wish to support these efforts by making the information more accessible.

Dr. Shingo is the Thomas Edison of Japan, a great creative thinker and I am proud and honored to represent the body of his work to the western world. I hope others will recognize his genius and join me in supporting his work and the spreading of his ideas by contributing to and competing for the Shingo Prize. America must improve its productivity, and Dr. Shingo's ideas are the best weapons for this fight.

Many people have contributed their efforts and expertise to this project. Special thanks go to Dr. Andrew Dillon, our translator, who brought new clarity to the highly complex subject matter. Constance Dyer and Camilla England worked tirelessly to present the information in easily accessible language. Esmé McTighe and David Lennon lent the considerable expertise of the production department. Susan Cobb designed the cover, and helped the rest of the dedicated staff of Rudra Press, Caroline Kutil, Michele Seery, and Gayle Joyce, to put it all together. My thanks to all of them.

Norman Bodek, President
Productivity, Inc.

Preface for the Japanese Edition

Despite the slow growth of the economy after the oil crisis of 1974, the achievements of Toyota Motors, "Japan's number one profit maker," drew wide attention and admiration from the industrial community. The secret of Toyota's success is generally considered to be the "Toyota production system" and the "kanban method," and numerous books have been published on the subject with titles such as *The Secret of Toyota's High Profits* and *Toyota — Secrets of the Kanban Method*.

Most of these books were written by journalists specializing in economics whose treatment of the subject matter is usually not technical in style. I was concerned that this might be misleading their readers; fortunately, Mr. Taiichi Ohno, the former Vice President of Manufacturing for Toyota, published two books on the subject, *The Toyota Production System* (Toyota seisan hōshiki) and *Workplace Management* (Nihon Nōritsu Kyokai).*

In the preface for *Toyota Production System*, Mr. Ohno expresses the hope that his book will enable many people to understand the Toyota production system correctly and implement it successfully in their own plants. At the same time, he admits that because of his emphasis on concepts, only a few case studies are provided. After reading his book, I have to agree with him.

Mr. Ohno's *Workplace Management* is well written. It is based on knowledge and experience accumulated during his long association with Toyota. While the book emphasizes methods, it is still primarily a description of the Toyota production system rather than an in-depth study.

Since 1955, I have been conducting so-called "production technology seminars" at Toyota that had been attended by more than

---

* Both these books are available in English from Productivity Press, Cambridge, MA.

3,000 people in 78 such seminars by July 1980. In addition, I have developed a long-standing relationship with Toyota Motors through my work as a consultant in plant improvement.

Management consultants are not allowed to disclose any confidential or proprietary information. Yet, many Japanese industries have a strong desire to learn about the Toyota production system since it is considered superior. It is, therefore, very important to provide correct and comprehensive information. *Workplace Management* and the *Toyota Production System* were both published to satisfy this demand. As a result, I was able to conduct, in public, a detailed study of Toyota production based upon published material.

It is natural for other Japanese companies to attempt to learn the Toyota production system. I have been afraid, however, that with access to superficial descriptions only, they might misapply the system or copy it uncritically.

Only a detailed study of the subject can prevent this from happening and ensure that the reader understands what conditions are necessary for successful implementation. My study will:

- Explain the philosophy behind the Toyota production system
- Provide additional information where required
- Criticize weaknesses and give credit where it is due
- Highlight the system's important aspects

Most of the existing publications are filled with flowery descriptions of the Toyota production system and Toyota's "kanban method." Yet, no effort is made to reveal the true essence of the systems. In my book, I plan to treat the subject in such a way that special features will stand out.

A reading of the *Toyota Production System* showed me that it is written in the language peculiar to Toyota. While the terminology may be clear to Toyota people, for the general public there are only sketchy explanations that can lead to misunderstandings. The following are examples of what I mean:

Waste due to overproduction. "We needed only 1,000 pieces, but because we assumed that there would be some defects, we manufactured 1,200. In fact, however, we needed only 1,080 pieces. This created a surplus of 120 pieces."

In the Toyota production system, overproduction is generally considered undesirable and many people regard it as an evil and make efforts to minimize it. When I make the statement, "You certainly have a large inventory, perhaps you've overproduced," I might get the answer, "No, it's not overproduction. We can use it for next month's requirements." Or, when I ask: "What do you think if you've completed production by March 15 for a March 20 delivery?" they'll reply, "That's good." When I ask why it's good, they might say: "It's much better than being late." Yet, in the Toyota production system, overproduction is out of the question.

These are clear cases of people misunderstanding Mr. Ohno's theories. It is important to be clear on this point; otherwise, one will not understand what the Toyota production system emphasizes with the statement "Waste due to overproduction is a question of 100 percent early production."

Lower machine operating rates are acceptable. Nowhere in the Toyota production system is there a statement claiming that it is necessary to improve machines' operating rates, only that machines must be ready for operation when needed. In other words, it is essential to have enough capacity to operate under conditions of increased demand. This is quite different from the conventional concept of machine efficiency.

Under the Toyota system, the emphasis is on multiple machine handling, where an operator works a number of machines.

How does the Toyota system decide between the following alternatives?

- The efficiency level of a machine is reduced because it is idle when its operation is completed and an operator is not available to attend to it.
- When the number of machines is reduced for an operator, she will become idle since the machine will still be operating when she returns to it.

Toyota, in most cases, will choose the first situation where lower machine operating efficiency is tolerated so that excess waiting time by operators can be eliminated. How is this choice justified? Toyota's logic runs like this: Machines and facilities will be depreciated to zero, whereas wages for labor must be paid forever, generally at an increasing rate. Also, when their respective costs per hour are compared, the ratio of labor to machine is 5:1. Thus, the Toyota production system addresses the basic economic issue: Instead of being concerned with machine efficiency, it makes improvements in that area in which the greatest cost reductions can be achieved.

Visual control. The Toyota production system emphasizes what it calls visual control. On my visits to Toyota, I was very impressed with the number of visual control devices, such as "kanban" and "andon" (lighted control boards).

Many people believe that the unique feature of the Toyota production system is visual control. Hence, many plants have adopted this system, the only function of which it is to report occurrences of abnormalities in a speedy manner.

Obviously, it is better to be informed by a speedy report than a slow process or not at all. Yet, there is something more important than being informed, namely, deciding what action must be taken if and when abnormal situations arise. According to Mr. Ohno's explanation in the *Toyota Production System*, it is crucial to prevent recurrence. This simple statement is very significant: If you suffer from appendicitis, mere alleviation of the pain through external application of an ice pack will not be enough; the appendix will have to be removed surgically so that it cannot make you suffer again. In a manufacturing context, this means that you need decisive action when abnormal situations occur. You must respond promptly by stopping the production line or machine and not restart production until the cause of the abnormality has been eliminated.

I have visited some plants where visual control was used even though the concept was not fully understood. Such companies do not attain its full benefits. An understanding of the basic principles of the Toyota production system is necessary if we are to apply them correctly. It is also risky to implement the system by merely copying superficial techniques. Failure is a likely outcome. It is, therefore, necessary to proceed with caution.

One of my concerns after reading several books on the Toyota production system is that, while such books do outline principles and techniques with detailed explanations, their treatment of the subject is specific and anecdotal rather than systematic. For example, just-in-time is frequently emphasized, but there is no discussion of what has to be done in order to achieve JIT. You may begin to get the idea after reading these books several times, but many do not tell you straight out *what* needs to be done. On the subject of autonomation, another mainstay of the Toyota production system, these books often don't contain specific explanations beyond a description of the concept as "automation with self-tripping devices" or "machines with human functions."

Leveling is another concept that is often not fully explained. Books may simply state, "If the main assembly line load is not uniform, various problems at parts-producing processes or sub-contractor plants will result." No explanation of how to achieve leveling may be offered. Such treatment of the subject, I feel, is inadequate.

In order to successfully implement the Toyota production system, you must have a correct understanding of the basic ideas behind these principles and the knowledge of methods and techniques to be able to implement them in a systematic way; otherwise, I fear you are likely to make serious mistakes which will result in the failure of the system — even if you have a clear understanding of individual techniques.

Anyone who carefully analyzes the Toyota production system will arrive at the following conclusion: Reduction in setup times, achieved with the help of the SMED system (Single-Minute Exchange of Die) is essential. That is why we can say that the SMED system is a *sine qua non* of the Toyota production system.

The reader may be interested to know that the development of the SMED system occurred in three stages.

Stage 1

In 1950, we conducted a utilization analysis for an 800-ton press at Tōyō Kōgyō. Much valuable time was lost when we could not find a bolt for clamping the die to the press. This helped me to realize that setup changeovers had to be divided into two distinct groups of activities:

- *Internal setup* — procedures that can be performed only when the machine is stopped
- *External setup* — procedures that can be performed while the machine is in operation

Stage 2

In 1957, engine beds were machined by a large, open-sided planer at the Hiroshima shipyards of Mitsubishi Heavy Industries. It was our task to increase the machine's capacity. After struggling with the problem, we decided to add a second machine table since setup changeovers were taking too long.

While one engine bed was being machined, the next one was prepared on a standby machine table. When machining was completed, the standby table with the next part was mounted on the machine. In this way, we were able to increase machine utilization. The plant manager was very pleased with our accomplishment. In retrospect, I can see that what we did was to convert internal setup into external setup.

If I had treated this improvement as the conceptual advance that it was, I could have introduced the SMED system 13 years earlier than I did. I regret this very much.

Stage 3

In 1970, die changeovers on a 1,000-ton press took four hours to complete. After learning that Volkswagen in West Germany routinely changed equivalent dies in two hours, the department head requested that we reduce our changeover time similarly. We had to work hard to accomplish this, but six months later our changeover time was one and a half hours. This reduction was facilitated by:

- Dividing die changeover elements into internal and external setup
- Improving techniques and methods for other internal and external elements

Three months later, the department head again contacted me about improvements in the die setup procedure. He had been instructed by his management to reduce press setup time to three minutes!

At first, I thought it was impossible — we had spent a great deal of time and worked extremely hard to reduce setup times from four to one and a half hours. But then I had an inspiration:

Why not convert internal to external setup? I immediately wrote the eight techniques for achieving SMED on the blackboard. Then I explained to Mr. Sugiura, the manager, Mr. Ikebuchi, the supervisor, and Mr. Ota, the foreman, how we could achieve our objective by using the SMED system.

To this day, I am convinced that my experience at Mitsubishi had been percolating in my subconscious as a latent idea all this time. It exploded into this revolutionary system because of my keen interest in die setups — an interest generated by inspiration and persistent demands for improvement from Mr. Ohno, then Executive Managing Director of Toyota.

This *Study of the Toyota Production System from an Industrial Engineering Viewpoint* has brought me to the following conclusions:

- The elimination of the waste of overproduction cannot be achieved without SMED.
- Shortened cycle times demand small lot production (SMED is crucial here as well).
- SMED must be achieved if we want to be able to respond to changes in consumer demand.

Mr. Ohno must have realized that there is a close connection between the principal aspects of the Toyota production system and the SMED system. This is what led him, in his pursuit of the ideal production system, to the conviction that drastic reductions in setup times were essential. This conviction prompted him to demand that his people achieve three-minute die changeovers. Fortunately, his demand and my latent idea, coupled with my keen interest in setup reductions, all came together in a timely manner. It was this serendipitous convergence of circumstances, I am convinced, that made the invention of the SMED System possible. I would, therefore, like to express my sincere appreciation and highest respect to Mr. Ohno for his inspiration and guidance.

Many Japanese industries have implemented or are now implementing the Toyota production system and the SMED system to significant benefit. Federal-Mogul Corp. in the United States and H. Weidmann in Switzerland have also adopted these systems successfully. I believe that the SMED system concept will, in the near future, spread throughout the world.

Many people believe that when implementing a new system, only know-*how* is required. However, if you want to succeed, you must understand know-*why* as well.

With know-how, you can operate the system, but you won't know what to do should you encounter problems under changed conditions. With know-why, you understand why you have to do what you are doing and hence will be able to cope with changing situations. Thus, if you acquire only know-how about the Toyota production system, you may not be able to implement it effectively in your operation where production characteristics and conditions most likely differ substantially from those at Toyota. Consequently, even though Toyota will benefit from the system, you may suffer negative results. It is, therefore, necessary to have an overall understanding of the Toyota production system. In this regard, it is important to exercise special care with most of the older publications on the subject since they treat concepts and techniques separately, without apparent coordination.

For example, some of the publications on the subject describe the Toyota production method and the seven types of waste, as waste due to inventory, waste due to overproduction, waste due to process delays, etc. These are obvious and everyone will understand them. Waste due to inventory in itself can be recognized as a mode of waste. On the other hand, there are many people who consider excess inventory acceptable since it allows unexpected orders to be filled quickly. The problem now is how to overcome this apparent contradiction. In order to deal with this situation, it is important to present specific methods, such as drastic reductions in the production cycle, small lot production, and the SMED system.

This book was written by a production engineer and is based on a detailed study of the Toyota production method. Hence, it may differ from the book written by Mr. Ohno, the originator of the system.

As long as the Toyota production system is seen as merely a production control system, it will not differ in essence from other production control systems. However, the Toyota production system is an extrapolation of an idea I have stressed in my seminars, a way of thinking about production management in terms of a fundamentals-oriented view of plant improvement. This basic concept has been emphasized to Toyota engineers at the many seminars I have conducted since 1965. Consequently, my concepts and the Toyota production system have much in common. It is also natural that my thinking has been influenced a great deal by the Toyota production method.

I believe that the significant principle and unique feature of the Toyota production system lies in the following: In order to eliminate inventory (previously thought to be a necessary evil), various basic factors must be thoroughly explored and improved. Relentless efforts must be made to cut manpower costs. Total elimination of waste is the basic principle of the Toyota system, and if one cannot understand the basics, correct understanding of the whole is impossible. (I have further explored the concept of waste elimination in my book, *Systematic Thinking for Production Improvement — a Scientific Thinking Mechanism for Improvement*, (published by Nikkan Kōgyō Shimbun.)

The biggest problem I discovered while studying the Toyota production system from an industrial engineering viewpoint is that the system is often considered to be synonymous with the kanban system. Mr. Ohno writes:

- The Toyota production system is a production system
- The Kanban method is a technique for its implementation

Many publications are confused on this issue and offer an explanation of the system by saying that kanban is the essence of the Toyota production system. Once again: *The Toyota production system is a production system, and a kanban method is merely a means for controlling the system.*

Superficial reviews of the Toyota production system draw special attention to the kanban method because of its unique characteristics. Consequently, many people conclude that the Toyota production system is equivalent to the kanban method. The following points lie at the heart of that method:

- It applies only to production that is repetitive in nature
- Overall inventory levels are controlled by a number of kanban cards
- It is a simplified clerical system

A kanban method should be adopted only after the production system itself has been rationalized. That is why this book repeatedly emphasizes the fact that the Toyota production system and the kanban method are separate entities.

My *Fundamental Approaches to Plant Improvement* (Nikkan Kōgyō Shimbun, 1976) focuses on basic approaches to plant improvement and production control. I believe it has been very helpful in promoting better understanding by making comparative studies between a fundamental system and the Toyota production system.

Throughout my studies, I have emphasized the following points:

- It took Toyota Motors twenty years to develop the Toyota production system fully, and others will require at least ten years to obtain satisfactory results by copying it.
- It is possible to apply kanban methods successfully within six months.

Let me add that 90% of Toyota's excellent management performance was attributed to the Toyota production system itself and only 10% to the kanban method — a clear demonstration of the superior importance of the Toyota production system.

In writing this book, I have quoted from and referred to Mr. Ohno's book *Toyota Production System*. I would like to express my respect and appreciation to Mr. Ohno; at the same time, I want to ask for his understanding and approval of the critical comments and opinions I expressed after my detailed study of the subject matter.

I have arranged the contents of this book around the Toyota production system as an integrated system. However, I have repeated some explanations in several chapters so that each one can be read as complete in itself.

In closing, I would like to acknowledge the contributions, assistance, and cooperation rendered by many people, particularly Mr. Morita, the editor of *Plant Management*, and Mr. Hashimoto, who was in charge of the actual publication of this book.

Shigeo Shingo

Preface for the Original English Translation

The Japanese economy successfully weathered the oil crises of the seventies without suffering serious damage — probably to the wonder of other countries. This success has been attributed primarily to Japan's high productivity, which explains why many Westerners have visited Japanese factories and implemented Japanese management practices. Small group activities, such as QC (Quality Control) circles, and Japan's unique Toyota production system have been the center of attention.

Human action is supported by both the working will and the working method. That is why I think the success of the Japanese would be more correctly attributed to their unique labor-management situation, in particular:

- The loyalty of Japanese employees to their companies
- The non-adversarial relationship between labor and management (based upon life-time employment and only one labor union in a company)

The idea and method of quality control originated in the United States from where they were transmitted to Japan. There, they were developed further by linking them with the peculiarly Japanese small group activities, or circle activities, which significantly contributed to some remarkable improvements. The Japanese then extended the scope of quality control to include overall improvement activities regarding cost and safety, thus improving results even more. Japan's unique labor-management relations were the supporting base for these developments.

Readers outside Japan should not expect simple imitation of the external characteristics of Japanese QC circle activities to bring satisfactory results. Rather, they should carefully study Japanese QC circles until they grasp their essence and then adapt them to the conditions of their particular country.

Some problems occur simply because of different labor relations in different countries. Consider the example of multiple machine handling operations: In some countries, one worker could run five automatic processing machines but would not be able to take charge of five different machines if workers are unionized by work function. Yet, the ability to have one worker take care of several machines — removing and fitting product on one machine while another one is processing product automatically — is an important feature of the Toyota production system that results in significant labor savings.

In my preface to the Japanese edition, I explained why it was so important to differentiate between the Toyota production system and the kanban system. My objective in publishing this book was to clarify the distinction between the two so as to put an end to the misunderstandings. I hope my foreign readers will also guard against confusion.

Incidentally, the prevalence of robots in Japanese manufacturing is often cited as one of the reasons for our high productivity. It is an important factor, but the increase in productivity is not as great as one would expect from such a large investment. Rather, the most important function of robots is to liberate workers from unpleasant working conditions. For the most part, Japanese productivity is high because of our efficient production systems and highly qualified work force. This is an important point to understand.

I want to recommend *Toyota Production System: Beyond Large-Scale Production* by Mr. Taiichi Ohno, formerly Vice President of Toyota Motors, to American managers who want to gain an understanding of the ideology of the Toyota production system. This book, however, is not particularly well-suited to plant superintendents, industrial engineers, or management consultants who will be called upon to apply the principles of the system in a manufacturing setting. It is primarily for the second group of people that I wrote the present volume to supplement Mr. Ohno's book.

Since this book was written for a Japanese audience, there will be sections that are somewhat difficult for Westerners to understand that may also be difficult to apply in a non-Japanese setting. In my opinion, however, the concepts underlying the system are clear regardless of where they are studied and can be applied if the needs of the particular situation are evaluated carefully.

I do wish to ask the reader's indulgence regarding my use of certain terms in a manner that differs from common usage because of the particular function these terms have within the Toyota production system. For example:

Process and Operation

1. *Process* — The course by which material is transformed into product. This consists of four phenomena: processing, inspection, transport and storage.
2. *Operation* — The actions performed on the material by machines and workers.

In Europe and America, the term "operation" may be used for processing in process, but in this book it will be confined to the meaning expressed in 2.

Two Phenomena of Storage

As explained below, there are two types of storage:

1. Storage that occurs between two processes could be referred to as "ahead of operation." In this book, however, the term "processes delay" will always be used for storage which occurs because processes are not synchronized or because of bad timing.

   Short-term storage between processes is sometimes referred to as temporary storage. However, if such storage is necessary because processes are not synchronized or because of bad timing, I will call it "process delay" regardless of the length of the storage. In our system, storage is defined in terms of its character, not its length.
2. In the case of lot production, storage occurs between processes and prolongs the production cycle. The only way to eliminate it is to use transport lots of one. Such storage is here referred to as "lot delays."

In other books, process and operation often seem to be used interchangeably. As indicated in Figure 1, however, the recognition that the mechanism of production is a network of processes and operations is the understanding on which all phenomena of production rest. Processes lie along the y axis, representing the flow from raw materials to finished goods, and operations lie on the x axis, representing the flow in which a succession of workers work on items.

The Toyota production system is explained based on this recognition. Consequently, processes and operations are not in a parallel relationship, as considered formerly, but in a perpendicular one. Operation, therefore, corresponds to the four phenomena of process. The following types of operation exist:

- Processing
- Inspection
- Transport
- Storage

For 26 years, beginning in 1955, I was in charge of the training course for industrial engineering technology at Toyota Motors, training approximately 3,000 persons during that time. It is fair to say that the production control system that I emphasized in the course was similar to the Toyota production system in many ways.

Viewed as a fundamental production control system, the Toyota production system must be applicable to factories in any country, only having to be adapted to the characteristics of each situation. I believe that careful implementation will result in major improvements.

I sincerely hope that businesses throughout the world will understand the essence of the Toyota production system and apply it effectively.

Shigeo Shingo

Preface for the
Revised English Translation

When my friends heard that I had received an honorary doctorate in management from Utah State University, they said, "That's terrible! It means that the American people have begun understanding and disseminating your ideas. Soon, they will be producing better and less expensive goods, and we will start suffering from reverse trade friction."

Actually, America has led the world in production management for the last 200 years. And looking toward the future, all of us, including Japan, will run into trouble if the United States cannot continue in its leadership role. Everyone must participate in continuous improvement. Countries must share their skills and technology to keep our "global village" functioning smoothly.

When Toyota's production system started receiving international attention in the seventies and business leaders in different parts of the world began to implement it in their companies, it became clear that many wrongly understood it to be the "kanban method." To correct this mistake, I decided to publish, in English and at my own expense, the book now before you in revised form. Wishing to keep publishing costs to a minimum, I used local Japanese translators who lacked the skill to render a satisfactory English version. The writing was criticized as being "Janglish" rather than readable English, and justifiably so.

Thanks to the efforts of Mr. Norman Bodek, President of Productivity, Inc., the book was favorably reviewed despite that criticism. One reviewer wrote, "This green book is the Production Bible." A significant number of copies was sold, more than 30,000, which is a real tribute to the dedication and determination of American manufacturing personnel.

Wishing to make the book more accessible and useful for American readers, we decided to have it translated once more. Fortunately, the very capable Dr. Andrew Dillon was willing to perform this work.

I believe that this new translation will help many people come to a correct understanding of the Toyota production system. Too many superficial explanations and perspectives on the system have been published. What is needed is a systematic explanation of

- The principles of the Toyota production system
- The system of practicing these principles
- The practical application of the methods following these principles

Last year, Productivity, Inc., published my latest book, *Non-Stock Production: The Shingo System for Continuous Improvement*, which describes the principles of the Toyota production system and is based on my original points. It was evaluated highly as a book to guide the evolution of production systems through the 1990s and into the year 2000. I strongly urge you to read both these books and hope that they will help improve both your company and the prosperity of your nation.

Shigeo Shingo

A Study of the
Toyota Production System
From an Industrial Engineering Viewpoint

Part I

A Fundamental Approach
to Improving Production

1
Introduction

THE PRODUCTION MECHANISM

Before studying the Toyota production system, you must understand the production function in general.

Production is a network of processes and operations. Figure 1 illustrates how a *process* — transforming material into product — is accomplished through a series of *operations*.

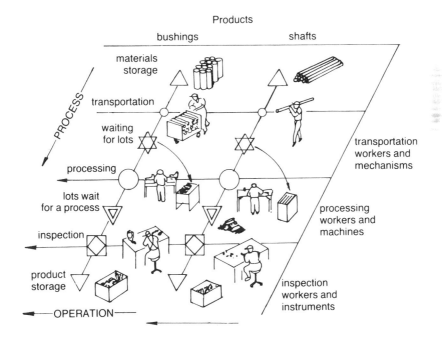

FIGURE 1. **The Structure of Production**

When we look at *process*, we see a flow of material in time and space; its transformation from raw material to semi-processed component to finished product. When we look at *operations*, on the other hand, we see the work performed to accomplish this transformation — the interaction and flow of equipment and operators in time and space.

Process analysis examines the flow of material or product; operation analysis examines the work performed on products by worker and machine. Consider a typical product, a shaft cut on a lathe, for example: The shaft is drilled, then rough cut and finally finished. This series of changes in the shaft is process. The lathe drills holes, rough cuts the outer surface, and finishes cutting the surface. This series of actions is operation.

To make fundamental improvement in the production process, we must distinguish product flow (process) from work flow (operation) and analyze them separately. Although process is accomplished through a series of operations, it is misleading to visualize it as a single line (Figure 2) because it reinforces the mistaken assumption that improving individual operations will improve the overall efficiency of the process flow of which they are a part. As discussed later, operation improvements made without consideration of their impact on process may actually reduce overall efficiency. Chapters 2 and 3 describe the very different measures that must be taken to improve process and then operations.

Summary

All production, whether carried out in the factory or the office, must be understood as a functional network of process and operation. Processes transform materials into products. Operations are the actions that accomplish those transformations. These fundamental concepts and their relationship must be understood in order to make effective improvements in production.

2
Improving Process

In order to maximize production efficiency, thoroughly analyze and improve process before attempting to improve operations.

PROCESS ELEMENTS

Five distinct process elements can be identified in the flow of raw materials into products:

- *Processing* — (○) — A physical change in the material or its quality (assembly or disassembly)
- *Inspection* — (◇) — Comparison with an established standard
- *Transportation* — (○) — The movement of material or products; a change in its position
- *Delay* — A period of time during which no processing, inspection, or transport occur

  There are two types of delay:
- *Process delay* — (▽) — An entire lot waits while the previous lot is processed, inspected, or moved
- *Lot delay* — (✿) — In lot operations, while one piece is processed, the others wait. They wait either to be processed or for the rest of the lot to be done. This phenomenon occurs in inspection and transport as well.

Basic Process Analysis

All production activities, regardless of differences in form, number, or combination, can be analyzed using these five symbols. Consider this sequence:

1. Steel bars are delivered from S Steel Works and stored (▽) for acceptance inspection.

2. The acceptance inspector inspects ($\Diamond$) the bars and they are again stored ($\triangledown$). Here, ($\Diamond$) is better symbolized as ($\maltese$) — ($\Diamond$) — ($\maltese$).
3. An entire lot is transported ($\circ$) to a shearing machine by forklift and stored ($\triangledown$).
4. The bars are processed ($\bigcirc$) and cut into 150mm lengths. This is more precisely symbolized as ($\maltese$) — ($\bigcirc$) — ($\maltese$).
5. Five boxes on the pallet are stored between processes ($\triangledown$).
6. One box at a time is transported ($\circ$) by forklift to the materials yard for forging. Each repetition should be symbolized as ($\maltese$) — ($\circ$) — ($\maltese$).
7. One box of sheared material is transported ($\circ$) to the forging press and stored ($\triangledown$).
8. Pieces of sheared material are successively heated ($\bigcirc$) at the oil furnace, transported ($\circ$) by chute to the press for forging ($\bigcirc$), then sent ($\circ$) to the trimming press for trimming ($\bigcirc$), and finally loaded on pallets. This flow can be symbolized as ($\maltese$) — ($\bigcirc$) (heating) — ($\circ$) — ($\bigcirc$) (forging) — ($\circ$) — ($\bigcirc$) (trimming) — ($\maltese$) — ($\triangledown$). Since there is a one-piece flow between heating, forging, and trimming, there is no additional ($\triangledown$).

Subsequent heat treatment, machining, and assembly can be symbolized as ($\bigcirc$) — ($\Diamond$) — ($\circ$) — ($\triangledown$) — ($\maltese$).

This example demonstrates the need to focus on these five elements in making process improvements:

- process
- inspection
- transport
- process delays
- lot delays

Figure 2 (pp.8-9) illustrates another example of a practical process analysis using this methodology.

PROCESS IMPROVEMENT

Processes can be improved in two ways. The first improves the product itself through value engineering. The second improves the manufacturing methods from the standpoint of industrial engineering or manufacturing technology.

Value engineering is the first stage in process improvement. It asks the question, "How can this product be redesigned to maintain quality while reducing manufacturing costs?" For example, after value analysis, two components formerly assembled with screws may be processed by a press in one piece; a product that used to be assembled by tightening eight screws may now require only four and a hook or catch at one side; and a product that used to be cast and machined may be produced by welding steel plates instead.

At the second stage of process improvement, the question is, "How can the manufacturing of this product be improved?" Improvements related to manufacturing technology involve such factors as proper melting or forging temperatures, cutting speeds, tool selection, etc. Improvements based on industrial engineering might include the adoption of vacuum molding, high-speed plating, instantaneous drying, etc.

Example 2.1 — Eliminating Flashing. "Flashing" occurs in conventional die casting because openings in the molding die are necessary to allow air to escape as the molten metal is poured in. It is almost impossible to finish pouring in time to prevent small amounts of the molten metal from entering these openings.

In the past, flashing was an inevitable side effect of die casting and eliminating it was a common improvement goal. For example, removal of circumferential flashing in one press operation was considered an improvement over hand-filing.

Obviously, as long as air is present in the molding die, flashing is likely to occur. In West Germany, however, Daimler Benz developed a low pressure casting method which removed air from the molding die with a vacuum pump before introducing the molten metal, an approach that eliminates flashing altogether.

We successfully applied the vacuum molding method in our own production processes at Toyota. Later, with the help of President Tsukamoto of Dia Plastic Co., it was applied in plastic molding to improve product quality and reduce defects and shot-cycles, for example (Figures 3 through 5C, beginning on p. 10).

Example 2.2 — Removing foam. This case involves an innovation for high-speed plating. Spraying or "showering" the surface to be plated resulted in a 75 percent reduction in plating time by forcing off undesirable air bubbles. In addition to speeding the plating operation, this new method reduced power consumption dramatically.

Process no.	451	Manuf. pcs.	600
Part name	Transmission & crankcase	Part no.	G60-IE
Material	AC-2	Pcs./set	1
Inspector	Furuyama	Date of inspection	24-3-24

Skeleton drawing

Pcs.	Distance	Time	Symbol	Process (place)	Operator	Machine	Tool, jigs, etc.	Storage	Operating conditions, developments, etc.
200-300kg			△	Warehouse				Stack on floor	
50kg	70m	0.1 hr.	C	To smelting shop	Smelter (furnace man)				
50kg	3m × 3 / 9m		▢	Weighing	Smelter	Floor scale			
50kg		2 hrs.	◯2	Smelting	Smelter				
50kg	(75)m × 4		m	To molding shop	Foundry worker				

Pieces	Distance	Time	Symbol	Operation	Worker	Notes
6 pcs.		3 hrs.	③	Casting	Foundry worker	Pouring gates / Flashes
6 pcs.	40m	4 hrs.	▷	Flash removal shop	Transport man	
	$\frac{10m \times 28}{280m}$	72 hrs.	Ⓒ	ditto		Stack on floor at corner
			▷			
55 pcs.		2 hrs.	Ⓜ	Cutting open pouring gates	Operator	
55 pcs.		56 hrs.	④	Flash removal	do:	
55 pcs.	$\frac{3m \times 28}{84m}$		⑤		do:	
			Ⓜ		do:	
55 pcs.	$\frac{2m \times 28}{56m}$	5 hrs.	◇ 6		Inspector	Sample inspection with caliper
			Ⓜ		do:	

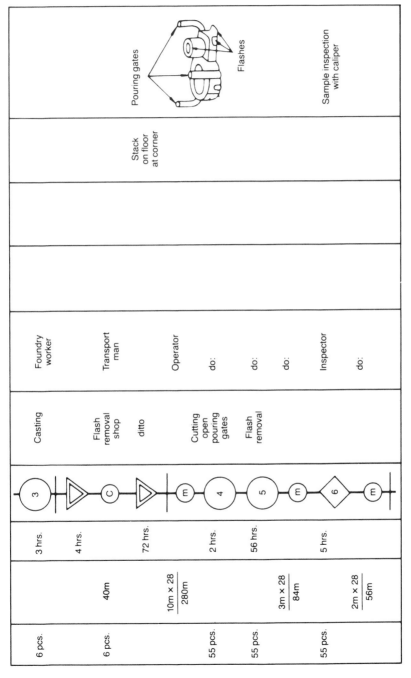

FIGURE 2. Analytical Process Chart

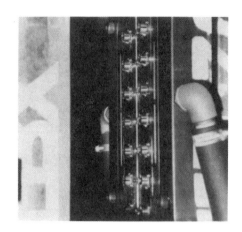

FIGURE 3. Vacuum Molding   FIGURE 4. Vacuum Molding Die
           Equipment

Example 2.3 — Drying plastic resin. In yet another case, the idea of drying a shot's worth of plastic resin during the molding cycle was explored. Letting the resin dry a little at a time by allowing it to float to the surface resulted in a 75 percent reduction of electric power consumption, a significant energy saving.

Clearly, once traditional processing methods are questioned and studied, new and more effective methods can be devised. Fundamental improvement can occur whenever we look for ways to prevent problems instead of fixing them after they occur. Figure 5, the case study described on pages 11 through 13, concludes this section on process improvement.

IMPROVING INSPECTION

Judgment Inspection and Informative Inspection

At most companies, a product quality report usually includes the total percentage of defects as well as a statistical breakdown by type. Reports typically look like this:

Total Defects:	**6.5%**
Flaws	2.8%
Dimensional defects	1.8%
Eccentricities	0.8%
etc...	

POINTS

- Impossible to limit quality fluctuation of product during forming. Tried to control temperatures of molding die, injection speed, etc. and other serious problems
- Standardized air and gas escape slits, hose diameters, and pump horsepower

PROBLEMS

- Functional quality of knob fluctuated
- Visible defects in formed product caused by gas burns, flashes, and short shots
- Had to conduct 100% inspection to guarantee quality
- Monomer paste from the gas generated by melting plastics was deposited at gas relief holes, increasing molding die maintenance time

IMPROVEMENTS

- Improved die by enlarging air and gas relief slits from .03 to the optimum size of .07mm
- Changed hose diameter from 3mm to 25mm
- Replaced 3HP water-sealed pump with 7.5HP oil-sealed pump, increasing capacity from 720mmHg to 760mmHg
- As quality stabilized, inspection time was reduced; quality could be guaranteed by first piece inspection
- Fluctuation in retentive force disappeared

RESULTS

Item	Before Improvement*	After Improvement*
Material cost	$928	$154
Labor cost	$825	$275
Value added	$377	$471
Defect rate	0.021%	0.009%
Spreading effects		17% up $1,503
Results of entire enterprise	$5,624/month	
Results of division	$1,965/month	
Total profit	$7,589/month	

*Dollar amounts are at 1980 yen/dollar conversion rates.

FIGURE 5. Improving Quality and Productivity through Vacuum Molding

Before Improvement

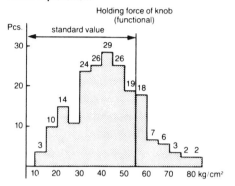

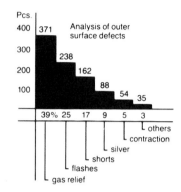

After Improvement

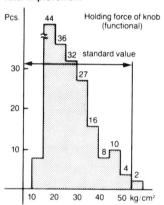

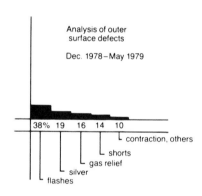

A. Quality Improvement through Vacuum Molding

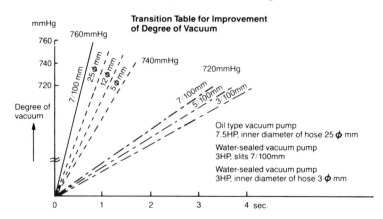

Transition Table for Improvement of Degree of Vacuum

Oil type vacuum pump
7.5HP, inner diameter of hose 25 φ mm

Water-sealed vacuum pump
3HP, slits 7/100mm

Water-sealed vacuum pump
3HP, inner diameter of hose 3 φ mm

B. Horsepower of Pump and Degree of Vacuum

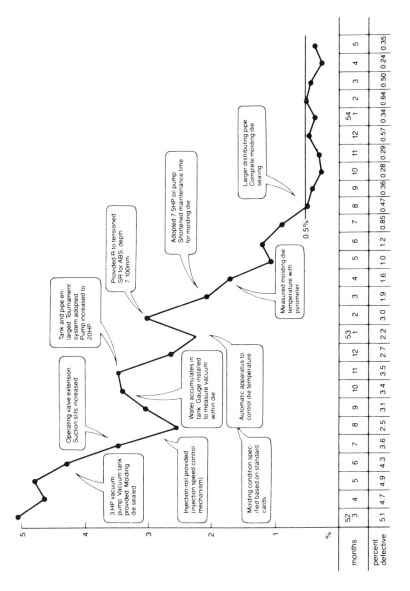

C. Reduction of Defect Rate by Vacuum Molding

months	52 3	4	5	6	7	8	9	10	11	12	53 1	2	3	4	5	6	7	8	9	10	11	12	54 1	2	3	4	5
percent defective	5.1	4.7	4.9	4.3	3.6	2.5	3.1	3.4	3.5	2.7	2.2	3.0	1.9	1.6	1.0	1.2	0.85	0.47	0.36	0.28	0.29	0.57	0.34	0.64	0.50	0.24	0.35

Operating valve extension Suction slits increased

Tank and pipe enlarged Tournament system adopted Pump increased to 20HP

Provided R to tensioned SR for ABS, depth 7 100mm

Adopted 7.5HP oil pump Shortened maintenance time for molding die

Larger distributing pipe Complete molding die sealing

0.5%

Measured molding die temperature with pyrometer.

3 HP vacuum pump Vacuum tank provided Molding die sealed

Injection-roll provided (injection speed control mechanism)

Water accumulates in tank Gauge installed to measure vacuum within die

Automatic apparatus to control die temperature

Molding condition specified based on standard cards

These figures are based on a "post-mortem" of quality defects discovered at final inspection. This type of inspection is called *judgment inspection* because it simply distinguishes defective from non-defective products and issues a "post-mortem certificate." Improving judgment inspection (by increasing the number of inspections, for example), may increase the reliability of the inspection process but will have no effect whatever on the actual defect rate. The number of defects discovered may go up or down, but the sources of the defects remain unimpaired. This form of inspection will reduce *inspection* errors, that is, overlooked defects or erroneously rejected non-defective products, but it cannot prevent defects from occurring during processing.

To actually reduce the defect rate, processing must be informed whenever a defect is discovered, so that steps can be taken to correct the processing method or condition and prevent a recurrence. Inspection that performs this function is called *informative inspection* because it feeds information back to processing; it is like a medical examination instead of a post-mortem. The sooner a symptom (defect) is identified, the more quickly and effectively the problem can be treated, and the greater the reduction in defects. In sum: Judgment inspections discover defects, while informative inspections reduce them.

Example 2.4 — High-speed plating. In Matsushita Electric's vacuum cleaner packing process, the cleaner, attachments, and instruction leaflets were placed in a box that was then weighed to determine whether any parts were missing. Despite this check, complaints that small parts and leaflets were missing continued to crop up, although not frequently enough to justify the expense of a more sensitive scale. Observation of the process established that inspection occurred after the defects happened. The production manager set about making improvements to prevent defects. Within two months, complaints dropped to zero. Here is what he arranged:

- A spring was installed under a stand that held the instruction leaflets. Pushing down on the stand to remove a leaflet activates a limit switch that lights up a sign reading "instruction leaflet inserted" (Figures 6 and 7).
- A bow-shaped spring was installed on the edge of the parts box. Removing parts from the box depresses a spring activating a limit switch that lights up a sign reading "all parts inserted" (Figure 8).
- After the "all parts inserted" sign is activated, a stopper on the conveyor retracts and the box is allowed to pass to the next process (Figure 9).
- If any items are missing, a buzzer sounds when the box arrives at the stopper and the conveyor comes to a stop. When this happens, the box is rechecked and the problem corrected.

These improvements made it impossible to send incomplete boxes on to the next process. Before the improvements, an error could be detected only after it had already occurred. Now, errors can be detected and corrected at their source within the same process.

FIGURE 6. Poka-yoke for
Instruction Manual

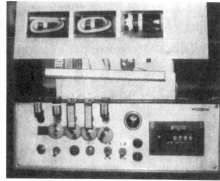

FIGURE 7. Lamp Indicates Insertion of
Instruction Manual

FIGURE 8. Poka-yoke Using
Bow-shaped Spring

FIGURE 9. Stopper on Conveyor

This example illustrates an important principle: The purpose of inspection must be prevention; however, for inspection to have that function, we must change our way of thinking.

Many companies employ impressive defect detection devices but fail to ask the most important question, that is, "What kind of inspection is being conducted?" If prevention is not the primary objective, no matter how excellent the methods and equipment, satisfactory results are not likely.

Sampling versus 100 Percent Inspection

Around 1951, quality control methods based on random sampling were introduced in Japan. New methods, including the cause and effect diagram, frequency distribution diagram, control chart, sampling inspection, experiment and planning method, and others were adopted. These statistical methods later had a major impact on quality control in our country.

The techniques were welcomed because they provided quality assurance that was less costly and time-consuming than 100 percent inspection. Sampling inspection appeared to assure quality more efficiently than 100 percent inspection.

In 1965, however, Mr. Tokizane, Managing Director of Matsushita Electric, made a profound observation. Each customer, he realized, purchases only one television set out of the company's total production of one million. If that one set is defective, the customer's faith in the company is destroyed. Under Matsushita's sampling inspection, one defect in a million sets produced probably could not be prevented, and, in fact, would have been an excellent result.

But how could Mr. Tokizane's ideal of 100 percent quality, or "zero defects," be realized through sampling inspection? It became clear that although sampling inspection may be the most rational method of inspection, it does not necessarily assure quality. Using statistics, an acceptable quality level (AQL) can be established; however, this is useful only in the context of sampling inspection. When the objective is zero defects, the concept imposes unrealistic and unnecessary limits on the level of improvement that can be achieved.

What is needed are methods that can assure quality with the same thoroughness as 100 percent inspection but with the ease and efficiency of sampling techniques. They are the first steps in statistical quality control.

Quality Control and QC Control Charts

Control charts are an important tool in statistical process control. They delineate two kinds of limits:

- Standard limits, which specify the range of permissible error allowed for products
- Control limits, which specify the range of variations in quality arising at the processing stage

Once control limits based on actual data have been established, samples are collected regularly. Any sample that deviates from the limits is considered an abnormal value, and action is taken to identify and correct the cause.

Relying on the control chart for quality assurance, however, has several drawbacks. First, it is most often used as part of a judgment inspection system which is aimed at finding rather than preventing defects. When data collected with the control chart method generates actions aimed at eliminating the causes of defects, the system becomes a kind of informative inspection. Feedback generated by the control chart method, however, is usually reviewed at the next monthly quality meeting. As a rule, this is too late to be effective. In any case, action is always taken *after* the fact; what is needed is preventive action *before* the defect occurs.

A second drawback of the control chart is that it can be used only in cases where a standard deviation is allowable, for example, machined shaft dimension of 120mm ± 0.05mm; it is not helpful, on the other hand, when a broken punch press produces a stream of parts without holes. Typically, continuous defects are discovered through sampling inspection. When one is found, the machine is stopped and the problem corrected. One hundred percent inspection is then conducted on parts previously processed to remove the defective items.

Using statistical QC methods, this problem would be dealt with by increasing the frequency of sampling inspection and perhaps introducing more efficient feedback and response procedures. These measures may reduce defects at final inspection but will not eliminate them.

In the case of occasional defects, the control chart method may be even less effective. For example, T Die-Cast Company, supplier for N Optical, has a problem with flow defects in their camera bodies. According to their QC requirements, a sample is taken out of every 100 pieces; if a flow defect is found, 100 percent inspection is conducted to remove any other defects. If the sample is perfect, however, the entire lot is considered acceptable and the products are delivered to N Optical. That company, in turn, may inadvertently accept the defects in the T Die-Cast lot if the products pass its own sampling inspection. Following this procedure, there is a significant possibility of defects reaching a customer.

Why doesn't the die casting company take measures to prevent defects at their source? Here's part of the problem. Quality control advocates progressive, rational concepts, such as building quality into the process and performing informative inspections to promote feedback to processing operations. Nonetheless, statistically-based sampling inspections receive most of the attention, while sampling inspection is nothing more than a logical *means*, a practical tool of quality control. Somewhere along the line means and ends became confused; the notion that you cannot have quality control without using statistics supplanted the original, legitimate concepts.

Moral: Quality can be assured reasonably only when it is built in at the process and when inspection provides immediate, accurate feedback at the source of defects.

Types of Informative Inspection

If you are committed to achieving zero defects, judgment inspection is not appropriate since it discovers defects only after they occur. Informative inspection is better because it helps reduce defects by checking close to their source and immediately feeding back information that can be used to prevent recurrence. A simple form of 100 percent inspection that is easy to administer should also be adopted. There are several types of preventive inspection.

Self Inspection and Successive Inspection

The inspection that provides the most immediate feedback is self-inspection where the worker inspects the products he/she processes. This method has two drawbacks. The worker may

- Make compromise judgments and accept items that ought to be rejected
- Make inspection errors unintentionally

This type of autonomous inspection is often promoted, but its efficiency is offset by the potential for lack of objectivity. A *successive inspection* system, on the other hand, provides both objectivity and immediate feedback.

In successive inspection, workers inspect products passed along from the previous operation before processing them themselves. Products processed by worker A flow to worker B who inspects A's work and then processes the product herself. B's work is inspected by worker C, who then performs her operation, and so on (Figure 10).

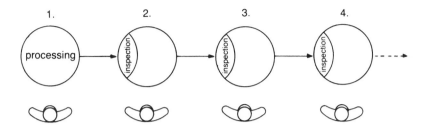

FIGURE 10. Successive Checks

Example 2.5 — Successive inspection. The television division of Moriguchi Electric Company adopted successive inspection with the following results: Using control charts and QC circle activities, they had reduced their rate of process defects from 15 to 6.5 but achieved no further improvements as a result of these activities. Then, they adopted successive inspection. A month later, process defects had dropped to 1.5; after three months, to 0.65 and then to 0.016.

These are excellent achievements that are consistent with results at other companies. On average, an 80 to 90 percent reduction in the number of defects can be achieved within one month of adopting the successive inspection system.

The system, furthermore, has been very successful in reducing process defects during the early stages of model changes. Since it is easy to implement quickly, its use under these circumstances should be encouraged.

Enhanced Self Inspection

Despite the potential for errors in judgment and careless mistakes, self inspection provides the fastest feedback. A self-inspection system that eliminated these problems would be even more efficient than successive inspection. Self inspection can be enhanced with the use of devices that automatically detect defects or inadvertent mistakes. Such systems give the individual worker immediate feedback, achieve 100 percent inspection, and prevent defects.

For example, an automobile component processed for left and right side assembly has identical contours except for the position of a hole on either the left or right side (Figure 11). The part was designed to be bent on the right side but occasionally, right- and left-handed components were accidentally interchanged. To prevent this from happening, a limit switch was installed on the press at the point where the hole should be located. If the hole is not in that position, the limit switch is activated, the press shuts down, and a buzzer alerts the worker. The power will not come on again until the part is placed on the press correctly.

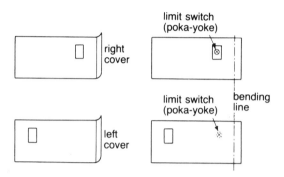

FIGURE 11. **Poka-yoke for Bending Cover Edges**

In this case, the limit switch not only performs a 100 percent informative inspection but also prevents the defect from occurring. Physical detection devices like this one are called poka-yoke, or "mistake-proofing" devices. (This term is used instead of the more common "fool-proofing" because even the best workers make mistakes inadvertently.) By installing in-process inspection devices, zero defects can be achieved.

Source Inspection

Source inspection prevents defects by controlling the conditions that influence quality at their source. *Vertical source inspection* traces problems back through the process flow to identify and control external conditions that affect quality. *Horizontal source inspection* identifies and controls conditions within an operation that affect quality.

Some quality inspections require subjective sensory judgments — paint hues, for example. In such inspections, however, we look for defects after they occur, which makes the goal of 100 percent inspection difficult to achieve. Also, we tend to rely on subjective judgment because we focus on defective outcomes or results rather than defective conditions or causes. Unacceptable color *is* a defect, but it is merely a symptom of the defective conditions that produced it. We use sensory inspection to identify such defects, but their causes will be controlled by physical methods.

Horizontal source inspection achieves 100 percent inspection by controlling the factors that produce a defective condition. For example, color tone can be controlled by regulating the factors that affect quality — controlling the quantity and density of the paint and the amount of air pressure discharged.

Poka-yoke Inspection Methods

Successive, self, and source inspection can all be achieved through the use of poka-yoke methods. Poka-yoke achieves 100 percent inspection through mechanical or physical control.

The Regulating Functions of Poka-yoke

There are two ways in which poka-yoke can be used to correct mistakes:

- Control type — when the poka-yoke is activated, the machine or processing line shuts down so the problem can be corrected
- Warning type — when the poka-yoke is activated, a buzzer sounds or a lamp flashes to alert the worker

The control poka-yoke is the strongest corrective device because it shuts down the process until the defective condition has been corrected. The warning poka-yoke allows defective processing to continue if workers do not respond to the warning. How frequently defects occur and whether or not they can be corrected once they have occurred will influence the choice between these two functions.

In general, occasional defects are corrected automatically. For example, a flaw in a portion of the material causes defects in the parts made from it, but subsequent parts will be good. More frequent occasional defects usually require a control poka-yoke. If the defect frequency is low and the defect can be corrected, a warning poka-yoke is appropriate. When the defect is impossible to correct, on the other hand, a control poka-yoke is preferable, regardless of frequency.

Continuous defects will continue to be produced until human or mechanical intervention occurs (for example, a broken punch press that causes continuous rejections), and the control poka-yoke is always most effective for them.

In every case, the decision to implement a poka-yoke must be made on the basis of a cost-benefit analysis. The control poka-yoke is the more effective in most cases.

Setting Functions of Poka-yoke

There are three types of control poka-yoke:

- The *contact method* identifies defects by whether or not contact is established between the device and some feature of the product's shape or dimension. (Small changes in product shape or dimension are sometimes introduced deliberately to make defects easier to identify.) Color differences are also used. Techniques based on them are considered extensions of the contact method.
- The *fixed-value method* determines whether a given number of movements is made.
- *The motion-step method* determines whether the established steps or motions of a procedure are followed.

Choosing a Poka-yoke Method

The poka-yoke device itself is not an inspection system but a method of detecting defects or mistakes that can be used to fulfill a particular inspection function. Inspection is the object, poka-yoke is merely the method. For example, a jig that does not accept an incorrectly processed part is a poka-yoke that performs the function of successive inspection. If successive inspection (which catches defects after they occur) is not the most effective way to eliminate the defects in that particular process, another system should be used. And, of course, the poka-yoke methods that fulfill another inspection system's functions may be quite different.

Therefore, the first step in choosing and adopting effective quality control methods is to identify the inspection system that best satisfies the requirements of a particular process.

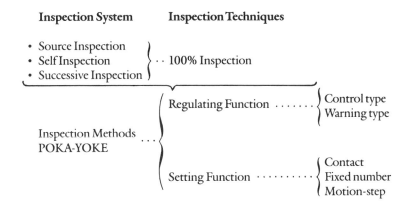

Inspection System   Inspection Techniques

- Source Inspection
- Self Inspection
- Successive Inspection   ·· 100% Inspection

Inspection Methods ...
POKA-YOKE

Regulating Function .... { Control type / Warning type

Setting Function ········· { Contact / Fixed number / Motion-step

Next, a poka-yoke method capable of fulfilling the particular inspection function must be identified: a control or warning type. Only after this has been done should the type or design of the device be considered, whether to use a contact, fixed value, or motion-step poka-yoke.

> *Example 2.6 — Poka-yoke applications at a Toyota supplier.* At Arawaka Shatai, makers of auto bodies, the back lining plate of car doors consists of a board covered with leather which is attached by 20 retainers. Several times a month, defects occurred when one or two of these retainers were left off. Workers were advised to be more careful and the rate of defects dropped for a while but then returned to its former level.
>
> Since this appeared to be a chronic defect, a warning poka-yoke was installed to alert workers in the event that a retainer was left off. Twenty proximity switches were installed on the jig of the press in the next process. If a retainer is missing, a buzzer sounds and the workers stop the press. The defective lining plate is immediately returned to the previous process and the missing retainer(s) attached.
>
> The reject rate dropped to zero. In this case, a contact type poka-yoke performs 100 percent successive inspection.
>
> In another process at this plant, metal fittings were attached to car seats. The production system called for mixed production, which meant that eight kinds of seats for the Corona, Mark II, Celica, etc., were fabricated in the same line flow. Workers followed the instructions on the accompanying kanban and attached the appropriate metal fitting to the seats.* Several times a month, however, the wrong metal fittings were attached. A poka-yoke was introduced to solve the problem.

---

* Note: The word *kanban* refers to the signboard of a store or shop but at Toyota, it simply means any small sign displayed in front of a worker. The term is discussed in detail in Chapter 9.

FIGURE 12. Poka-yoke for Retainers

Small foil disks are now attached to the lower portion of the kanban for each model. When the kanban arrives with the car seat, the worker inserts it in a specially designed box that is fitted with a reflector-type photoelectric switch for each model. The foil disks activate the switch. This lights a lamp and opens the cover on the parts box that contains the fittings for that model. The worker takes the necessary parts from the box and attaches them to the seat. Since the boxes remain closed unless they are activated by the kanban, it is impossible to accidentally take fittings from the wrong box.

This method entirely eliminated the defect. When one of the workers was asked what he thought about it, he replied in the local slang, "Poka-yoke? Oh, it's 'anki'" — meaning, "it's a breeze." In this case, a motion-step poka-yoke device performs the self-inspection function and relieves workers of the need to pay attention to the metal fitting selection. This allows them to concentrate fully on the fastening of the screws.

It is important to realize that there are two kinds of forgetfulness. Since we are not infallible, everyone forgets or overlooks things now and then. This is the first kind of forgetting. The second is "forgetting that we might forget" — when we forget to make sure that we have not overlooked something. To guard against this, we make checklists. Poka-yoke methods incorporate the function of a checklist into an operation, so we don't "forget what we forgot."

FIGURE 13. Poka-yoke for Attaching Metal Fittings (only opens the cover of the box containing the required metal fittings)

TRANSPORT IMPROVEMENT

Transport, or movement of materials, is a cost that does not add value to a product. Most people try to improve transport by using forklifts, conveyors, chutes, etc., which actually only improves the *work* of transport. Real improvement *eliminates* the transport function as much as possible. The goal is to increase production efficiency, which is accomplished by improving the layout of processes.

Example 2.7 — Improving layout. Tokai Iron Works is a small press plant that produces small quantities of a wide variety of products. The company experienced low productivity and chronic delivery delays; fundamental improvements were needed.

Although used for many products, Tokai's presses performed only three simple types of processing: hole punching, bending and embossing, and occasionally marking. The machines were arranged by type and grouped to maximize capacity. As a result, the company produced in large lots and invested far more labor than necessary in transporting different products from one machine group to another.

There was a simple solution to Tokai's problem: First, they rearranged the machines according to the flow of the products. Then they installed a 60cm wide belt conveyer and placed ten presses on either side of it.

> With this layout, they achieved a one-piece flow operation which eliminates transport and significantly increases the operating ratio of the machines. Work-in-process is reduced, production time shortened, and the plant is spacious and airy. Productivity is up 200 percent, and the chronic delivery delays have been eliminated.

It is essential to recognize that transport improvement and transport *operations* improvement are two distinctly different problems. Transport only increases costs, it never adds value. Typically, processes consist of 45 percent processing and 5 percent each inspection and delays, with transport representing the remaining 45 percent of labor costs. Even when manual transport is mechanized, work costs are simply shifted from manual to mechanical — an investment without returns. With this in mind, the absolute elimination of transport through layout improvement is not an unreasonable objective.

Only after opportunities for layout improvement have been exhausted should the unavoidable transport work that remains be improved through mechanization.

ELIMINATING STORAGE

As noted earlier, there are two types of delays related to storage: storage between processes (*process delays*) and storage for lot size (*lot delays*).

Eliminating Process Delays

Process delay refers to both lots of unprocessed items waiting to be processed and accumulated excess inventory that sits waiting to be processed or delivered. (For example, a supplier may hold stock for the customer company.) Excess inventory is created in two ways:

- Quantitative process delays result when defect rates are overestimated, when there is excess production. The surpluses have to wait between processes.
- Scheduling process delays result when production proceeds ahead of schedule, when too much is produced too soon, causing additional delays between processes.

There are three types of accumulations between processes:

- E storage. From a production engineering perspective, certain accumulations result from unbalanced flow between processes.
- C storage. From a production control perspective, buffer or cushion stocks are allowed between processes to avoid machine breakdowns or rejects delaying succeeding processes.
- S storage. "Safety stock" — overproduction beyond that required for current control purposes — to allow managers to feel "secure."

Eliminating E Storage

Two factors of process flow can affect the accumulation of material between processes: leveling quantity and synchronization.

Leveling quantity. Leveling quantity means that equal amounts are produced at each process; it involves balancing production quantities and processing capacities. Typically, processing capacity, especially machine processing capacity, is not balanced among processes. As a result, inventory can build up between a high and a low capacity process if both are operated at 100 percent capacity.

At Toyota, the quantity to be produced is determined solely by order requirements. If the lowest capacity processes can produce the quantity required, operation of higher capacity processes is kept at the same level by either slowing the processing down or operating intermittently. If the lowest processing capacity is insufficient to produce the required quantity, it must be improved.

This approach defies the conventional wisdom that each process must be operated at maximum efficiency. Balancing the capacities of the entire process to eliminate accumulation between steps, however, is the more efficient approach overall. Although unused or excess capacity, while it does not add to the bottom line, can be assigned a dollar value, eliminating the hidden costs of overproduction actually saves money.

There are three ways to level quantity:

- Standardize (level) processes in a production line at the highest process capacity
- Standardize processes in a production line at the lowest process capacity

- Balance production quantities at the level necessary to fulfill order requirements

Of course, in a plant that uses C-type storage (buffer inventory), there is less need to be concerned about balancing capacity among processes.

> *Example 2.8 — Eliminating storage.* At the Iida Metal Company, a 90 stroke-per-minute blanking machine preceded a 60 stroke-per-minute punching and bending press. As a result, surplus blanked products accumulated on pallets and were stored in a corner of the plant from where they were supplied to the press line as needed. In addition, the blanking machine was shut down for about one third of the monthly production hours because of its high production capacity.
>
> To eliminate this storage, three steps were taken. First, the blanking and press machines were linked closely. Second, a magazine was installed between the two machines to hold blanked products. The blanking machine now runs for the approximately two minutes it takes to fill the magazine and then shuts down automatically. Third, pressing continues while the blanking operation is shut down, until only a few blanked products remain in the magazine. The blanking machine automatically resumes operation after about one minute to refill the magazine.

Note that there was actually no change in the operation of the blanking machine — resting for one out of every three minutes is equivalent to shutting down for one third of the monthly production hours. Leveling process capacity between the two machines, however, eliminated overproduction and accumulation of blanked materials and produced real cost savings.

In Example 2.8, the blanking machine still had excess capacity which was utilized by having the machine supply products to two press lines. For such a situation, there are other techniques to level production between processes.

- *By-pass flow operation.* Where press line A was used for large volume production, it was linked directly with the blanking machine. Surplus products were re-routed to the pallet during the flow process and then fed into the press line when it was complete.
- *Mixed flow operation (with one-touch die change).* The blanking machine processed 500 pieces of product A that flowed to line A. With a one-touch exchange of die (p. 43), it could then begin immediately to process 300 pieces of product B for line

B, thus establishing a mixed flow. In this situation, suitable storage had to be set up between the blanking machine and the press line.

- *Low-cost material feeder.* Another success was achieved through the purchase of a second-hand press, the only purpose of which was to feed products to the A line. The addition of a material feeder transformed the press into an inexpensive homemade blanking machine that was then linked directly to feed into the A line.

These examples demonstrate that the presence of high capacity machines should not be used to justify lot processing and unprocessed product storage. The principle involved is simple: process capacity should *serve* production requirements, not *determine* them.

In addition, direct process flow is often a key element in leveling production quantity. A smoother flow prevents storage and reduces labor time and the production cycle. It also improves quality by enhancing feedback on defective products.

Synchronization. The second way to eliminate E storage is by synchronizing the flow between operations. Even when the quantity of production is leveled, unnecessary storage can still occur between operations if they are not synchronized.

From a practical standpoint, however, once quantities are leveled, synchronization is simply a matter of efficient production scheduling. In the past, synchronization has been promoted as a way to prevent storage between processes, without recognition of the primary importance of leveling quantity. Leveling must be done first, however, because it helps eliminate the process delays that make synchronization so difficult. This fact also underscores the importance of synchronizing the *entire* process flow. To do so, production quantity must first be leveled at every stage, including pressing, spot welding, painting, and so on.

Eliminating C Storage

C-type accumulations (cushion stocks) compensate for chronic problems such as machine breakdowns, defects, downtime for tool and die changes, sudden changes in production schedule, and the like. It is when such problems are not properly understood as causes of overproduction that cushion stocks come to be seen as a necessary evil and are consciously maintained by production control. This is not a true perception; C storage can be avoided by eliminating the following:

Machine breakdowns. When a machine breaks down, cushion stocks are fed into the next process so the flow of production is not interrupted. This stopgap measure, however, increases the costs of production without reducing the number of breakdowns. To reduce this type of storage successfully, the cause of the breakdown must be thoroughly investigated, even if that requires shutting down the line and implementing careful measures to prevent similar breakdowns. Through these actions, the need for cushion stock is eliminated. (Another approach to preventing breakdowns, discussed in Chapter 3, is to use pre-automation devices to detect pre-failure conditions.)

Defective products. When defective products occur, they disrupt the flow of production. That is why semi-processed products are often stored between processes and substituted for defective units as they occur. This approach is based on the assumption that a certain number of defects is unavoidable. They can be reduced to zero, however, through preventive inspection and the simple 100 percent inspection techniques which make C storage unnecessary.

Process delay storage as compensation for lengthy setup. When tool and die changes cause extended delays, it makes sense to reduce the apparent per-unit processing time by increasing lot size. This does, however, increase storage and handling costs. The economic order quantity (EOQ) system was developed to help determine the lot size that would balance these factors, but this approach is useful only when attempts to reduce changeover times are unsuccessful.

In most cases, however, setup times can be reduced significantly through such techniques as single-minute exchange of die (SMED). (Please refer to the general discussion on pp. 42-57. For in-depth applications, see Shigeo Shingo, *A Revolution in Manufacturing: The SMED System* [Cambridge, MA: Productivity Press, 1985.])

At Mitsubishi Heavy Industries, the application of SMED has led to significant improvements: changeover for an 8-arbor boring machine was reduced from 24 hours to 2 minutes and 40 seconds in the course of one year. And, at Toyota, changeover for a bolt maker was reduced from eight hours to 58 seconds. I could cite over 400 cases in which changeover times have been reduced to approximately one-twentieth of the original. Not surprisingly, the EOQ is vanishing as a theme in engineering economics.

Change in production plan. Buffer inventories help meet unexpected increases in production demands or advance deliveries. These buffers are not necessary, however, when:

- Production changes can be facilitated by a single minute set-up
- Short production cycles permit advance delivery despite short lead time
- Flexible production capacity, derived through pre-automation (Chapter 3), helps meet unexpected increases in production.

Example 2.9 — Advance deliveries. Togo Industries manufactures automobile springs. Occasionally, a customer will call to request that an order scheduled for some future date be delivered the next morning. In such emergencies, the die can be changed in three minutes and the springs formed after working hours on machines equipped with automatic start and stop mechanisms. The springs are heat-treated the next morning and delivered by 10 a.m. Although such requests are infrequent, Togo is prepared to respond without relying on reserve stocks.

Accumulation between machines of different capacity. When a high-capacity machine supplies products to, or receives them from, several lower capacity machines, accumulation between processes is inevitable. Two measures can be taken:

- Several inexpensive, lower capacity machines can be linked directly to the succeeding machines to avoid accumulation
- Quick die change and small-lot production can be implemented to ensure minimum storage between processes

Here, the moral is that investing in expensive, high performance machines is not always the best solution to fulfill a factory's production requirements.

Accumulation as a result of different operating times. Accumulation occurs when, for example, all machining is done on one shift but heat treatment and plating are done in three. To eliminate storage between processes:

- Adopt pre-automation for the machining process and conduct the three-shift operation without workers.
- Increase the efficiency of the heat treatment or plating process to produce the required quantity in one shift or add overtime to balance the two operations.

Eliminating S Storage

S-type storage is not created to deal with any imbalance or predictable problem; rather, it is intended to simply increase one's sense of security. This is why such accumulations are sometimes referred to as "safety stock" or "safety valves." In addition to the above general reason, they result from four causes:

- Elimination of the potential for delivery delays
- Scheduling errors
- Overestimates of the need for buffers against breakdowns and defects
- Indefinite production schedules

Example 2.10 — Eliminating safety stock. At Asahi National Electric, components delivered from outside plants and suppliers were first stored in a warehouse and then redelivered for assembly. I told the managing director that this seemed a lot like depositing a paycheck in a savings account only to withdraw it the next day to pay daily living expenses. "Why don't you use today's salary directly for tomorrow's expenses?" I asked. "We put money in a savings account for such things as buying a car or to cover unexpected medical costs. When those types of expenses arise we must pay. Why don't you reserve your savings for just such special expenses as a cushion? Similarly, why don't you have the items you receive from your suppliers delivered to assembly directly instead of first storing them in the warehouse?"

The managing director asked suppliers to deliver only the number of items required for one day's production and to deliver them directly to the assembly plant. Stock in the warehouse is now designated as safety stock and set aside. Only when defects are found are good parts "borrowed" from the warehouse to replace them. Similarly, shortages due to breakdowns are made up out of the safety stocks. The next day, parts equal to the number borrowed are produced and the safety stock is replenished. In this way, everyday requirements are met directly while unexpected requirements are handled by "withdrawals from savings," which are later restored.

After using this method for two months in the assembly of washbasin units, 24 units out of 60 did not require parts from the warehouse. The remaining 36 units used up an average of one third of the warehouse stock as defective parts were taken there to be exchanged for good ones. Due to this additional control factor, work was performed more carefully and processing defects dropped by 50 percent.

During the experiment, a chronic problem was identified. While being secured within the frames, mirrors frequently broke because of an error in the fitting operation. This made it necessary to stop the line twice. It was determined that the worker performing this operation pushed the bottom edge of the mirror down against the rubber packing material to create enough clearance at the top of the frame to allow the mirror to slip into place. To make this happen, the worker had to push against the face of the mirror with her hand at a crucial moment. If the timing was off, the mirror broke. Furthermore, the breakage problem worsened whenever an experienced worker in charge of the operation was absent and had to be replaced by another.

Since broken mirrors had been easy to replace, no one had considered improving the operation to eliminate the problem. But the new stricter control over the replacement of defective parts made improvements essential. After analyzing the operation, changes were made that allowed even new workers to fit mirrors without breakage. A device with a special cam was installed. By tilting its handle, the mirror is pushed downward and into the frame with moderate but consistent force.

This controlled use of safety stock led to three important improvements:

- Stocks were reduced by 80 percent at the new control level
- More careful work on the assembly line reduced processing defects by 50 percent
- Controlling the replacement of defective units helped uncover hidden problems and focused attention on their root causes. This resulted in additional reductions of sporadic defects and safety stock through improved tooling.

I call this two-step approach to quality improvement the safety stock system: Current levels of stock are frozen and used only as safety stock; daily requirements are supplied directly as they are needed. This method reveals the actual safety stock requirements of the existing control level as well as the problems typically hidden by excess inventory. Both can be dealt with through improvements that will further reduce the level of safety stock.

To use this method successfully, production control must first answer these questions:

- How much safety stock is necessary at the current control level?

- Which stocks currently exceed the requirements for particular safety functions, such as defects, breakdowns, etc.; which safety stocks are actually unnecessary, resulting from early or excess production?
- What are the causes of actual safety stock requirements?

This method of reducing safety stock can also smooth the transition to stockless production. Work-in-process is frozen at existing levels; reduction occurs gradually as improvements are made and actual requirements become clearer.

Conclusion

Process delays occur as a result of imbalances and instabilities among processing, inspection, transport, and other elements in related processes. Stock accumulates as we try to compensate for these weaknesses. Unfortunately, the more it increases, the more it also masks underlying problems and keeps us from attacking them directly. Merely removing the accumulation, however, does not solve these fundamental problems. The causes of the instability must themselves first be eliminated. As poor production flow, defects, machine break-downs, excessive set-up times, etc., are corrected, accumulations gradually diminish and are eventually eliminated.

Eliminating Lot Delays

Whenever parts are processed in lots, the entire lot, except for the one piece being processed, is delayed "in storage" in either an unprocessed or a processed state until all pieces in the lot have been processed. Each piece must be held; each piece is delayed.

Improvements in Large Lot Production

Little attention has been paid to such delays because they are typically concealed within processing times. They have also generally been overlooked when the efficiencies of large lot production were analyzed. The reason for increasing lot size is the assumption that this will compensate for delays caused by long set-ups. For example, when it takes four hours to do a die change and the operating time for one piece of product is one minute, apparent processing time can be reduced considerably by increasing the lot size from, for example, 100 pieces to 1,000 (Table 1). The truth is that lot delays prolong the production cycle considerably (Table 2).

Setup Time	Lot Size	Principal Operation Time Per Item	Operation Time	Ratio (%)	Ratio (%)
4 hrs.	100	1 min.	$1 \text{ min.} + \frac{4 \times 60}{100} = 3.4 \text{ min.}$	100	
4 hrs.	1,000	1 min.	$1 \text{ min.} + \frac{4 \times 60}{1,000} = 1.24 \text{ min.}$	36	100
4hrs.	10,000	1 min.	$1 \text{ min.} + \frac{4 \times 60}{10,000} = 1.024 \text{ min.}$	30	83

TABLE 1. **Relationship between Setup Time and Lot Size — I**

Setup Time	Lot Size	Principal Operation Time Per Item	Operation Time	Ratio (%)	Ratio (%)
8 hrs.	100	1 min.	$1 \text{ min.} + \frac{8 \times 60}{100} = 5.8 \text{ min.}$	100	
8 hrs.	1,000	1 min.	$1 \text{ min.} + \frac{8 \times 60}{1,000} = 1.48 \text{ min.}$	26	100
8 hrs.	10,000	1 min.	$1 \text{ min.} + \frac{8 \times 60}{10,000} = 1.048 \text{ min.}$	18	71

TABLE 2. **Relationship between Setup Time and Lot Size — II**

If lot production is nT, with T = 5 hours and number of processes n = 3, then the production cycle (L) = 15 hours. If, however, one piece of product is transferred to the next process as soon as it is completed, then:

$$\text{production cycle } (l) = T + (n - 1)t*$$

$$= 5 + (3 - 1) \times 1 \text{ min.}$$

$$= 5 \text{ hours and 2 minutes}$$

---

* t = 1 minute − processing time for one piece

Therefore:

$$\frac{l}{L} = \frac{T + (n-1)t}{nT} = \frac{1}{n} = \frac{5 \text{ hrs} - 2 \text{ min}}{15 \text{ hrs}} = \frac{1}{3}$$

As shown, $(n - 1) \times t$ is usually negligible compared with T. In this case:

$$\frac{l}{L} = \frac{1}{n}$$

Thus, if three processes were changed to a one-piece flow operation, the length of the production cycle would be reduced by two-thirds. If ten processes were changed, the production cycle would be one-tenth the original length.

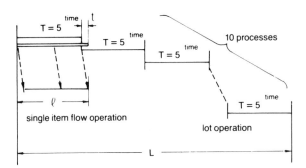

FIGURE 14. **Improvement of Lot Delays**

Improvements through Transport and SMED

Production cycles are reduced significantly by eliminating lot delays. Yet many plants tolerate the delays caused by lot production, because they believe that it reduces the relative setup costs and saves man-hours.

This thinking, however, is based on faulty assumptions. In the first place, *processing lots* reduce man-hours, while *transport lots* shorten production cycles. It follows then, that the greatest reduction in production time is obtained, even with processing lots of 1,000, when each item is transported individually to the next process. Yet, one-piece transport lots involve increased transport from one process to the next, a problem solved by improving layout. After layout is improved, more efficient transport means should be considered, such as placing succeeding processes next to one another or connecting them by conveyors. This allows processed material to flow easily from one process to the next. In this way, layout improvements both shorten production cycles and cut transport man-hours dramatically.

In the second place, by adopting SMED, setup times can be reduced to such an extent that there is simply no advantage to increasing the processing lot size. Reductions from four hours to five minutes, for example, are not uncommon.

The Order-Delivery Relationship and Shortened Production

Reducing production time, as noted above, requires the elimination of storage between processes. As the production cycle is shortened, storage decreases. It is the understanding of the relationship of this cycle to the order-to-delivery period, however, that is the most useful in the reduction of storage delays.

The period from order to delivery is symbolized by D and that from first process to last (production cycle) by P. Their relationship is most critical when D is less than P ($D < P$). For example, if a product is ordered for delivery within ten days but takes 20 days to produce, it obviously cannot be delivered when it is required. To make certain that D is always greater than P, sufficient inventory must be produced and carried to fulfil all those orders that must be delivered in less than 20 days (Figure 15). This is typically accomplished by carrying semi-processed stock to reduce the production time (P') which, however, results in increased storage between processes. If product order forecasting is incorrect, these accumulations may be larger than necessary or may need to be held for excessively long periods. To avoid these excess accumulations, the absolute production cycle from start of process to finish (P_0) must be less than D, i.e., $D > P_0$.

Generally, semi-processed parts are held between processes anywhere from half again to four times as long as the actual processing period. If that period is eliminated by quantity leveling and synchronization, the production cycle can be reduced by as much as 80 percent.

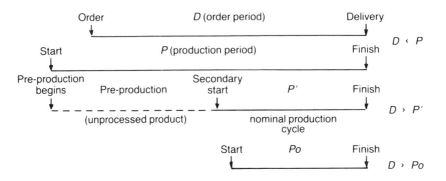

FIGURE 15. Relation of $D:P$

Another important factor in determining the length of the production cycle is storage for lot size. Its elimination can also reduce P significantly, depending on the number of processes. For example, when three processes are involved:

- Eliminating storage between processes results in a 60 to 80 percent reduction
- Eliminating storage for lot size results in a 70 percent reduction

The combined impact of these two strategies can reduce the production cycle by 86 to 93 percent. When ten processes are involved, the reductions can reach 96 to 98 percent.

This method of reducing production time delays is the foundation of the Toyota production system. When coupled with the practice of SMED, deliveries can be made even on very short notice without any inventory.

Example 2.11 — Shortening production. R Manufacturing produces refrigeration trucks. During the oil crisis, the company's orders and profitability slumped, leaving them with 23 unsold units in inventory. At this company, D was much shorter than P. Although final specification for orders was determined seven to ten days before delivery, the production cycle lasted three weeks. Standard vehicles were produced in advance and special features added to order. When orders dropped, these standard vehicles became stock.

To regain profitability, the company had to reduce its production cycle dramatically, and several steps were taken to accomplish that: The plant layout was changed to permit a one-piece flow and eliminate storage between processes. During this transition, many opportunities for improvement became apparent. For example, materials were sheared in ten-unit lots; by installing a one-touch method for exchanging the fixture, a one-piece flow was established. In another instance, injecting insulation into the refrigerator walls and then baking on the enamel required nine days, most of which was taken up by baking them in lots of ten side walls, ten rear walls, ten tops, and so on. This period was reduced to one and a half days by baking all the walls of each unit together.

Within a year and a half, the production cycle had been reduced to five days and stocks of finished vehicles were cleared, eliminating the need to produce ahead. The company recovered from the oil crisis and gained in efficiency as well.

We have already stated that there are many managers and supervisors who think that lot production is advantageous or that their own production requirements cannot be adapted to a one-piece flow operation. This kind of thinking is not correct, however, when viewed from the standpoint of fundamental production. The above example clearly demonstrates the importance of the relationship between D and P in production management and that it should be thoroughly investigated and improved.

In a 1979 interview in *Plant Management Magazine*, Taiichi Ohno, former vice-president of Toyota Motors Company, was asked whether applying the Toyota production system in the future to multi-product, small lot production would provide good results. He replied:

> Toyota Motors started with small lot production of a variety of products. So we looked for effective methods for multi-type, small-lot production in order to catch up with the U.S. What kind of production system could we adopt? We decided on the SMED system, created by Mr. Shingo.
>
> When die changes are performed skillfully, it is not costly to produce in small quantities. The Japanese had to find a way to produce a variety of products in small, medium, or even large quantities — who else would consider it? Was the excellent production equipment used in the United States suitable for Japanese factories? The more we studied the situation, the more factors militated against its use. Because they were developed to handle fewer types of products, larger lots, and enormous sales, U.S. facilities are not appropriate for Japan. But they are of such high quality, we tend to purchase these expensive machines and use them anyway.

Summary

Mixed-model, small lot production was introduced at Toyota in an effort to catch up with American automobile manufacturers. Toyota's approach was to first remove inefficiencies in processing, inspection, and transport. Then, it attacked storage problems to eliminate accumulations of work-in-process and finished goods throughout the production process.

3

Improving Operations

COMMON FACTORS IN OPERATIONS

In Chapter 2, I described the four activities that make up any process: processing, inspection, transportation, and delay operations. In this chapter, we will look at operations (p. 42).

Although actual operations may vary widely, they can be classified as follows:

Setup operations. Preparation before and after operations, such as setup, removal and adjustment of dies, tooling, etc.

Principal operations. Performing the work required. This includes *essential operations* (those actions which actually accomplish the principal operation), that is:

- Processing — machining a product
- Inspection — measuring quality
- Transportation — moving material
- Storage — holding or storing parts

It also includes *incidental operations* (actions that help achieve the essential operation), for example:

- Processing — attaching material or parts to the machine and removing them when the operation is completed
- Inspection — fitting product into the gauge and removing it
- Transportation — loading and unloading material
- Delay — placing parts in the storage area and removing them

Margin allowances. Activities indirectly related to the operation, for example:

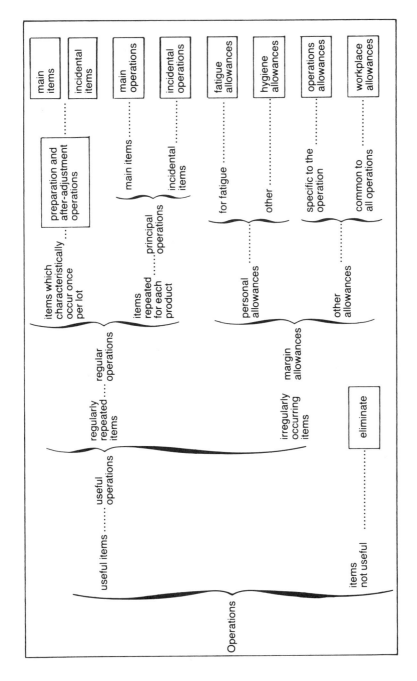

FIGURE 16. Structure of Operations

- Operation allowance — work indirectly related to the job, e.g., lubricating, applying coating mold removal agent, removing chips, attending to defective products, machine breakdowns, etc.
- Workplace allowance — indirect work common to a number of different operations, e.g., supplying materials, replacing products on pallets

Personal allowances. Activities not related to the operation that serve the needs of the operator. They are of two types:

- Fatigue allowance — rest period between operations
- Physical allowance — drinking water, going to the toilet, etc.

IMPROVING SETUP (Exchange of Dies and Tools)

Adopting single-minute exchange of die (SMED) or one-touch exchange of die (OTED) is the most effective way to improve setup.

At Mitsubishi Heavy Industries, for example, setup time on an eight-arbor boring machine was reduced from 24 hours to two minutes and 40 seconds in a year. In the same time period, setup on a bolt-forming machine at Toyota Motors was reduced from eight hours to 58 seconds. Outside Japan, at H. Weidmann Co. in Switzerland, setup on a 50-ounce plastic molding machine was reduced from two and a half hours to six minutes and 35 seconds. And, at Federal-Mogul Co. in the United States, exchange of tools on a milling machine was reduced from two hours to two minutes.

These examples are typical of the kind of improvements achieved using SMED and OTED techniques. On average, reductions are around 80 to 95 percent.

Example 3.1 — The birth of SMED: Distinguishing between the two types of setup. In 1950, I was asked to conduct an efficiency improvement survey at Toyo Kogyo's Mazda plant to eliminate the bottlenecks caused by three large body-molding presses. After visiting the workplace, I asked the section manager to authorize a week-long stopwatch production analysis so I could get an idea of the current performance of the 350-, 750-, and 800-ton presses, none of which was working at capacity.

The section manager told me this would be a waste of time since he had already put his most skilled and conscientious workers on the presses around the clock. In his opinion, the only way to improve productivity further was to buy more machines, but management had denied his request.

"I can understand your situation," I said, "but let me do the analysis anyway. If there's really no other way to eliminate the bottlenecks, I'll advise management to buy the machines." That argument persuaded the section manager to agree to the survey.

A die change was scheduled for the 800-ton press on the third day. After removing the old die, the worker began rushing around frantically. I ran after him with my logbook in order to record his activities. Finally, I asked him what was going on and he replied that he was searching for a missing mounting bolt for the new die. "I'm sure I put them all on the tool shelf, but now I can't find the last one." I told him I'd wait by the press until he found it.

More than an hour later, he returned brandishing a bolt in his right hand. "You found it!" I said.

"No," he answered, "I didn't. I finally had no choice but to take one from the next machine. I'm so late because I had to shorten and thread it."

I gave him a few words of encouragement, but to myself I thought: "What is he going to do when it's time to set up the other machine?"

The die change took most of the day to complete. When it was over, I asked if it always took that long. "Oh yes," the operator said, "it's like this most of the time."

The results of the study done on the 800-ton press are shown in Figure 17. The press was engaged in actual molding operations only three percent of the day. The die change and job and workshop allowances added up to 67 percent.

The above example suggests that there are two types of setup operation:

- Internal setup (IED)* — setup operations that can be performed only when the machine is stopped, such as mounting or removing dies
- External setup (OED)* — setup operations that can be completed while the machine is running, such as transporting dies to or from storage

---

* These are Mr. Shingo's original designations: IED stands for "internal exchange of die," OED for "outer exchange of die."

Content of Operation / Machine	Setup: Preparation After-Adjustment	Main Operation: Essential Operation	Main Operation: Auxiliary Operation	Margin Allowances: Hygiene	Margin Allowances: Fatigue	Margin Allowances: Oper.	Margin Allowances: Workplace	Important Points for Reexamination: Preparation & After-Adjustment			Important Points for Reexamination: Workplace Allowances		
									sec.	%		sec.	%
800-ton press / Main Operator	47.0%	3.0%	24%	1.0%	5.0%	6.0%	14.0%	die transportation	869	3.5	material transport.	574	2.3
								securing die	2940	11.7	waiting crane	776	3.1
								adjusting	5475	21.7	material cooling	902	3.6
								removing die	1789	7.2	assist adjacent press	34	0.1
								miscellaneous	610	2.4	miscellaneous	1162	4.6
750-ton press / Main Operator	46.3	4.27	23.6	0	1.84	7.34	16.65	die transportation	1469	5.3	material transport.	2231	8.3
								securing die	2033	8.2	waiting crane	356	1.4
								adjusting	5968	23.5	misc.	1599	6.4
								removing die	307	1.2			
								misc.	1963	7.9			
750-ton press / Assistant	23.5	0	15.8	0	13.2	4.9	42.6	die transportation	1633	6.5	loading & unloading (material & products)	3711	14.8
								preparing and securing part	727	2.9	waiting for preparation & after-adjustment	5635	22.0
								adjusting	1912	7.6	waiting for main operation	701	2.8
								removing die	507	2.0	misc.	380	1.5
								misc.	224	1.0			
300-ton press / Main Operator	40.0	9.0	27.0	0	2.0	13.0	9.0	die transportation	2000	7.9	material transport.	105	0.6
								securing die	2849	11.3	waiting crane	1220	4.8
								adjusting	3424	13.6	misc.	56	0.2
								removing die	799	7.2			
								misc.	1699	6.7			

FIGURE 17. **Production Analysis of a Large Press**

In any analysis of setup operations, it is important to distinguish between the work that can be conducted while the machine is running and that which must be done when the machine is shut down. Using this principle at Toyo Kogyo, internal setup time was reduced by 50 percent.

> *Example 3.2 — A Second Encounter with SMED.* In 1957, I was asked to increase the capacity of a large, open-sided planer used to machine ten-ton diesel engine beds at Mitsubishi's Hiroshima shipyard. Because of the size of the engine beds and the difficulty of exchanging tools, the net operating rate of the planer was below 50 percent.
>
> Analysis revealed that the marking off to center and dimension the engine bed was being done on the planer table while the machine was down, causing a considerable reduction in operating rate. While discussing this with the plant manager, I suddenly had an idea: Why not do the setup operations for the next engine bed on a second planer table? By doing so, we could switch the tables as we shifted from one lot to the next and significantly shorten the interruption in the planing operation.
>
> This improvement increased the productivity of the planing operation by 40 percent.

What we had actually done was to convert an *internal* setup operation to an *external* one. This is a fundamental principle of setup improvement. If I had seen it as such, rather than as a solution to a particular operational problem, the SMED system would have been born 13 years earlier.

> *Example 3.3 — A third encounter with SMED: Converting internal to external setup.* In 1970, I visited the body shop at Toyota Motors' main plant. Management had asked the division manager, Mr. Sugiura, to cut the four-hour setup time on their 1,000-ton Scheoler press by 50 percent. (Apparently, Volkswagen in West Germany was able to change the die on the same press in just two hours.)
>
> I made two suggestions: First, clearly distinguish internal and external setup operations; second, improve operations in both categories. Within six months, setup time had been reduced to one and a half hours.
>
> When I returned several months later, however, Mr. Sugiura told me that management now wanted setup time reduced to three minutes! For a moment I was dumbfounded by their request, but then I remembered the improvement at the Mitsubishi shipyard. Why not convert internal to external setup? A number of ideas followed in rapid succession and I quickly noted eight techniques based on this principle on a conference room blackboard. The new approach allowed us to achieve the three-minute goal within a few months.

Expecting to find that *any* setup could be performed in less than ten minutes, I named my concept "single-minute exchange of die," or SMED. It was later adopted by Toyota Motors as one of the principal elements of the Toyota production system.

Mr. Taiichi Ohno, formerly a vice-president at Toyota Motors and now a consultant, wrote as follows about SMED in an article entitled, "Bringing Wisdom to the Factory."

> Until about ten years ago, production in our firm took place as much as possible during regular working hours. Changing cutters, drills, and so on was done during the noon break or in the evening. We had a policy of replacing the cutters after every fifty items, but as production rose over the past decade, machine operators resented these time-consuming changes. The multigrinder caused one of the worst delays: replacing its abrasive wheels took half a day. Since this task would halt production for the entire morning if performed during working hours, we brought workers in for half a shift on Sundays to do it.
>
> This is an uneconomical and therefore unacceptable way of running a production facility. Maintenance activities had to be carried out during regular working hours. We began, therefore, to look for ways to perform setup changes much more quickly. Shigeo Shingo of the Japan Management Association had been advocating "single-minute setup changes" to increase productivity. We felt this method might be useful in our situation and began to implement it.
>
> In the past, after spending half a day on setup, a machine might end up being used for only ten minutes. There was a tendency to think that production ought to go on for at least as long as the setup. This, however, would have given us far more finished product than we could ever sell.
>
> We are now working to cut setup times to a matter of seconds. Of course, this is easier said than done. Nonetheless, we are determined to further reduce the amount of time needed for setup changes. (*Management*, Japan Management Association, June 1976)

As Mr. Ohno's remarks illustrate, reducing setup time helps improve production as a whole. For this reason, the SMED system has been an essential element in the development of the Toyota production system.

SMED Techniques

Setup time is typically comprised of the following four functions:

- Preparation of material, dies, jigs and fixtures, etc. — 30 percent

- Clamping and removing dies and tools — 5 percent
- Centering and determining dimensions of toolings — 15 percent
- Trial processing and adjustment — 50 percent

The eight principal SMED techniques for reducing setup time in each of these areas are discussed below.

Technique 1 — Separate Internal from External Setup Operations

Clearly identify which of the current setup operations must be performed while the machine is shut down (internal setup or IED) and which can be performed when the machine is running (external setup or OED). For example, all preparation and transportation of dies, jigs, fixtures, tools, and materials to and from the machine can be done while the machine is running. Internal setup should be limited to removing the old die or tool and securing the new one.

By simply separating and organizing external and internal operations, internal setup time (unavoidable machine shutdowns) can be reduced by 30 to 50 percent.

Technique 2 — Convert Internal to External Setup

This is the most powerful principle in the SMED system. Without it, single-minute setup times could not be achieved. Making this conversion involves reexamining operations to see whether any steps have been mistakenly assumed to be internal and finding ways to convert those steps to external setup.

To avoid the internal setup time involved in shut height adjustments, for example, die heights can be standardized by attaching blocks or shims to smaller dies. Another simple conversion is to preheat dies for die-casting, which eliminates heating the die by trial shot.

Technique 3 — Standardize Function, not Shape

Standardizing the shape and size of dies can reduce setup times considerably. Shape standardization is wasteful, however, because all dies would have to conform to the largest size used, which would increase costs unnecessarily.

Function standardization, on the other hand, requires only uniformity in the parts necessary for setup operations. For example, adding a plate or block to the attachment edge of the die standardizes the dimensions of that part only and makes it possible to use the same clamps in different setups.

Technique 4 — Use Functional Clamps or Eliminate Fasteners Altogether

A bolt is the most commonly used clamping device, but securing it can be very time-consuming. For example, a bolt with fifteen threads must be turned fourteen times before it is actually tightened on the last turn. As a practical matter, the last turn tightens the bolt and the first loosens it — the other thirteen are wasted motion. If the purpose of the bolt is simply to fasten or unfasten, it should be just long enough to fasten in one turn. This would make the bolt a functional clamp. One-turn functional clamps include the U-slot method, the pear-shaped hole method, and the external clamp (Figure 28, p. 49).

Threaded screws are by no means the only way to secure items, nor should we assume that a fastener is always necessary. One-touch methods using wedges, cams, and clamps or springs reduce setup times considerably, as do interlocking improvements that simply fit and join two parts together. These methods can reduce setup times to seconds. They are explained in greater detail in my book *A Revolution in Manufacturing: The SMED System* (Cambridge, MA: Productivity Press, 1985).

In clamping methods, the direction and magnitude of force required are critical considerations. Threads can secure in three directions: X (side to side), Y (front and back), and Z (up and down). Since we do not always know the amount or direction of the force required, analysis of these criteria is essential.

At Mitsubishi Heavy Industries, for example, stoppers were screwed to each of the spindles of a boring machine. Setup operations were difficult and time-consuming because the stoppers had to be tightened in extremely cramped conditions. There was no real need, however, for the stoppers to be screwed on in that manner. Although they bore a considerable force from the opposite direction, they were supported by the end of the spindle, and only very little force was needed to remove them.

Once we had reached this understanding, we could improve the operation by removing the threads to make cylindrical fits. We cut grooves near the end of the spindles and attached three springs around the edge of each stopper (Figure 18). When we placed the stopper over the end of the spindle, the springs snapped into the groove, and the spring tension held the stopper in place. This shortened the time for securing and removing stoppers considerably.

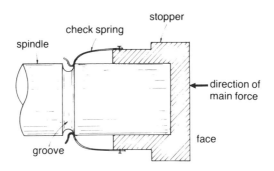

FIGURE 18. **Securing a Stopper**

Technique 5 — Use Intermediate Jigs

Some of the delays due to adjustment during internal setup can be eliminated by using standardized jigs. While the workpiece attached to one jig is being processed, the next workpiece is centered and attached to a second jig. When the first workpiece is finished, the workpiece attached to the second jig is easily mounted on the machine for processing.

For example, a profile milling machine produced form blocks for television picture tubes. Marking off for centering and setting heights for the template and the material was done as internal setup on the bed of the machine. Because of the many curves in the blocks, this was a complicated and time-consuming operation. Two intermediate jigs were constructed that were slightly smaller than the milling table. While one item is machined, a template and the next workpiece are attached to the other jig on the table surface, then centered and set for proper height.

Since the jigs are standardized, centering and positioning take less time, reducing external as well as internal setup time. Clamps are used to mount the jigs quickly and easily on the table.

Intermediate jigs can also be used on large presses with multiple dies of different sizes and heights. In that situation, they are used to move the internal centering and securing operations off the machine. With this improvement, the press needs to be turned off only while a forklift switches the intermediate jigs with the dies already mounted.

Technique 6 — Adopt Parallel Operations

Operations on plastic molding or die-casting machines and large presses invariably involve setup work on both sides or at both the front and back of the machine.

If only one worker performs these operations, much time and motion are wasted as he goes from side to side or back and forth around the machine. But when two people perform the parallel operations simultaneously, setup time is usually reduced by more than half, due to the economies of movement. An operation, for example, that takes one worker 30 minutes to complete may take two workers only ten.

When such parallel operations are employed, setup man-hours are the same as or less than they were with one worker and the operating rate of the machine is increased. The method is often rejected, unfortunately, by managers who think they cannot spare another worker to assist with the setup. When setup is reduced to nine minutes or less, however, three minutes assistance is all that is required; and with these simplified setups, even an unskilled worker can provide the necessary assistance effectively.

Technique 7 — Eliminate Adjustments

Typically, adjustments and trial runs account for 50 to 70 percent of internal setup time. Their elimination produces tremendous time savings.

Eliminating adjustments begins with the recognition that *setting* and *adjustment* are two distinct and separate functions. Setting occurs when the position of a limit switch is changed; adjustment occurs when the limit switch is tested and repeatedly adjusted at a new position. The assumption that adjustment is unavoidable leads to unnecessarily lengthy internal setup times and requires a high level of skill and experience on the part of the operator. Adjustments can be eliminated, however, if a gauge is used to precisely determine the correct position of the limit switch. Then, setting will be the only operation required.

Adjustment is progressively less of a factor as setting becomes more accurate. The first step in doing away with it is to make calibrations which eliminate the need to rely on intuition. If an approximation is all that is required, a graduated scale may be sufficient, but it cannot do away with adjustments altogether. Greater precision is achieved using a dial gauge, magnescale, or numerical control device.

At Togo Manufacturing, a dimension-setting stopper was moved by means of a threaded spindle. Whenever the stopper setting was changed from 50mm to 60mm, the spindle had to be turned through all the increments in between. But what was the point of all this turning if the stopper was never set at any other positions but 50mm and 60mm? Why couldn't it be moved directly from one position to the other? To eliminate the wasted turning, the threads on the spindle were removed and a U-type gauge was installed underneath so the stopper could slide up to the gauge and be secured with a set screw. This made the resetting of the stopper a quick and easy task.

This example highlights a frequent obstacle to eliminating adjustment: We use devices that permit unlimited and continuous settings, when what we really need are limited or stepped settings.

Of course, the best kind of adjustment is no adjustment at all. For example, the "least common multiple" (LCM) system is based on the principle that adjustment can be eliminated entirely when the number of settings is limited and unvarying.

In one plant, a limit switch was used to set the end point in machining shafts. Since there were five shaft lengths, the switch had to be moved to five different locations. It could not be positioned correctly without as many as four trial adjustments every time the setup changed. By installing limit switches at the five sites, each equipped with an electrical switch that is supplied with current independently of the other switches, this problem was eliminated (Figure 19). Now, setup is performed by flipping a switch.

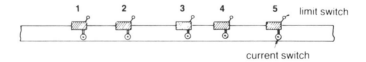

FIGURE 19. **Changing Limit Switches**

A second example of the LCM approach is illustrated in Figure 20. In this operation, a drill was used to countersink a hole for a stationary screw in a motor core shaft. Stoppers had to be repositioned for eight different lengths which made repeated test runs and adjustments necessary. The adjustments were eliminated by mounting stopper plugs of eight different heights on a single plate. To change operations, the plate is simply rotated to set the stopper at the desired height and then secured. This one-touch method reduced internal setup to a matter of seconds.

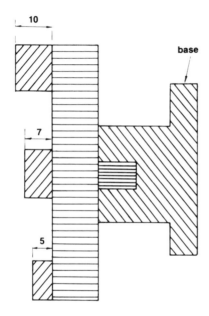

FIGURE 20. A Rotary Stopper

The LCM approach as well as the one-touch and interlocking methods simplify setting or positioning and eliminate adjustment. This latter objective must be kept in mind if we are to avoid missing the obvious. For example, some presses are sold with adjustable shut heights because different companies have different requirements. This does not mean, however, that any one of them actually operates with dies of varying shut heights. These companies should either standardize die heights or purchase presses customized for their needs. The same faulty logic is evident when expensive presses are equipped with motorized adjustable shut height and highly accurate adjustment functions. Why invest in such functions when it is much more economical to eliminate adjustments through standardization?

Technique 8 — Mechanization

Although changing small blades, jigs, dies, and gauges does not pose much of a problem, mechanization is often essential to efficiently move large dies, casting dies, and plastic molds. Oil and air pressure can be used for convenient one-touch attachment of dies. And, of course, the motorized shut height adjustment mentioned earlier is also helpful.

Investment in mechanization should, however, be considered very carefully. Recently, many companies have standardized the dimension of clamping plates and finished them to a high degree of precision. One-touch clamping is then performed by inserting these plates into special clamping fixtures. However, only the die actually forms the product. Considering the purpose of the operation, it is wasteful to finish clamping plates to a high degree of precision.

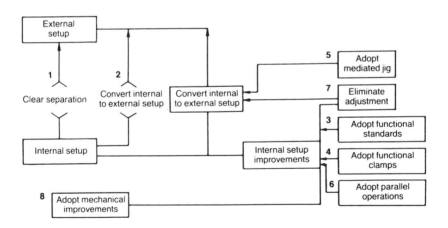

FIGURE 21. Flow Chart for Applying the Eight SMED Techniques

Mechanization should be considered only after every effort has been made to improve setups using the techniques described. The first seven principles can reduce a two-hour setup to three minutes, and mechanization will probably reduce that time only by another minute.

SMED is an analytical approach to setup improvement of which mechanization is only one component. Attacking such improvement with mechanization may reduce setup time initially but will not remedy the basic inefficiencies of a poorly designed setup process. It is far better to mechanize setups after they have first been thoroughly streamlined by applying the SMED principles.

Four Conceptual Stages of SMED

SMED takes a progressive approach to setup improvement. In doing so, it passes through four basic stages. Each is discussed below.

Stage One

In this preliminary stage, no distinction is made between internal and external setup. Many actions that could be performed as external setup, such as searching for tools or repairing the die, are instead executed while the machine is down. This lengthens the setup period unnecessarily.

Stage Two

This is the most crucial stage in the implementation of SMED. It involves the separation of internal and external setup operations. Make a checklist that includes all the parts, operating conditions, and steps that need to be taken while the machine is running. Then check functioning of all parts to avoid delays during internal setup. Finally, research and implement the most efficient method for transporting dies and other parts while the machine is running.

Stage Three

Analyze the current setup operation to determine whether any of the activities conducted as internal setup can be converted to external setup. For example, preheating a casting die while the machine is still running eliminates the need for preheating with trial shots of molten metal during internal setup.

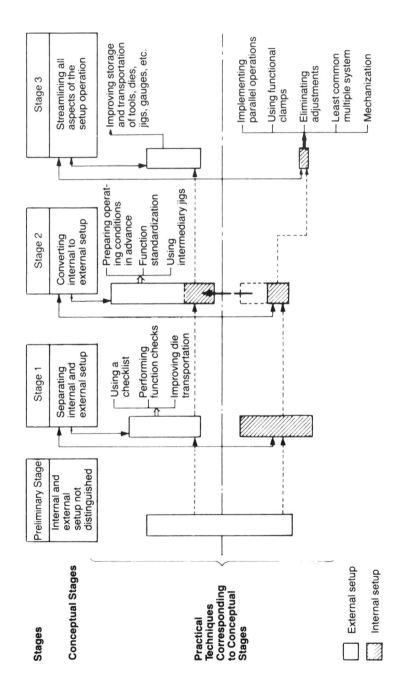

FIGURE 22. The Single-Minute Setup (SMED): Conceptual Stages and Practical Techniques

Stage Four

Examine both internal and external setup operations for additional opportunities for improvement. Consider eliminating adjustments and streamlining clamping methods.

Out of several hundred SMED improvements achieved over the years, the following proved most effective:

- Clear separation of internal and external setup
- Thorough conversion of internal to external setup
- Elimination of adjustments
- Clamping without screws

These methods can reduce setups to less than one-twentieth of their previous times. In fact, changes can sometimes be completed in seconds by eliminating adjustments and using the least common multiple system described earlier. *The quickest way to change a tool is not to change it at all.* In the five limit switch example, page 52, only the machine function was changed — from switch to switch, without mechanical or manual adjustment. To make SMED a reality in the workplace, simply demonstrate its basic methods to workers and let them start a SMED revolution.

IMPROVING PRINCIPAL OPERATIONS

As noted earlier in this chapter, principal operations consist of essential and incidental operations.

To improve essential operations means to advance production technology, that is, to change machining or forming techniques used or automate the operation. To improve incidental operations is to simplify or automate the loading and unloading of parts or material from the machine. Toyota Motors has improved principal operations by separating workers from machines wherever possible through the techniques of multi-machine handling and pre-automation.

Separating Worker from Machine

Modern industries have prospered by gradually transferring the work that was done by humans to tools and machines. Machinery drives the tools once guided by workers' hands, and electrical or other power sources now replace the power of the human body. Throughout this evolution, however, machine reliability remained low, requiring workers to closely tend their machines. Human judgment was required to identify and correct machine problems.

In Japan, the separation of worker from machine began in the mid-1920s. At that time, parts were typically mounted and turned on machines but machined manually with cutting tools. As mechanization increased, cutting tools were applied automatically, which transferred the functions and power of human hands to machines to a considerable degree.

Over time, the reliability of machines increased, and fully automated mechanisms can now detect and correct problems in their own operation. But workers continue to stand watch by the machines because this practice, like other old habits, is not an easy one to give up.

At Toyota Motors, however, worker and machine have been separated as much as possible to promote production efficiency as well as effective and meaningful use of human resources. Since the late 40s, Toyota workers have not been tied to a single machine but are responsible for five or more, feeding one while the others work automatically.

These multi-machine handling operations are supported by two important principles. First, while depreciation eventually results in "free" machine use, workers must be paid indefinitely. Thus, from the standpoint of cost reduction, idle machines are preferable to idle workers. Second, cost reduction is more important than high machine operating rates.

DEVELOPMENT OF PRE-AUTOMATION OR AUTONOMATION

Further evolution of these ideas led to the adoption of pre-automation, what I called autonomation in the Toyota production system, or "automation with a human touch." It completely separates workers from machines through the use of sophisticated mechanisms to detect production abnormalities. Many of the machines used by Toyota are equipped with this capacity.

There are said to be twenty-three stages between purely manual work and full automation. Up to the twentieth, however, hand work has simply been mechanized. To be fully automated, a machine must be able to detect and correct its own operating problems. It is technically and economically feasible to build equipment that *detects* problems (pre-automation), but to also have it *correct* them would be both very expensive and technically difficult and therefore not cost-effective. Ninety percent of the results of full automation (the first twenty stages) can be achieved at relatively low cost if machines are designed to merely detect problems, leaving the correction of problems to the workers.

Thus, pre-automation or autonomation is the stage before full automation. In terms of necessary steps, it can be divided as follow:

Mechanizing Hand Work	Mechanizing Brain Work
1. Automate essential operations	
2. Automate auxiliary operations	5. Automate trouble
3. Automate job allowances	detection
4. Automate workshop allowances	

6. Worker selects an appropriate solution and executes it

Example 3.4 — Pre-automation. At Matsushita Electric, five sets of 500-ton presses were equipped with pre-automation devices with the result that 43 percent of total production could be accomplished without workers in attendance. They applied the following methods:

- Production of product A continues through the lunch period with machines that require no attendance.
- Product B is made from hoop stock. By the end of the workday, 80 percent of a roll of material has been used. At that time, a SMED changeover is done to produce product C, which requires much less material and can be produced during the evening hours from a single coil of material without a worker present.
- Next morning, the die for product C is replaced with that for B to continue producing from the remaining 20 percent of coiled material.

This arrangement involved the installation of a large-scale product storage unit at a cost of 6 million yen for all five presses. New equipment to attain the same level of production, however, would have cost ten times as much and required five additional operators.

This is how Matsushita takes advantage of both the SMED system and pre-automation. The cost of products produced with pre-automation is half of what it was with conventional production methods.

With its concept of autonomation, the Toyota production system, too, advocates the use of mechanical devices to detect abnormalities. The idea, however, is not necessarily integrated into a comprehensive system.

IMPROVING MARGIN ALLOWANCES

Even when main operations, such as fixing, machining, and removing products, have been automated, many time-consuming indirect operations, such as removing chips, feeding materials, and stocking products, are still done by hand. Allowances for marginal activities that are related to a specific job or work area should be examined carefully for improvement opportunities. Automation could be applied in many of them. Here are a few examples:

- Lubrication — Consider automatic lubrication, use of oil-impregnated metals, etc.
- Cutting oil — Consider automatic oiling or cutting without oil
- Chip removal — Consider powdering chips or automatic lubrication and chip removal

Workshop allowances, which consist of indirect work common to a number of different operations, can also be streamlined. For example, consider the following:

- Automatic feeding for materials, especially when dealing with large quantities
- Automatic product storage, especially automatic replacement of pallets to store large quantities of products

Keep in mind that little is accomplished by automating main operations if marginal activities are still performed manually.

In the area of *personal allowances*, higher labor productivity is achieved by improving work methods and increasing worker motivation and involvement. No matter what the level of automation, people will always be an essential and vital part of production.

Summary

By adopting the SMED system, Toyota achieved dramatic reductions in setup time. Adding multi-machine handling and autonomation further increased productivity.

4

Conclusions on Developing Non-Stock Production

The principal feature of the Toyota production system is its emphasis on stockless, or non-stock, production. To comprehend the system, it is first necessary to understand the meaning of "stock."

In the past, stocks or inventory have been considered a "necessary evil," with the emphasis on "necessary" and the "evil" thought to be inevitable and perhaps even useful. There are two types of stock: that which occurs naturally as the result of certain production practices, and "necessary" stock. Both are discussed below.

Naturally Occurring Stock

Stock may accumulate because of:

- Incorrect market demand forecasts
- Overproduction just to be on the safe side
- Lot production
- Differences in shiftwork; for example, performing annealing in three shifts and finishing in one shift

"Necessary" Stock

Stocks may build up because of inefficiencies in both process and operations. Inefficient *process* results in three types of stock build-up:

- Stock created by advance production undertaken when production cycles are longer than order cycles ($P > D$)
- Stock produced in advance in anticipation of demand fluctuations

- Stock produced to compensate for poor production management and the delays caused by inspection and transport

Inefficient *operation* results in two types of stock buildup:

- Stock to compensate for machine breakdowns or defective products
- Stock generated when operations are carried out in large lots to compensate for long setup times

The word "necessary" in the concept "necessary evil" referring to stock has come to mean "for safety's sake." This interpretation has caused managers to hold quantities of safety stock.

But both naturally occurring and so-called necessary stocks are wasteful, unprofitable phenomena that should be studied carefully and eliminated completely. Stock reduction should not become an end in itself, however, since cutting stock blindly may cause delivery delays or a drop in machine operating rates. Rather, the conditions that produce or necessitate stock must be corrected so that stock can be reduced in a rational fashion. There are three strategies that must be pursued to approach the ideal of non-stock production:

- Reduce the production cycle dramatically
- Eliminate breakdowns and defects by detecting and responding to their causes
- Reduce setup times to single minutes or even seconds by adopting SMED which makes small lot production and rapid response to demand fluctuations possible.

Part II

A Study of the
Toyota Production System
from an Industrial Engineering
Viewpoint

5

The Principles of the
Toyota Production System

WHAT IS THE TOYOTA PRODUCTION SYSTEM?

When asked this question, most people (80 percent) will echo the view of the average consumer and say: "It's a kanban system"; another 15 percent may actually know how it functions in the factory and say: "It's a production system"; only a very few (5 percent) really understand its purpose and say: "It's a system for the absolute elimination of waste."

Some people imagine that Toyota has put on a smart new set of clothes, the kanban system, so they go out and purchase the same outfit and try it on. They quickly discover that they are much too fat to wear it! They must eliminate waste and make fundamental improvements in their production system before techniques like kanban can be of any help. The Toyota production system is 80 percent waste elimination, 15 percent production system and only 5 percent kanban.

This confusion stems from a misunderstanding of the relationship between basic principles of production at Toyota and kanban *as a technique* to help implement those principles. In the preface of his book, *The Toyota Production System* (Cambridge, MA: Productivity Press, 1987), Taiichi Ohno makes this distinction clear. Kanban, he says, is simply a means of achieving just-in-time. The confusion arose because the term "rules of kanban" had been used to refer to principles of production as well as to kanban. For example, one important kanban rule requires that all materials and products be accompanied by a kanban card; another emphasizes that defective products should not be passed along to succeeding processes. This latter rule, however, is not properly a function of kanban — rather, it is one of the basic principles of the Toyota production system.

67

This distinction becomes more obvious when we consider it in terms of the three functions of management:

- Planning — establishes the system and objectives, e.g., plant layout, process lines, and standard operations, etc.
- Control — ensures correct execution of the plan
- Inspection — compares execution to plan so that one or the other can be corrected or adjusted if necessary

The above cycle of organization, control (including execution), and inspection moves forward like the steps on a stairway (Figure 23). The Toyota production system is the planning function; kanban is a control function.

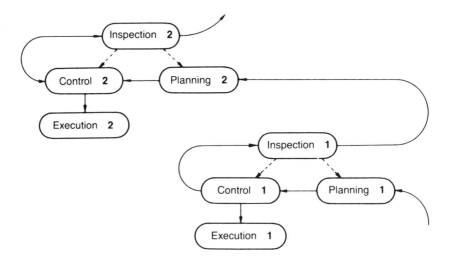

FIGURE 23. Flow of Planning, Control, and Inspection Functions

BASIC PRINCIPLES

Much has been written about the Toyota production system in "dialect"; that is, terms particular to the system are used without explanation, as if they were generally understood. This has caused some confusion and misunderstandings. To avoid similar problems in this book, I will explain some basic principles and terms.

Waste of Overproduction

There are two types of overproduction:

* *Quantitative* — making *more* product than is needed
* *Early* — making product *before* it is needed

For example, a product is made for export with a very short lead time before shipment. To prevent shortages due to defects, the company produces 100 pieces more than the 5,000 ordered. When only a few defects occur, the remaining extra pieces must be discarded. This is *quantitative overproduction*.

On the other hand, if 5,000 pieces are ordered for delivery on December 20 but produced by December 15, that is *early overproduction*.

Many managers are concerned only about preventing quantitative overproduction — they don't care that 20 days' worth of inventory is being held and managed, as long as products are produced to order. At Toyota Motors, early overproduction is not tolerated. The method used to eliminate it is just-in-time production.

Just-In-Time

In Japanese, the words for "just-in-time" mean "timely," "well-timed," or "just *on* time," exactly at the appointed time. The term connotes much more than *timeliness*, however, because concentrating on delivery time alone might encourage early overproduction and so result in unnecessary delay. But Toyota's production system is also *non-stock* or stockless. This means that each process must be supplied with the *required items* in the *required quantity* and at the *required time* — just-*on*-time, with no accumulation.

Separation of Worker from Machine

The progressive change in the relationship between worker and machine is an important feature of the Toyota production system. As mentioned in Chapter 3, worker and machine have been separated to increase production efficiency as well as promote effective, more meaningful use of human resources. This separation began as machines gradually replaced the power and work of human hands. Table 3 illustrates the progressive transfer from handwork to automation. The transformation involves the six stages discussed below.

Stage 1 — Handwork. Workers shape and finish articles by hand, without any assistance from machines.

Stage 2 — Manual feeding with automated machining. Workers attach and remove products from machines and feed the tools by hand. Only the machining is performed by machines.

Stage 3 — Automated feeding and machining. Workers attach and remove products from the machines and start the machines. Machines perform tool feeding and machining. Workers detect abnormal conditions and correct them. (This last function is also carried out in the first two stages.)

Stage 4 — Semi-automatic. Automated attachment and removal of products; automated feeding and machining. The only work carried out by workers is the detecting and correcting of abnormal conditions.

Stage 5 — Pre-automation. All functions, including the detection of defects, are performed by the machine; workers merely correct the defects.

Stage 6 — Automation. Entirely automatic processing, trouble detection, and correction.

Toyota progressed through these six stages in gradually converting manual to machine operations. Even so, it was a very difficult decision to fully separate workers from machines. Even at stage 3 (automated feeding and machining), workers were expected to stay with their machines, to supervise or observe, watching for and correcting abnormalities.

The textile industry was the first to use pre-automation to completely separate worker from machine. Before coming to Toyota Motors, Mr. Ohno worked at Minsei Textile Company (now Toyoda Autoloom Company) with the automatic looms invented by Sakichi Toyoda. There, he observed machines stop automatically and send out a signal when they detected an abnormal condition.

Type / Stage	Hand Functions				Mental Functions			
	Principal Operations				Marginal Allowances			
	Main Operations		Incidental Operations		(Usual Method)		(Toyota Method)	
	Cutting	Feeding	Installation/ Removal	Switch Operation	Detecting Abnormalities	Disposition of Abnormalities	Detecting Abnormalities	Disposition of Abnormalities
1 Manual operation	worker	worker	worker	worker	worker	worker	worker	worker
2 Manual feed, automatic cutting	machine	worker	worker	worker	worker	worker	worker	worker
3 Automatic feed, automatic cutting	machine		worker	worker	worker	worker	Machine that stops automatically (worker oversees more than one machine)	worker
4 Semiautomation	machine		machine	machine	worker	worker	Machine (worker oversees more than one machine)	worker
5 Preautomation (automation with a human touch)	machine		machine	machine	machine	worker	Machine (automation with a human touch)	worker
6 True automation	machine		machine	machine	machine	machine	machine	machine

TABLE 3. Separation of Worker from Machine

At Toyota, he equipped machines with automatic stops so that an operator could move between machines, attaching and detaching products and starting the machines. This permitted multi-machine handling. The ability to detect abnormalities was later also built into the machines.

Generally, this function is added at stage 5, after all mechanical work has been automated. At Toyota, however, automatic stops and trouble-detecting functions were incorporated at a much earlier stage. This facilitated the separation of worker from machine, a concept that is very well developed in the Toyota production system and an essential component of it.

Low Utilization Rates

The machine-output ratio at Toyota Motors is two to three times that of similar companies. Indeed, for the same level of production, Toyota has far more equipment than most other companies and this is one of its strengths.

This is what a cursory examination of the statistics tells us; however, it represents a superficial understanding of the situation. Why? Many people estimate the average capacity-utilization or operating rate to be about 40 percent. At that level, Toyota's actual machine-output ratio ends up being either the same as, or somewhat better than, that of other companies.

Multi-machine Handling and Low Operating Rates

This lower operating rate is the natural result of the separation of worker from machines in multi-machine handling operations. In 1955, 700 workers were handling 3,500 machines for an average of five machines per worker. In this type of situation, one machine may finish cycling while the worker tends to another and the operating rate decreases.

If the number of machines per worker were reduced, the operating rate would go back up; but workers might then have to wait for machines to finish.* In sum, at Toyota lower machine operating ratios are preferred to idle time for operators.

---

* Waiting (by workers) is one of the seven cardinal wastes at Toyota and is eliminated wherever it is found, pp. 191-194.

There are two reasons for this: First, once machines and equipment have been depreciated, they are essentially cost free. Second, operator cost per hour is generally much greater than machine cost; from the standpoint of cost reduction, an idle machine is preferable to an idle worker.

For example, a $60,000 press is fully depreciated in ten years at a rate of $6,000 per year, or $500 per month. The cost of a worker, on the other hand, including wages, benefits and indirect costs, is three to five times that over a period of ten years. Machines *seem* more expensive because of their high purchase price; in most cases, however, the cost of a worker is much higher. Multi-machine handling at Toyota has resulted in their productivity per worker being 20 to 30 percent higher than that of other companies.

Equipment Planning and Low Operating Rates

What does all this mean in terms of equipment planning? First, if low operating ratios can be anticipated, less expensive, lower capacity equipment can be purchased up front. Furthermore, a company can:

- Design and produce its own machines
- Design machines for others to produce
- Improve low-cost machines from outside sources to suit company needs

There are thousands of machines at Toyota, and each one has been improved to suit the specific needs of the company. Expensive, special-purpose equipment or robotics made outside the company are not considered a good investment.

"Sunk cost" is an expression used at Toyota in the context of equipment investment. Their thinking is that equipment should be depreciated as soon as it is purchased, regardless of whether or not it is being used. It is always more profitable to use machines that produce at low cost, and equipment that actually increases costs should be taken out of service no matter how expensive it was to purchase. New equipment should be purchased only after all the reasons for its acquisition have been studied carefully. Once a purchase has been made, the cost of the machine is "sunk" and management must conduct experiments to find ways to keep production costs low.

The large number of machines has a second benefit: Production can be increased quickly during peak demand periods by simply hiring temporary workers. Since the machines have typically been improved for easy handling, temporary workers can work independently after only a brief training period.

Perform an Appendectomy

At Toyota, machines are equipped to detect production problems and shut down immediately when one occurs, indicating what type of problem it is on an indicator lamp. Also, workers are allowed to stop the production line when they notice a problem. When the line is stopped, an *andon* (indicator panel) lights up informing everyone in the area of the type of problem and where it has occurred.

The andon is a visual control that communicates important information and signals the need for immediate action by supervisors. There are some managers who believe that a variety of production problems can be overcome by implementing Toyota's visual control system. At Toyota, however, the most important issue is not how quickly personnel are alerted to a problem, but what solutions are implemented. Makeshift or temporary measures, although they may restore the operation to normal most quickly, are not appropriate. Nor is the best response, when defects occur, to work overtime to produce the scheduled number of good units. These solutions are like using an ice pack to cure appendicitis — it may relieve the pain for a while, but only an appendectomy will prevent a recurrence. This is Toyota's approach — to discover and implement solutions that permanently prevent a problem from recurring.

Once, parts delivery from a supplier was delayed and a line stopped for two hours. The parts acceptance chief apologized for the delay, but the plant manager would not accept his apology since the parts acceptance department was in no position to prevent the problem. This story illustrates an important point: If you want to prevent the recurrence of a problem, you must first identify and acknowledge its root cause. If the problem here lay with the method of communicating orders to suppliers, the procurement chief should explain the delay and develop a plan to prevent recurrences. If the supplier caused the delay, the responsible party at that plant should explain and rectify the problem.

Toyota's visual control system can facilitate this problem-solving process, but only an understanding of this principle can make it successful. At Toyota, there is only one reason to stop the line — to ensure that it won't have to stop again.

FUNDAMENTALS OF PRODUCTION CONTROL

Adopting a Non-Cost Principle

Many companies determine the price of their products by using this basic cost principle:

$$\text{Cost} + \text{Profit} = \text{Selling Price}$$

Using this formula, when the cost of oil goes up, for example, the product selling price is raised to reflect the higher energy costs and maintain the desired level of profit. Similarly, if the price of iron ore goes up, the price of steel must go up to reflect the higher cost of raw materials. Even the government finds it easy to raise prices in response to increased costs. Some even argue that the profit added should be large enough to cover potential losses if the product does not sell. Toyota accepts neither this formula nor these arguments. Since the market (the consumer) always determines the appropriate selling price, Toyota uses a "non-cost" principle instead:

$$\text{Selling Price} - \text{Cost} = \text{Profit}$$

Applying this formula, since consumers decide the selling price, profit is what remains after subtracting the cost from it. The only way to increase profit, then, is to reduce costs. Consequently, cost reduction activity should have the highest priority. Adoption of the non-cost principle and the elimination of waste have permitted Toyota to often take the lead in reducing the selling prices of its cars over the past 35 years.

Any company can make an effort to eliminate waste, but as long as it operates by adding profits to cost to determine price, its efforts are likely to be superficial. Only when cost reduction becomes the means for maintaining or increasing profits will a company be motivated to eliminate waste thoroughly.

Similarly, if people decided how much it should cost to run the government machinery, many "necessary" expenditures could not be justified and real waste elimination would occur. Wouldn't it serve the public interest if the government operated on this principle?

Elimination of Waste

The Toyota production system is said to be so powerful that it could squeeze water from a dry towel. This is actually a good description. For example, to dry powder, we must not only remove the moisture on its surface; we must also eliminate the invisible moisture crystallized within. Similarly, at Toyota, we search for the waste that usually escapes notice because it has become accepted as a natural part of everyday work.

The movements of operators can be classified as operation and waste. *Waste* is any activity that does not contribute to operations, such as waiting, accumulating semi-processed parts, reloading, passing materials from one hand to the other, and the like.

There are two types of *operation*: those that add value and those that do not. Operations that do not add value, such as walking to get parts, unpacking supplied parts, and operating switches, may be considered waste. Without work improvements, however, they cannot be eliminated entirely.

Value-adding operations actually transform materials, changing either form or quality. These transforming activities are the *processing* discussed in Part 1. They turn raw materials into parts or products and increase their value through activities like assembling parts, forging raw materials, stamping steel plates, welding, heat-treating gears, or painting the body. The greater the value added, the higher the operating efficiency.

At the production site, of course, other non-value adding activities, such as those caused by poor equipment maintenance and repair and rework, reduce the net operating efficiency. Observation tells us that the percentage of work actually adding value to a product is lower than expected. This means that workers must change movement into work. *Work* advances a process and adds value while merely *moving* quickly and efficiently may not accomplish anything.

Man-hours must be reduced if the net operating ratio is to be increased and, at Toyota, the ideal is to achieve a 100 percent operating ratio. Table 4 lists waste elimination improvement activities at Toyota between 1976 and 1980 as reflected in suggestions submitted and adopted during that period. Table 5 illustrates the impact of these activities by comparing Toyota's assembling man-hours per car to those of American, Swedish, and West German automobile manufacturers.

Year	Total Number of Suggestions	Number of Suggestions per Person	Adoption Ratio
1976	463,000	10.6	83%
1977	454,000	10.3	86%
1978	527,000	11.9	88%
1979	575,000	12.8	91%
1980	860,000	18.7	94%

TABLE 4. Number of Improvements Suggested at Toyota Motors

		Toyota Takaoka Plant	Plant A (America)	Plant B (Sweden)	Plant C (West Germany)
1	Number of employees	4,300	3,800	4,700	9,200
2	Number of cars produced (daily)	2,700	1,000	1,000	3,400
3	Time per car (number of people)	1.6	3.8	4.7	2.7
4	Ratio	1.0	2.4	2.9	1.7

TABLE 5. Assembly Time per Vehicle by Country *

*From the thesis of M. Sugimori

Eliminating Waste through Fundamental Process Improvements

As discussed in Part I, process consists of four components: processing, inspection, transport, and delay operations. Of these, only processing adds value; the others can be viewed as waste. In the past, the typical approach to process improvement was to "improve the waste." Instead, fundamental improvements must be made because they eliminate the waste itself and thus the need to "improve" it.

Consider the following examples of this methodology applied to inspection, transport and delay.

Inspection improvement. Without inspection, defects will cause problems, so we adopted sampling inspection. However, fundamental improvement through preventive inspection eliminates the inspection operation altogether. Poka-yoke devices eliminate defects and reduce inspection man-hours to zero.

Transport improvement. Forklifts improve transport of product through time and labor savings. Fundamental improvement in plant layout, however, eliminates the need for transport altogether.

Delay improvement. As long as cushion stocks are used to keep the operation running smoothly, new methods will be generated to improve the flow of items to and from the warehouse and to control inventory. Automatic warehousing techniques and computer-driven inventory control programs are very popular. Synchronizing each process, however, eliminates process delays (storage between processes); and implementing one-piece flows eliminates lot delays (storage for lot size).

In addition, assigning to machines the function of detecting trouble and providing them with the ability to shut down automatically minimizes problems and helps prevent their recurrence. It also reduces the need for cushion stocks. Finally, achieving zero defects eliminates the need for buffers altogether.

Unfortunately, positive permanent solutions like these are often not even considered.

Eliminating Waste Through Fundamental Operations Improvement

Taking a look at operations in the same way reveals that only essential operations add value. Others, such as die changes, auxiliary operations, and margin allowances can all be viewed as waste. Operational improvement, therefore, is also a form of "waste improvement." Consider the examples that follow.

Setup improvement. Die changes are essential but very time-consuming. Lot size is often increased to offset man-hours spent in changeover. By comparison, adoption of the SMED and OTED systems reduces changeover times dramatically and eliminates the economies of large lots.

Auxiliary improvement in operations. Because their attachment and removal is troublesome, products are aligned in one direction in a magazine and attached and fed into the machine automatically. By adopting a one-piece flow in the prior process, however, products can be removed automatically and transferred in one direction to the succeeding process. With such an arrangement, individual products can be attached automatically for processing.

Similarly, one-touch switch operation reduces operating time. If, however, equipment is modified to start machining automatically as soon as the product is attached, the manual labor of switching is eliminated.

Job allowance improvement. Automation is used to improve the application of cutting and lubricating oil and chip removal. Fundamental improvement, however, in the form of oil-less bearings and machining, might eliminate the need for lubricating and cutting oils altogether. Furthermore, an oil mist cools tool blades ten times more effectively than other methods, eliminates false cutting edges, removes chips to extend blade life by 30 to 60 percent, and reduces lubricant consumption by 90 percent.

Chips and scraps are eliminated when more precise forging and casting methods are used. A second-best solution is forced removal of chips away from the machine to make their disposal easier.

Workshop allowance improvement. Typically, product feeding and storage operations are improved by using continuous materials and large volume pallets for products. Automatic changeover mechanisms, however, may effect fundamental improvement. Such devices bring new coils or batches of material into position for continuous feeding or supply fresh pallets, for example, eliminating the need for workers to perform these tasks. Furthermore, connecting successive processes eliminates process delays, minimizes unfinished parts inventories, and eliminates the need for special storage equipment.

These are all examples of positive, permanent — *fundamental* — improvement, but when someone suggests that they implement them, many people respond by saying: "Our methods may not add value, but without them, the work would not go forward, so we have no choice. They are evils — but necessary evils." Unfortunately, as time goes by, the "evil" is forgotten and only the "necessary" remains. This is why so much waste remains hidden in process and operation.

The ability to eliminate waste in production is developed by giving up the belief that there is "no other way" to perform a given task. It is useless to say, "It has to be done this way," or "This can't be helped!"

At Toyota, we have found that there is *always* another way. We look for the waste that people take for granted or don't consider a problem. When we discover a wasteful practice, we don't say, "This can't be helped." Instead, we say, "This doesn't add value, so we'll have to change it — but we'll tolerate it until we can find a way to eliminate the waste completely."

A positive attitude is absolutely essential to waste elimination. As long as we affirm the present condition by saying there is no other way, we will miss opportunities for improvement. We cannot find and eliminate waste if we are not looking for it.

> *Example 5.1 — One-touch press switches.* OSHA regulations demand that operators be protected from potentially harmful contact with machinery through lock-out devices unless machines are equipped to shut down automatically when any part of the operator's body enters the danger zone.
>
> For the sake of safety then, press operation requires that switches be pushed continuously with both hands to ensure that both hands are out of the danger zone. If one hand is removed, the machine stops automatically. Most people say, "If it's a safety regulation, it can't be helped." However, it is a wasteful practice that slows the work considerably. How can both safety and productivity be served?
>
> Figure 24 shows how multi-machine handling or multi-process handling is performed at Toyota. A one-touch switch for the first press is placed near the second, the switch for the second press is placed near the third, and so on. When the operator starts the press, she is already safely outside the danger zone for that machine. This improvement alone doubled productivity! (It does not, however, protect a third person from accidentally entering the danger zone, so additional protective measures must be taken.) But think how much we can accomplish when we stop thinking that "something can't be helped."
>
> *Example 5.2 — Eliminating the waste of oiled scrap.* At T Industry, coiled material was used with progressive dies on the press. I asked the plant manager why the material was oiled with a felt roller. He told me that oil

was necessary when extruding the material. Then I asked, "Why do you oil the scrap?" After some reflection he replied, "The roller covers the entire surface of the material, so it can't be helped."

I told him that the words "it can't be helped" were the real problem. Once we acknowledge that oiling scrap is wasteful, we are ready to consider another oiling method. Some time later, the oiling method was changed. Spraying oil mist on the upper and lower part of the press die has eliminated oiled scrap.

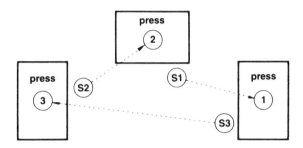

FIGURE 24. Remote Control of Press

This is a simple example of a powerful principle: Search actively for waste!

Example 5.3 — One-touch start up for several machines. At Taiho Industry, one worker performed a multi-process handling operation with fourteen cutting machines and had to manually start the machines at each process. To improve this procedure, a one-touch button for machines 1 through 7 was installed near the eighth machine so all seven machines could be started at once; another button for machines 8 through 14 was installed near the first machine so all those machines could also be started at once.

This improvement reduced the cycle time from 35 to 4.2 seconds. They had thought that there was "no other way" but to start each machine separately. This wasteful procedure could not be improved upon until they realized that the timing for each machine to run and finish its process was not important as long as all of them finished before the next cycle.

Improving Processing and Essential Operations

As noted earlier, only those aspects of process that transform material or improve quality, the essential operations that actually produce the changes in form and quality, i.e., machining, etc., add value to a product. Inspection, delay, transport and other operations within processing (setup, auxiliary and margin allowance operations) only increase costs and should be eliminated.

Processing itself and essential operations, however, should be examined carefully for possible improvements. Are there better ways to increase the added value of products from the viewpoint of value engineering (VE) and value analysis (VA)? To help answer this question, we must reexamine the materials, methods, and products themselves. Vacuum molding to prevent flashing and reduce defects is an example of improving the processing method.

Ask the "Five W's and One H" and "Why?" Five Times

A key activity emphasized at Toyota is finding the true causes of problems or waste. We ask "Why?" again and again until the answer is found. Traditionally, "5W 1H" means:

- Who — subject of production
- What — objects of production
- When — time
- Where — space
- Why — to find the cause for each of the above because they are all important factors in unravelling a problem
- How — methods

At Toyota, the five W's really mean *five Whys* — asking "Why?" five or more times until the cause of a problem is discovered. For every factor — what, who, where, when, and how — we ask "Why, why, why, why, why?" Asking once is never enough. By asking "Why?" five times, *how* we should solve the problem is also clarified.

The pursuit of improvement is carried out along three axes:

1. The X axis — focuses on the goals of improvement
2. The Y axis — recognizes multiple goals
3. The Z axis — pursues goals systematically, working gradually toward underlying or fundamental goals

Asking "Why?" five times prevents us from ending our investigation before we reach the root cause of the problem, the fundamental goal of improvement. If we don't conduct our search diligently and systematically, if we don't keep asking "Why?" we may settle for an intermediate measure that does not really eliminate the problem.

Mass Production and Large Lot Production

Taiichi Ohno's book, *The Toyota Production System*, is subtitled *Beyond Large-Scale Production*, but what he means by this is not explained in the book. Although this title seems to argue for a more appropriate *scale* of production management, Ohno's position is that the Toyota production system is the antithesis of American mass production. In the preface he states:

> The Toyota production system evolved out of need. Certain restrictions in the marketplace required the production of small quantities of many varieties [of products] under conditions of low demand, a fate the Japanese automobile industry faced in the postwar period.

American markets, on the other hand, seemed to require mass production of fewer types of products. The production and management system developed at Toyota was the result of trial and error efforts to compete with the mass production already established in the American and European automobile industries.

But is the distinction between these two approaches as simple as that? The goal of American mass production is to lower both per-unit labor costs and overall costs by lightening the burden of depreciation. In turn, low selling prices stimulate demand, creating a favorable cycle of mass production and mass sales.

From this standpoint mass production is highly advantageous, particularly for specialized machinery and dies. For example, Volkswagen derived great benefit from producing the famous "Beetle" over a long period of time with little variation. Similarly, Toyota Motors produced more of its Corollas than any other car manufacturer did of a single model and realized substantial profits.

The potential for mass production (large quantity production), however, is a characteristic of the market and is not always an option an enterprise can choose. Although it has sometimes been referred to as "anticipatory" or "planned" production, it is actually only speculative in nature. Of course, production schedules are based upon past sales and market research, but actual demand often turns out to be quite different from projections.

In sum, the enterprise may not be free to choose between small, medium, or mass production because it does not control market demand. It can, however, choose between small or large lot production.

Large lot and mass production are really two different dimensions. Small lot production is preferred (even for mass production) because it reduces and controls the accumulation of excess inventory. Even when the total order quantity is large, orders can be filled on time in small quantities without accumulating stock. On the other hand, large lot production will always result in excess inventory over a period of time, regardless of total demand. The Toyota production system is the antithesis of large-lot production, *not* mass production — which is why setup time reduction is so important in it.

Toward Order-based Production

Toyota's order-based production schedule corresponds directly to actual demand. When demand increases, a seller's market develops. During such periods, anticipatory production can keep up with actual demand without losses. But in normal market conditions, actual demand must determine production.

Characteristics of Order-based Production

Mass production is speculative. At Toyota, production is based on confirmed orders and is geared to a market that demands fast delivery of a wide variety of models, each produced in small quantities. The SMED system made multiple models possible and, together with small lot production, facilitated production in small quantities. Small lot sizes and synchronized one-piece flow production shortened delivery times considerably.

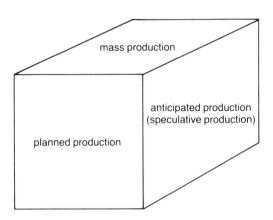

FIGURE 25. Characteristics of Mass Production

The chief difficulty with order-based production is fluctuation in demand. Daily fluctuations can be addressed through load and capacity leveling (Chapter 7); monthly or annual fluctuations, however, must be handled without carrying inventory to "level" total annual load. In order to respond to seasonal fluctuations in demand, Toyota sets basic production capacity at minimum demand level and handles increases through overtime and the use of excess machine capacity and temporary workers. These techniques work as follows.

Overtime. There are four-hour breaks between the two shifts during which an up to 50 percent increase in demand can be met.

Excess capacity and temporary workers. During average demand periods, many workers manage ten machines loaded at 50 percent of capacity. When demand increases, temporary workers are hired. This makes it possible to operate at 100 percent capacity, having each worker handle only five machines. To do this effectively, of course, machines had to be improved so that even temporary workers could work independently after no more than three days of training.

Thus, fluctuations in demand are managed by flexibility in production capacity. This is possible because Toyota employs 20 to 30 percent fewer workers than other automobile manufacturers and has greater reserve capacity as a result of waste elimination and work improvements.

Order-Based Production for Seasonal Demand

Unlike Toyota, S Electric Company produces products based on speculation about future demand. They manufacture seasonal goods and finish production for the whole winter based upon a demand forecast by October. After October, they become subject to the fluctuations of the market and often have to carry large amounts of inventory.

The company wanted to convert to order-based production but had no idea how to cope with the seasonal fluctuations in demand. They now produce 70 percent of the units for which sales can be reliably projected by the end of October. For November, December, and January, order-based production is carried out. To deal with the fluctuations in demand, they have adopted the SMED system and shortened their production cycle considerably. Several products can now be delivered within ten days of receipt of the order.

That year, the summer was very hot and meteorologists predicted a very severe winter. Other companies built up large inventories to meet the expected demand. When a mild winter followed, they were left with large finished goods inventories. At S Electric, they discovered a shocking difference of ¥4 billion between their earlier "planned" production and actual production. Had they gone ahead with planned production, they would have had that much surplus inventory; but since they had changed to order-based production, they carried only ten percent inventory — enough to meet actual demand.

The Relationship Between Production Cycle and Order Delivery Period

In Chapter 2, we saw that the relationship between delivery period and production cycle is very important. D (the period between order and delivery) must be greater than P (the period from the first production process to the last) — $D > P$. If a product is ordered for delivery within ten days but takes 20 days to produce, it cannot be delivered when it is required. To make certain that D is always greater than P, additional semi-processed stock is produced and carried to fulfill all orders for delivery in less than 20 days.

As we also saw in Chapter 2, incorrect forecasting leads to the excessive accumulation and storage of stocks between processes. To avoid that problem, the absolute production cycle (from start to finish) — Po must be less than D, that is, $D > Po$. Generally, this is accomplished by leveling and synchronizing production and by eliminating process delays and lot delays.

Speedy Delivery and Order-based Production

A Japanese trader was transferred to West Germany. When he went shopping for a wardrobe for his new home, he was told that they were not available ready-made but would have to be made to order and that the earliest possible delivery date was in six months. When he asked why it couldn't be finished sooner, the proprietor said, "My wardrobes are built to last a lifetime; why can't you wait six months for delivery?" The trader was amazed at the difference between the German and the Japanese marketplaces.

In America and Europe, expectations about delivery times are very different from Japan's. In England, for example, it may take from six months to a year for delivery of an Austin. And in America, you may have to wait three to six months for a special-order GM or Ford. Everyone, however, likes to take delivery on made-to-order goods as soon as possible.

Due to the recent appreciation of the yen, domestic cars cost about $500 less than Japanese cars in America. Even so, Toyota has continued to enjoy good sales because of their rapid delivery, good mileage, and low maintenance costs. Their market research in America indicated that these were the features American buyers are looking for.

Toyota fills demand in the export market with the same non-stock or stockless production system used for domestic sales. For example, a special-order Celica is ready for delivery in ten days. The salesperson informs the head sales office which places the order directly with Toyota Motors. There, the order is entered into the computer and re-layed to the assembly plant. The car is produced within two days; six days are allowed for delivery, and there is an additional two-day margin. In this way, customers anywhere in Japan can take delivery on ordered cars within ten days. For standard models, instant delivery is available.

Strong Market Research

Of course, the two-day production cycle mentioned above does not include processing of raw materials. The body, frame, and various other parts are produced according to a fixed production schedule. The two days are scheduled for the painting and final assembly re-quired to match customer order requirements.

That is why it is very helpful to be able to predict with a high de-gree of certainty how many and what kinds of cars will be needed. Twice a year, Toyota Motors surveys about 60,000 people to deter-mine demand trends, at a cost of roughly ¥ 120 million. Five or six additional surveys are conducted each year. The total annual marketing budget of around ¥ 600 to 700 million, allows Toyota to develop highly accurate market forecasts. Another of its data-gathering techniques is to stay informed, from day to day, about how many cars by model are registered with the Japanese department of motor vehicles. Based on this information, the production schedule can be changed at any time. This practice confirms Toyota's dedication to order-based production and its determination to manufacture only those cars that can be sold.

Production Planning for Order-based Production

Production planning must be viewed from two perspectives. First, how precisely can demand be identified? Second, how closely can demand be met through the production plan? If production is based merely on speculation, these requirements are easily met; if the goal is non-stock or stockless production, however, planning is much more of a challenge. Toyota's approach is illustrated in Figure 26. It is also important to coordinate production planning with information systems.

Production figures in the annual plan are based on market research. Monthly and weekly production are planned to conform to forecasts, but daily production schedules are determined entirely by orders. Customers prefer to take delivery very soon after placing their orders, but total production takes longer, so Toyota's system is actually a combination of anticipated and order-based planning.

As the year progresses, long-term plans are broken down into monthly production projections. At many companies, adjustments to the monthly schedule are permitted only during a limited period after which the schedule is fixed until next month's plan is set. With this approach, excess inventory can build up over time. Toyota's method is similar but is applied in a more precise and flexible manner. As daily production approaches, the plan is tuned more and more precisely to accepted orders. The production sequence plan of final assembly is adjusted daily to customer orders and changes are relayed to preceding processes via kanban.

Early processes, such as raw materials forming, drilling, boring, and machining, are common to all models. As materials move from parts processing and assembly to sub-assembly and then final assembly, customer model or color preferences determine specialized parts requirements. As Figure 27 shows, however, order-based production becomes essential only at that stage in processing where individual customer requirements must be taken into consideration. This includes, for example, exterior painting and fittings.

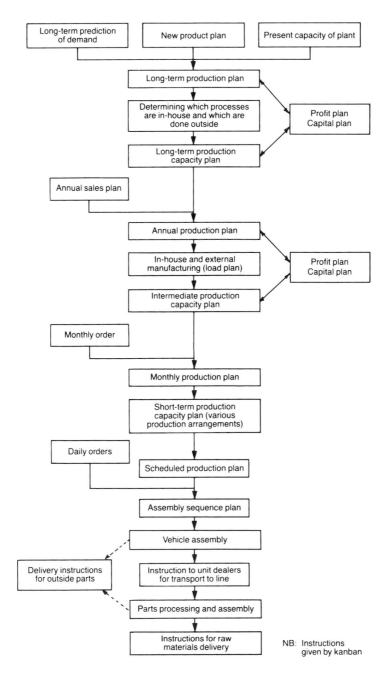

FIGURE 26. Production Plan of Toyota Production System*

*From the thesis of M. Sugimori

In sum, Toyota integrates accurate anticipatory production planning with order-based planning as production nears final assembly. This flexible planning, combined with daily fine-tuning of the final assembly production sequence plan, permits true order-based production that also satisfies the requirements of stockless production.

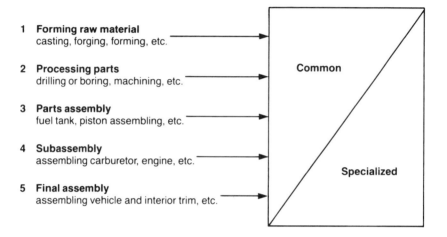

FIGURE 27. Common and Specialized Nature of Production

Toyota's "Supermarket" System

The Toyota production system is sometimes compared to a supermarket. It has the following advantages: Supermarket customers (processes) buy what they need, when they need it. Since they may go to the shelf and take what they want, sales man-hours (materials management) are reduced. Finally, the shelves are refilled as products are sold (parts withdrawn), which makes it is easy to see how much has been taken and avoid overstocks.

Of course, in the supermarket there is no guarantee that products sold today will also sell tomorrow, so some products may sit on the shelf for a prolonged period. How much of a problem is this at Toyota? This analogy to baseball may give you an idea: If a batter with a one-for-three average grounds out in the first inning and ends the second inning with an easy pop fly, will he have a hit in the third inning? To answer that question, all you can do is play the odds. One person might say, "He has a .333 batting average, so he gets one out of three — he'll have a hit for sure this time!" Another might say, "He's not feeling well today, so there's a good possibility of another easy pop fly in the third inning." I'd go along with the second guess, because the rating process is a matter of averages.

At Toyota, however, when assembly withdraws parts from process Z, Z's workers simply process an equal number taken from the preceding process which, in turn, takes an equal number of parts from the process before it, and so on. In this way, very little is left to chance. This is equivalent to surmising that a batter who has a hit in the first inning will do so the next time he is at bat.

Some scholars have said that the Toyota production system increases work-in-process inventory because a store of unfinished parts is reserved at each process to supply the needs of the subsequent process. In actuality, however, that inventory is produced only to replace parts used in products actually sold, not those that might be sold. A clear distinction must be made here between stock that results from a discrepancy between forecast and actual demand, and stock that accumulates temporarily in response to actual demand. Overstocks are far less likely to occur when parts are processed only in response to actual daily demand.

Thus, the most important feature of a supermarket system is that stocking is triggered and maintained by actual demand. Toyota has used this concept to create a flexible production system in which later processes take from earlier ones like customers in the supermarket. This is often characterized as the "pull" system of order-based production. But push and pull are only effects or measures to be taken. Toyota adopted order-based production and used a pull system to make it work efficiently.

The Ford and Toyota Systems Compared

When asked to compare the Ford and Toyota production systems and to state which company he thought was in the dominant position, Mr. Ohno said:

> New developments and improvements occur daily in both systems, so it is hard to judge, but I am confident that Toyota's system is particularly suited for production in a low growth period.

As we shall see, there are a number of reasons for this conclusion.

Many companies, like Ford, mass produce parts in large lots to avoid changeovers. The Toyota system takes the reverse course. On page 95 of *The Toyota Production System*, Mr. Ohno says: "Our production slogan is 'small lot sizes and quick setups.'" He also states that the stockless (or non-stock) approach is another significant feature of the Toyota system:

> Even though today, some manufacturers — Volvo, for instance — have one person assemble the entire engine, in general, the manufacturing mainstream still utilizes Ford's work flow, or automation, system. Although the events described by Sorensen took place around 1910, the basic pattern has changed very little.
>
> Like Ford's, the Toyota production system is based on the work flow system. The difference is that, while Sorensen worried about warehousing parts, Toyota eliminated the warehouse.*

Three Basic Differences

Toyota has three basic features that distinguish it from Ford: small lot sizes, mixed-model production, and continuous one-piece flow operation from processing to final assembly.

Large lot versus small lot production. It can be argued that the difference between Ford and Toyota is that Ford mass-produces a few models whereas Toyota produces many models in small quantities. This is true enough, but it doesn't give a complete picture. As mentioned earlier, the decision to adopt either mass production or production of small quantities of a wide range of models is not made in a vacuum; rather, it is a response to market conditions and user demands.

Similarly, high or low growth periods result from changing social circumstances beyond the company's control. In a high growth period, it is easy to create a seller's market; but during a low growth period, buyers determine the market. Enterprises must be flexible and ready to meet new and different demands.

Obviously, mass production has some advantages, such as depreciation for special or exclusive machines, toolings, and dies; but the key issue is whether to adopt small or large lot sizes. Traditionally, American automobile manufacturers have assumed that large

---

* *The Toyota Production System: Beyond Large-Scale Production*, pp. 94-95 (herein after referred to as *Toyota*).

lots and planned mass production would generate substantial cost savings. This approach resulted in:

- Large finished goods inventories (caused by gaps between production based on forecasts and actual demand)
- Work-in-process accumulations between processes (created by large lot production)

Although these phenomena often increase during low growth periods, they are tolerated for a number of reasons. First, large lots reduce delays caused by tool and die changes; second, they facilitate the division of labor and reduce man-hours and other costs; third, division of labor provides employment opportunities for unskilled laborers and this, when combined with lower product costs, adds the benefit of helping to boost consumption.

All these justifications break down, however, when setup times are shortened through SMED. What is more, even in small lot production many functions are common to more than one product or process. As long as the small lots add up to a large total production, the division of labor is maintained and unskilled workers can still be employed.

Small lots also shorten production cycles and reduce the need for speculative production. Under these conditions, it becomes possible to produce to actual demand.

Adopting mixed-model production in the assembly process. The very first automobiles were probably produced one at a time by a single group of workers. Ford's one-piece flow assembly operation made division of labor possible but it is based on large lot production. For example, 200,000 units of model X are produced in the first part of the month, followed by 300,000 units of model Y in the middle of the month and finally 400,000 units of model Z. At Toyota, however, leveled mixed-model production results in a final assembly sequence of 2X 3Y 4Z that is repeated throughout the day.

Mixed-model production eliminates work-in-process accumulation by using small lots. It responds rapidly to fluctuations in demand and facilitates planning by letting you know at the beginning of the process what the average load will be.

Consistent flow operation from parts to assembly. Assembly at Ford occurs as a one-piece flow, but the parts supplied to assembly are produced entirely in large lots. At Toyota, assembly and parts processing both are performed as one-piece flow operations, for example, frame-welding or parts machining. Moreover, Toyota uses a comprehensive system in which the various parts flow directly into final assembly. All parts, whether they are processed within the plant or supplied from outside, are produced in small lots and create a single continuous one-piece flow. This is a fundamental principle of the Toyota system and a significant difference between Ford and Toyota.

Figure 28 summarizes the differences between Toyota and Ford.

Feature	Ford	Toyota	Benefit
1. One-piece flow	only in assembly	processing and assembly linked	shorter cycles, reduced finished goods inventory, reduced work-in-process
2. Lot size	large	small	WIP reduction, order-based production
3. Product flow	single product (few models)	mixed flow (many models)	reduced WIP, adjusts to change, promotes load balancing

FIGURE 28. Differences between the Ford and Toyota Systems

- Both Ford and Toyota use one-piece flow in assembly operations.
- Ford, however, produces a few models in large lots, with a single product flow operation in assembly. Toyota produces many models, in small lots, in a mixed-model assembly operation.
- Assembly and parts fabrication are separated at Ford, but directly linked at Toyota.
- One-piece flow is used only in the assembly process at Ford; parts are processed in large lots. At Toyota, all production is in small lots.

The Toyota system is not opposed to the Ford system. Rather, it is a progressive enhancement — a system geared to the Japanese market that mass-produces in small lots with minimum stocks.

These are the principal features of the Toyota production system. The key to their achievement is the adoption of SMED, to reduce setup time and promote small lot production.

Summary

The primary goal of the Toyota production system is to identify and eliminate waste and reduce costs. Inventories are eliminated by addressing and overcoming the hidden conditions that cause them. Order-based production, or production to demand, rather than anticipatory or speculative production, helps control these conditions. Another important strategy, from the standpoint of operations, is the separation of man from machine — pre-automation to achieve multi-machine operation.

6

Mechanics of the
Toyota Production System

*Improving Process — Schedule Control
and Just-In-Time*

Process consists of processing, inspection, transportation, and storage operations, but only processing adds value. This is very well understood at Toyota where cost reduction through waste elimination, particularly the waste of overproduction, is the goal. They treat inspection, transportation, and especially storage, or the practice of carrying stock, as wastes and eliminate them wherever possible.

Many people consider just-in-time the most prominent feature of the Toyota production system, but it is actually no more than a strategy to achieve non-stock or stockless production. More important is the conceptual framework of stockless production.

Schedule and load control are two important concepts in the Toyota production system. Schedule control ensures that product is made on time. Load control ensures that product can in fact be made, that there is a proper balance between capacity and load. Here's an illustration: If you don't show up on time, you will miss the train (schedule control); but even if you are on time, you won't be able to get on if the train is already full (load control).

SCHEDULE CONTROL AND JUST-IN-TIME

Production Planning

Ordinarily, production planning occurs in three stages:

- Master schedule — long term (annual, biannual, or quarterly)
- Intermediate schedule — monthly

• Detailed schedule — practical production sequence for one week, three days, or one day

Toyota's master schedule is based on extensive market research (p. 87) and yields a rough production number for sales. Unofficial monthly production numbers are given to the plant and to parts suppliers two months in advance and then firmed up a month later. These firm numbers are used to plan detailed daily and weekly schedules and to level the production sequence. Approximately two weeks before actual production, each line is given projected daily production numbers for each model. A single leveled schedule is sent to the end of the final assembly line, as are all daily changes, to match the schedule to actual orders. Changes are communicated back down the line through the kanban system. Flexibility at the detailed schedule level is the feature that distinguishes Toyota's scheduling system from others. From day to day, precise changes can be made quickly and easily.

Schedule Control and Stockless Production

Chapter 5 introduced two distinguishing features of the Toyota production system: order-based production and non-stock or stockless production.

Non-stock and Just-in-time

As we saw in Chapter 5, the use of just-in-time merely to ensure final delivery within a prescribed period often results in overproduction and early production. At Toyota, however, just-in-time also means producing parts or products in exactly the required quantity — just when they are needed, and not before.

At Toyota, non-stock production means that stocks of finished cars must be zero, that is, production must equal but not exceed orders. To achieve this balance, Toyota adopted order-based production. Since it is not always possible to achieve a production cycle (P) that is less than the period between order and delivery (D), or $P < D$, the "supermarket" approach to planning and production was also adopted. (The supermarket works on the assumption that what was purchased today will probably also be in demand tomorrow.) Hence, planning for early processes is based on anticipated orders; the buildup of excess inventories, however, is prevented by gearing later processes and final assembly to actual customer orders. This flexibility and control is achieved through the kanban system. Finally, since it is an absolute rule to produce no more than required, machine capacity, or capacity utilization, are not considered factors in production control.

Seven Principles for Shortening the Production Cycle

At Toyota they say: "The cylinder block cast at Kamigo in the morning runs in a finished automobile by evening." How is this accomplished?

Reduce process delays. Process delays occur when an entire lot is waiting to be processed. To shorten the production cycle, it is far more effective to reduce process delays than to reduce processing time. Generally, the ratio of processing time to storage is between 2:3 and 1:4. In the most extreme cases, cutting process delays by one half will result in a 60 percent reduction in production time; eliminating it altogether can reduce the production cycle by 80 percent.

To achieve these results, one must level production quantities and processing capacity among processes and synchronize the flow of work throughout the plant. Whatever the lot size — be it 3,000, 300, three pieces, or only one — if processing times are identical at each process, they can be synchronized to eliminate process delays. When machines with different capacity follow one another, processing times will not be equal. Then, the faster machines have to be slowed deliberately to equalize nominal processing times. If lot sizes are large, however, lot delays will prolong the production cycle.

Reduce lot delays. Eliminating process delays through quantity leveling and synchronization can reduce the production cycle by 80 percent at the most. To reduce it further requires the reduction or elimination of lot delays.

Generally, the delays caused by lot delays are hidden in the shadow of processing time and are apt to be overlooked.

Figure 29 illustrates the difference in processing time between lot and flow operations. There, a lot of 3,000 pieces takes 15 hours to move through three 5-hour processes sequentially. If, however, the three processes are connected so that as soon as one piece is completed it is transferred to the next process, production time can be reduced substantially. For example, in the above example, if processing time per piece is six seconds, the production cycle will be reduced to five hours and 12 seconds. This is a two-thirds reduction. If five processes are conducted in a one-piece flow, the production cycle will be reduced to one-fifth; if ten, to one-tenth; and so on.

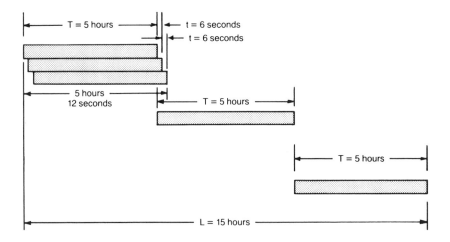

FIGURE 29. Production Period of Lot Operation and One-piece
Flow Operation

Breaking production into small lots can shorten production cycles dramatically. Many resist this idea, however, because producing large lots reduces the time spent in tool and die changes, thus reducing overall man-hours for processing. With small lot production, however, this advantage is offset because the increase in transportation lots shortens the production cycle.

In a one-piece flow, each transportation lot is equivalent to one piece. This reduces production time considerably. A lot of 3,000 pieces, for example, can be processed in a very short time if each piece is transferred to the succeeding process as soon as it has been processed. In order to realize this reduction, however, the plant layout must facilitate simple and speedy transportation between processes.

Reducing production time. Through the use of quantity leveling and synchronization, process delays can be eliminated, reducing the production cycle to one-fifth; and using one-piece flows for ten succeeding processes, for example, reduces the production cycle to one-tenth. The multiplier effect of eliminating both process and lot delays can reduce the production cycle to as little as $\frac{1}{50}$ ($\frac{1}{5} \times \frac{1}{10}$) when ten processes are involved.

This multiplier effect is further enhanced when one determines optimal lot size. The limiting constraint on the production cycle is the time it takes to run through one processing lot. The size of the processing lot, in turn, is determined principally by the amount of time needed for setup changeovers. This time can be cut by 90 percent if a one-hour setup can be cut to six minutes, so the net effect on the operating rate will remain unchanged even if the processing lot is reduced from 3,000 to 300 pieces.

If processing time is 0.5 hours and lot size is cut to one-tenth of what it was previously, these improvements, combined with the elimination of process and lot delays, make it possible to slash the production cycle dramatically:

$$\frac{1}{50} \times \frac{1}{10} = \frac{1}{500}$$

Production in lots of 3,000 units once included both process and lot delays and took ten days to accomplish. Switching to lots of 300 units, equalizing and synchronizing the ten processes involved, and instituting one-piece flows brought processing time to a mere 0.5 hours ($\frac{1}{500}$ of 240 hours).

There are four basic principles that must be followed in creating the one-piece flow that results in the dramatic reductions in production time shown above.

- Level production quantities between processes and synchronize all processes (to eliminate process delays)
- Reduce transportation lot size to one (to eliminate lot delays)
- Improve layout to compensate for the more frequent need for transportation
- Reduce lot size

By following these principles, the Toyota engine block cast in the morning runs in a finished automobile by evening.

Employ layout, line forming, and the full work control system. As noted above, one-piece flow production requires quantity leveling, small lots, and synchronization between processes. Since it greatly increases the number of transport operations, two strategies have been developed to reduce overall transportation time:

- Alteration of plant layout so that little or no transport is required
- Use of some other convenient method of linking processes, such as a conveyor

Since the latter method may be troublesome and expensive, layout improvement is generally preferable.

Several steps must be taken to improve layout. First, the various machines should be laid out to correspond to the product processing flow. Arranging production departments by type of machines (for example, press department or lathe department) only increases transportation. Consider the following arrangements:

- Single process line — For month-long production of a single product and a single model in large quantities
- Common process line — When production of a single product is not sufficient for a month's continuous flow but products A, B, C, and D have processes in common that can be arranged in a continuous flow
- Similar process line — Products A, B, C, D, E, and F have some but not all of their processes in common, so only partial lines can be formed of those common processes

At Toyota, the common process line is used most frequently. In general, however, many plants have fewer common process factors and must adopt the similar process arrangement.*

Line layout improvements result in the following benefits:

- Elimination of transportation man-hours
- Faster quality information feedback to help reduce defects
- Reduction of man-hours by reducing or eliminating process and lot delays
- Shortened production cycle

---

* For those cases, to determine the most efficient machine layout for your particular production requirements, see the section "Improving Layout" in my book *Non-Stock Production: The Shingo System for Continuous Improvement* (Cambridge, MA: Productivity Press, 1988), pp. 326-28.

Shortening the production cycle will hasten the implementation of order-based production and help reduce stocks of finished goods. And, by eliminating the two types of delay between processes, stockless production can become a reality.

Although line forming has a number of advantages, it does present some difficulties. The largest potential problem comes with differing machine capacities within a process or between processes. As noted earlier, however, machine capacity is not considered a factor in production control at Toyota. Under its stockless system, no more than the required quantity is produced during any cycle. Therefore, lower capacity machines are perfectly acceptable so long as they can produce the required amount; and even if machine capacity is high, overproduction is not permitted. Ideally, machine capacity should match production requirements; but in fact, high capacity machines are used even when they cannot be utilized fully.

The above problem has led to a further refinement at Toyota. A small quantity of stock is maintained between large and small capacity machines. When stock levels reach twenty pieces, operation of larger capacity machines is stopped. It resumes when the level drops to five pieces. Typically, large capacity machines follow low capacity machines intermittently to permit synchronization between processes and maintain minimum stock levels.

This is full work control which is defined as a control method where operations are halted when stocks are at a maximum. Under full work control, overall production output eventually matches the quantities required.

With this method, a high machine operating ratio is not necessary and, in fact, often not desirable. In order to work, the method requires a commitment to restrain machine operation even if it results in a low machine operating ratio. If this point is not understood, the full work system cannot be adopted.

When combined with production lines incorporating quantity leveling, synchronization, and one-piece flows, on the one hand, and SMED for small lot production, on the other, the full work control system geometrically shortens the production cycle.

Synchronize operations and absorb deviations. Synchronization or line balancing is essential in any series of flow operations. It follows that every effort should be made to segment tasks and establish standard operations in order to minimize balance-related losses.

In practice, however, no matter how scrupulously operations are planned and executed, some deviations from standard times will occur. For example, a screw may be too tight and a little more time than usual is required to loosen it; or a screw may be dropped and time is lost retrieving it or getting another. These little troubles inevitably occur, so some degree of deviation from standard times cannot be avoided.

Typically, we deal with these problems by placing buffer stock between workers. When they complete their work ahead of schedule, workers process stocked products; when one worker is delayed, the next draws from his or her buffer stock and the delayed worker tries to recover lost time by working faster in the next cycle. Thus, the product stocked between workers serves as a buffer to absorb and prevent delays between processes.

If stocks serve only as buffers, one piece should be sufficient between processes; in practice, however, several or many pieces are held.

- Parts boxes arrays — A good width for a work area is about 75cm. However, this standard is often ignored when many parts are needed and parts boxes are stored at some distance because there is no sense that it is inappropriate to keep large stocks. In situations like this, the size of the storage area between workers can often be halved through the use of three-dimensional arrays of parts boxes.

  In assembly operations, moreover, the fact that only a single unit of a given part is required at any one time suggests several approaches. Rotating parts boxes could be designed that release only the parts needed at the required time. Other devices could be made with the same characteristics as the above but arranged in three dimensions instead of just two — that is, stacked vertically as well as arranged side by side. Measures of this sort will prevent a proliferation of parts boxes and keep the work area from becoming too large.

- Absorbing deviations from standard times — Using the procedures described above helps minimize stocks between processes; but at Toyota, absolutely no stock is tolerated between processes. To absorb deviations from standard time, Toyota adopted a *mutual assistance system*. When a delay occurs, workers help one another rather than let stock accumulate.

For group operations, Toyota employs two relay systems as practiced in sports: *swimming relays* and *track-and-field relays*.

In a swimming relay, fast swimmers are not permitted to dive into the water until the preceding swimmer touches the pool wall — the faster swimmer (worker) works at the pace of the slower one. In track-and-field relays, on the other hand, a *relay zone* is established. If the preceding runner is fast, the baton can be passed to a slower runner at the end of the zone; if the succeeding runner is fast, the baton can be handed to her at the beginning of the zone — the fast swimmer (worker) helps the slow one.

This mutual assistance system absorbs deviations from standards between processes without building stock.

Establishing tact time. Tact is the time it takes to produce one piece of product. This time is equivalent to total working time divided by production quantity. Don't be fooled into thinking that reducing tact time necessarily has anything to do with productivity improvement. For example, ten workers may produce 100 pieces of product. After work improvement, they may be able to produce 120 pieces. This doesn't mean, however, that they should make 120 pieces per day. If 100 pieces per day are all that is required, real improvement is achieved if fewer than ten workers can produce them — producing unnecessary product does not represent a productivity improvement.

In sum, tact time can be calculated from either the required production quantity or the actual capacity of workers and machines. Making the correct choice may not seem problematic, but it is important to exercise caution. For example, it would be ridiculous to drive over the speed limit just because a car is able to go faster. Since the Toyota production system is based on the principle that overproduction is waste, tact time is calculated from the required production quantity.

Ensure product flow between processes. When taken to its logical conclusion, Toyota production methodology leads to an ideal system in which everything — from raw materials manufacturing (forging, casting, pressing) to machining, initial assembly, sub-assembly, and final assembly — is linked in a coherent one-piece flow. Although such total integration has not yet been achieved, Toyota has developed a system of frequent and continuous mixed small lot deliveries from fabrication plants (for example, framing, painting, and machining) to the assembly line.

Extremely frequent deliveries from processes adjacent to the final assembly plant create a flow of products that approaches the total system described above. At Toyota, one frequently encounters numerous tractor-trailers bearing the sign "Priority Vehicle." These vehicles carry parts in mixed small lots that are required by final assembly and may not be delayed. When they go by, even the company president yields the right-of-way. Similarly, forklifts transport parts from forging, casting, and stamping plants directly to machining.

All these activities are synchronized with tact times and managed through kanban. The work is so orderly and progresses at such speed that it is sometimes called the "whirligig system." The success is reflected in Toyota's remarkable inventory turnover rate. Table 6 compares this rate with that of other automobile manufacturers.

Year	Toyota	Co. A (Japan)	Co. B (USA)	Co. C (USA)
1960	41 times	13 times	7 times	8 times
1965	66	13	5	5
1970	63	13	6	6

TABLE 6. Inventory Turnover of Auto Manufacturers by Country *

*From the thesis of M. Sugimori

Adopting SMED

To say that the remarkable reduction in die and tool changeover times is a major factor in the success of the Toyota production system is no exaggeration. Order-based and stockless production absolutely demands reductions in setup time.

Early Days of SMED

By the time I visited Toyota in 1970, its changeover time for a 1,000-ton stamping machine was four hours — twice as long as

Volkswagen's. Nearly six months later, our efforts to improve this procedure had reduced the time to one and a half hours. Everyone was excited because we had beaten Volkswagen.

When I returned to Toyota two or three months later, however, top management demanded that changeover time be reduced to three minutes. Initially, I considered this an unreasonable request. After studying the Toyota production system, however, I gradually realized that these short times (which could not possibly be achieved without SMED) were essential to the achievement of order-based and stockless production.

I still did not know how to achieve such a drastic reduction. Then I had an inspiration — to convert *internal* setup to *external*. This fundamental SMED principle enabled us to reduce the time to three minutes after only a few months.

I read in a financial journal that it was possible to reduce a three-hour setup time at Toyota to three minutes because workers had been idle much of the time. This is an extremely superficial explanation that reveals the author's poor grasp of the Toyota production system. Reducing changeover time is never a matter of labor density; rather, it requires a change in thinking and the use of scientific methods derived from a revolutionary perspective on the problem.

Others have tried to explain SMED successes at Toyota in terms of skill engineering and calculated that it took 340,000 practice runs — which amounts to 30 man-years — to reduce a three-hour changeover to three minutes. According to this point of view, the

	Toyota	Co. A (USA)	Co. B (Sweden)	Co. C (West Germany)
Stamping machine stopped during die change	9 mins.	6 hrs.	4 hrs.	4 hrs.
Number of changes	1.5/shift	1 in less than 2 shifts	—	1 in 2 days
Lot size	1 day	10 days	1 month	—
Strokes per hour	500-550	300	—	—

TABLE 7. Comparison of Changeover Times of Stamping Machines by Country (hood and fender) *

*From the thesis of M. Sugimori

achievement was mainly the result of training, although the improved jigs, fixtures, and changing methods and the quick-wittedness and inspiration of Toyota workers were also acknowledged.

In fact, however, it took only three months to reduce the setup time from three hours to three minutes. And it was the scientific principles of SMED rather than skill engineering that provided the solution. I could cite thousands of examples from other Japanese enterprises to show that setup times for tools and dies can be reduced about 95 percent from former requirements in several months. It is only when compared with companies outside Japan that Toyota's reductions are remarkable (Table 7).

Important Aspects of the SMED System

As stated earlier, during ten years of practical application, eight basic techniques, or principles, of tool and die exchange emerged. The most important of these are:

1. Clearly distinguish internal (IED) from external setup (OED)
2. Convert internal to external setup
3. Improve functional clamps (consider "threadless" fasteners)
4. Eliminate adjustments

The last two principles require further discussion:

Functional Clamps

In fitting bolts and nuts, the following three actions must be performed:

1. Place nut on tip of bolt and turn once to secure it
2. Continue turning the nut
3. On the last thread, tighten it with the required torque

Of these three actions, the first is most difficult to perform: Unless the nut is centered and placed on the bolt at just the right angle, it will not be fitted to the bolt. Why not consider tightening and loosening it without removing it from the bolt? And how can we work with the fact that bolts and nuts are loosened at the first turn and secured at the final turn of the thread?

Surprisingly, these simple matters are generally not well understood. I once challenged the workers at a job site to perform a die exchange without turning any nut or bolt more than once. They had to pay me $500 for each extra turn! To avoid these penalties, they made the following improvements:

1. Twelve bolts secured the cover of a vulcanizing pan. They cut the bolt holes on the cover in the shape of old-fashioned keyholes (also called "dharma holes") and secured them with U-shaped washers (Figure 30a). After one turn of the nuts, the washers can be removed, and by turning the cover counterclockwise to the larger side of the dharma hole, the cover is removed without removing or even touching the nuts. This shortened the changeover time considerably.

2. In S Industry's wire winding operation, to remove the product, the nut was removed before the washer. This process was improved by using a nut with an outer diameter smaller than the inner diameter of the wound core and securing it with a U-type washer. (Figure 30b) Now, to remove the core, the nut is loosened with one turn and the U-type washer is pulled out. Then, without touching the nut, the wound core is pulled off. This improvement reduced the time between operations to one-tenth of what it used to be.

In response to a similar challenge, a two-hour changeover time was reduced to two minutes at F.M. Company in the United States. The solution they devised is shown in Figure 30e. It worked like this: Threads were sliced off at three points on the circumference of the bolt and at three corresponding points on the nut (which was a little thicker than usual). This makes it possible to slip the nut onto the bolt to the required depth and turn it once to tighten it, a one-touch tightening.

Functional clamps without threads. Another approach to consider is the clamp without threads, which can reduce changeover times even more effectively.

The purpose of tightening a threaded screw is *to secure an item*, but a screw is only one way to achieve that goal. Many engineers, however, regard the screw as the universal securing method and do not think

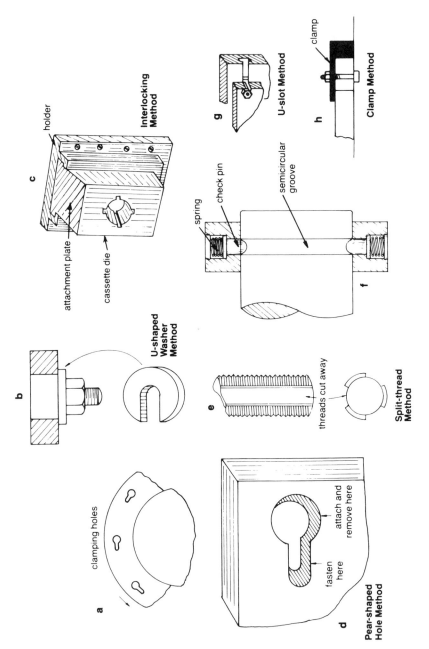

Figure 30. Functional Clamping Devices

to use others, such as cams or wedges, that do not employ threads. Interlocking schemes or the "cassette" method are other options.

In all these instances, it is important to consider the direction in which force will be applied. Three are possible: X = side to side, Y = front and back, and Z = up and down.

Stamping machine clamps. Press dies typically are not required to bear very heavy front and back or side to side loads — they simply need to be kept from moving. Vertically, however, the lower die is supported by the machine bed and the upper one must be held suspended so it won't fall of its own weight. The maximum load, therefore, is the compression force of the lower and upper dies.

The clamping solution is to standardize both sides of the upper and lower dies and to fit them together to a tolerance of ± 0.15mm with an L-shaped guide bar. Also, front and back movement must be prevented through the use of wedges. With this method, stamping machine dies of less than 50 tons can simply be inserted or pulled out, which makes die exchanges in about 15 seconds possible. It is, of course, necessary to standardize die heights.

Boring machine stoppers. On an eight-arbor boring machine, stoppers in each spindle were secured with screws that were difficult to reach for adjustment and tightening. In order to function properly, of course, stoppers must make contact with the product and determine its dimensions. A major improvement was adopted as follows:

- Threads on the bolts were machined off to make a cylindrical fit
- Grooves were cut at the end of each spindle and springs attached to the end of the stopper to slip into the grooves. The stopper was then held in place by spring tension

In this way, the stopper was supported by the cylindrical fit both on the sides and vertically. The force on the stopper from the opposite direction was borne by the spindle and only a small amount of force was required to pull the stopper out. This improvement reduced changeover time by 90 percent.

In general, when we want to improve clamping methods, we tend to consider expensive alternatives like hydraulic, pneumatic, or magnetic devices. Practical and inexpensive solutions are available, however, with a proper understanding of the clamping function.

Eliminating Adjustment

The most important principle for shortening the duration of tool and die changes is to avoid adjustment. To apply this lesson, we must understand the difference between setting and adjustment — two very different activities. In *setting*, the correct position is already set and adjustment is unnecessary. For example, if a limit switch is positioned correctly the first time, it does not have to be adjusted for succeeding jobs. In the same example, *adjustment* would mean moving the limit switch around to find the correct position for setting it. People commonly think that adjustment is an unavoidable part of setup, but it doesn't have to be.

The least common multiple system. The *least common multiple system* is an effective means to eliminate adjustment. Consider, for example, a process that requires adjustment with a limit switch at any one of five settings. The solution is to place a switch at each position but connect each one to a separate power switch. When, for example, the second setting is required, only the second power switch is activated. With such a one-touch switch-over of limit switches, the mechanism itself requires no adjustment — only the *function* is switched over. Three more examples follow.

Drilling. A securing screw in a motorshaft required a hole. Since eight different shaft lengths were involved, the position of the drilling stopper had to be moved accordingly and adjusted each time the position changed. To eliminate the need for adjustments, the workers prepared a circular plate with eight stoppers of different thicknesses. Whenever a different shaft length was required, the circular plate was turned to the required stopper with one touch.

Machining. Five standard jigs were used to position the tools used for the automatic machining of camera parts. To set the tools correctly took many hours of adjustment and great skill. The operation was improved by cutting five slots on the outer circumference of a cylinder corresponding to the five kinds of standard jigs. Adjustment was eliminated entirely by rotating this so-called "standard cylindrical jig" and inserting a pin at the required position. Changeover time was shortened considerably and the work can now be performed by unskilled workers.

Fabricating helical springs. A machine produced six helical springs of different heights for automobiles. The position of the stopper was changed by turning a guide screw. After setting, a trial product was produced and, depending on the result, adjustments were made. To eliminate adjustment, the threads on the guide screw were removed and six different positioning jigs fitted at its bottom. Now, when the stopper contacts the jig, the correct position can be secured without adjustment.

As these examples illustrate, many machines are provided with position changing devices that use screws, but the following point must be considered carefully. Most machines are designed to permit *continuous and unlimited* positions. What we usually need, however, are *limited and fixed* positions. In changing a setting from 100mm to 120mm, for example, we don't need to move to 100.1mm, 100.2, 100.3, 100.4, and so on to get there.

In reality, we need only a few settings. Since manufacturers do not know which settings will be required by the different companies, they provide unlimited positioning capacity. The particular plant using the machine must choose a method that is suitable for the work required (usually one that employs limited and fixed positions) and adapt the machine accordingly.

Surprisingly, most people don't understand this and do not customize the machine's functions to increase its usefulness for their specific situation. Often, they end up using unnecessarily difficult procedures. I have come to a new understanding about machine manufacturers: They consider the functions required for fabricating products in their design, but it is doubtful that they are also concerned with simplifying tool and die changes. Hence, those who actually operate machines must address these concerns in their own plants. While the basic principles of SMED always apply, different mechanical solutions may have to be developed to optimize machine function in particular circumstances.

Benefits of the SMED System

If SMED is adopted, the following benefits can be expected:

1. By shortening setup times, machine operating rates will be increased.
2. Small lot production significantly reduces finished goods inventories and the buildup of stocks between processes.

3. Finally, production can rapidly respond to fluctuating demand by adjusting to meet changes in model and delivery time requirements.

Most companies consider the first of these to be the most important. Since, at Toyota, producing only the amount required is the highest principle and cost reduction is a priority, low operating rates may be permitted. Consequently, Toyota attaches greater importance to the second and third items, with particular emphasis on reducing finished goods inventories and accumulated stocks between processes. If a one-hour changeover is reduced to three minutes, the product will most likely be produced in small lots with many tooling changes.

Incidentally, on many of my plant visits, top management comments on their successes with SMED. They discover that, in addition to providing the three benefits mentioned above, it solves other problems as well. Workers who, in the past, resisted changes because of fear of failure gain confidence from their success in reducing setup times and learn to enjoy challenges. As a result, a company-wide culture that supports improvement activities develops.

Flexibility of Capacity

Actual market demand will not be consistent from month to month throughout the year; nor will the quantities required from day to day be the same in a given month. It is natural for us to think that such fluctuations are unavoidable. A typical solution is to accumulate stocks of products and unfinished goods in order to lessen the impact of changes in demand.

The Toyota production system, by comparison, favors order-based production. This is a very different approach from anticipatory or planned production. If it is adopted casually, however, many wasted man-hours may result. Toyota handles this problem by maintaining flexible capacity production. This allows the company to respond quickly and efficiently to increases and decreases in demand.

Responding to Increases in Demand

Long-term predictions of demand. At bonus time,* demand can always be expected to go up. A number of solutions are undertaken to

---

* Editor's note: Twice a year, in April and October, Japanese workers receive substantial bonuses. The upper limit on payments is usually related to company profits; the lower is generally determined during the annual labor negotiations.

handle increases in demand that are certain and predictable over a long period.

- Multi-machine and multi-process handling normally allow machines to be loaded at only 50 percent of capacity, by having one worker handle ten machines, for example. At the time of the expected increase in demand, additional temporary workers can be hired to load machines at 100 percent capacity — by having each worker handle five machines instead of ten and thus doubling the normal production output. If a company wants to follow this production approach, it is important that machines be easy to handle, so that unskilled, temporary workers can generate full output after only a brief training period.
- Each regular assembly worker typically handles an operation with a one-minute tact time. By adding temporary workers, each operation can be broken down into two 30-second segments. With this shorter tact time, production output will double. As with machine handling, work methods must be improved so that temporary workers will be able to perform the work easily.

Short-term increases in demand. At Toyota, the first and second shift are separated by a four-hour period. This makes it possible to increase production capacity for short periods by working overtime between the two shifts. Overtime for day laborers can also be used occasionally to increase capacity. In addition, improvements in equipment and work methods can produce surpluses in capacity that can be used to meet increased demand. Finally, in some cases, workers who usually perform tasks that are not related to production can provide temporary assistance in production.

When Demand Decreases

Decreases in demand can be a difficult problem. Typically, companies assume that demand will increase. When actual demand is lower than projected, they overproduce and accumulate inventory since they equate machine idling with loss. At Toyota, overproduction is regarded as waste and inventory is not permitted.

There are several steps production management can take when demand decreases:

- In parts fabrication, workers can be given more machines to handle
- In assembly, tact time can be increased and the number of workers reduced

These measures may prevent overproduction, but how does one utilize the surplus man-hours that result? Toyota's basic philosophy is that it is better to allow workers to be idle than to overproduce. Furthermore, in Japan, management is responsible for protecting a worker's job — companies rarely lay off workers during slow periods and then call them back when demand increases.

Workers can be kept busy with the following types of tasks during low demand periods:

- Repairing small leaks throughout the plant that have been neglected (this saved one company close to $5,000 in water charges)
- Maintaining and repairing machines that have been neglected during the regular production cycle
- Practicing tool and die changes
- Fabricating jigs and fixtures for planned improvements
- Producing in the plant what was previously done by outside suppliers. (From an accountants' perspective, this might be viewed as a loss since labor costs for in-house fabrication are generally higher than a supplier's. On balance, however, since surplus man-hours constitute waste, it may be advantageous to produce some items in the plant.)

As these examples suggest, decreases in demand are far more difficult to handle than increases. Therefore, even during times of average demand, a company should continuously seek to make improvements so that demand can be met with the fewest workers possible. Toyota has followed this rule and, as a result, its labor costs are 20 to 30 percent lower than those of its competitors.

It would be wrong to assume that producing with the fewest workers also means producing with the smallest number of machines on the floor. Instead, excess machine capacity should be retained so that when demand increases, additional workers can be hired and production increased. Without this policy, machines are run at full capacity and operating rates become all-important. If demand increases under such circumstances, workers can be added but machines cannot. Therefore, to anticipate increases, we are forced to overproduce and carry a large inventory during low demand periods. This creates numerous burdensome and wasteful costs.

Elimination of Defects

Inspection to Prevent Defects

With conventional production control systems, a certain level of stock is maintained to prevent defective products from disturbing the production line. Since overproduction is not permitted for any reason at Toyota, defects must be prevented from occurring altogether. To do so, inspection must *prevent* defects, not merely *find* them.

Preventive inspection, described in detail in Chapter 2, involves three strategies:

- Source control — controlling defects where they occur
- Self inspection — workers are responsible for finding and correcting defects
- Successive inspection — workers check each other's work

100 Percent Inspection

For a complete elimination of defects, 100 percent inspection must be adopted. Sampling inspection is not enough. Although supported by statistical science, it assures only the highest quality inspection *methods*; it cannot actually guarantee product quality — that is, zero defects.

The following example explains the limitations of sampling inspection:

On a high-speed automatic press performing lot operations, 50 to 100 parts may pile up on the chute. The first and last pieces are checked, and if both are defect-free, the whole lot is removed to a pallet. If the last piece is defective, however, all the pieces are checked. The defective pieces are removed and steps are taken to prevent the defect from recurring. This is a kind of 100 percent inspection. We should not assume that sampling inspection is the only kind of inspection that can be performed in high speed operations. The example goes on to argue that pure sampling inspection is inappropriate for a continuous flow of products.

This approach seems to me to be mistaken on two counts: Defects are of two kinds, occasional and continuous. Thus,

1. When occasional defects occur in the middle of 100 pieces of product, they will be completely hidden among the acceptable pieces.
2. If the defect is continuous, as many as 99 pieces will have to be thrown out if, for example, the second of the 100 pieces turned out to be defective.

The above is essentially inspection to *find* defects. If, however, our goal is to eliminate defective products completely, we must find an inexpensive, high speed inspection device when high speed presses are used — and it must inspect not to *find* defects but to *prevent* them.

Poka-yoke Is Only a Means

The Toyota production system recommends the use of poka-yoke methods. A poka-yoke device is an improvement in the form of a jig or fixture that helps achieve 100 percent acceptable product by preventing the occurrence of defects. Poka-yoke is only an intervention, however, not a goal in itself. So, before designing and installing a device, we must first determine whether source, self, or successive inspection should be relied upon. Once this decision has been made, poka-yoke is available as a practical measure *to provide 100% inspection*. Here are some examples:

- Devices that prevent a part from fitting onto a jig if any operational mistakes have been made
- Devices that prevent a machine from beginning processing if there is anything wrong with the workpiece
- Devices that prevent a machine from beginning processing if any operational mistakes have been made
- Devices that correct operational or motion errors and allow processing to proceed
- Devices that stop defects by checking at one process for errors made at the previous process and preventing them from flowing to the next process
- Devices that prevent a process from starting if any part of the previous process was forgotten

Of the above examples, the first four are suitable for self inspection. The last two are designed for successive inspection. There are two types of inspection to consider when applying poka-yoke:

- Sensory inspection — depending on human judgment and senses; for example, concentration of color, degree of brightness in plating, etc.
- Physical inspection — not relying on human senses but using various detection instruments

If physical inspection measures are possible, they may be incorporated in a poka-yoke device or, better yet, in some means of source inspection or self inspection. Since successive inspection catches defects only after the first one has occurred, it should be reserved for cases where only sensory inspection is possible. Furthermore, it should be adopted only when neither source nor self inspection is feasible for significant technical or economic reasons.

In determining what sort of practical measure must be installed, we must consider the different functions and types of poka-yoke devices.

$$
\textbf{Correcting function} \left\{ \begin{array}{l} \bullet \text{ warning or} \\ \bullet \text{ control} \end{array} \right.
$$

$$
\textbf{Setting function} \left\{ \begin{array}{l} \bullet \text{ contact} \\ \bullet \text{ constant number} \\ \bullet \text{ motion step} \end{array} \right.
$$

Understanding the differences between these devices will help you successfully apply the concept of poka-yoke.* Finally, it is important to understand that simply implementing poka-yoke devices will not guarantee zero defects. The questions of which type of inspection to use and how to perform it have to be resolved. If they are not answered carefully, the absolute elimination of defects (defects = 0) cannot be achieved.

Eliminating Machine Breakdowns

The elimination of machine breakdowns is really a part of operational improvement and is discussed in that section of the book. It is,

---

* For a more detailed discussion of applications, see my book, *Zero Quality Control: Source Inspection and the Poka-Yoke System* (Cambridge, MA: Productivity Press, 1986).

however, also a form of process improvement in the Toyota production system because it makes stockless production possible. I will, therefore, address machine breakdowns here as well.

Visual Control

In most situations, some parts inventory is carried to assure continued production should a machine break down. Since the Toyota production system is a stockless system, it does not allow such a parts buildup. What solutions are implemented at Toyota when machines break down?

If there is trouble with either a worker or a machine operation, the operation or machine is stopped — all workers have been trained to respond to trouble in this fashion. Supervisors, on the other hand, are urged to try to keep machines and processing lines going. A conflict is thus created between workers and supervisors.

When problems occur, visual controls or *andon* (indicator lights) show supervisors and others where the trouble is. That troubles are immediately visually communicated to everyone is a remarkable feature of the Toyota production system; but when troubles arise, it is the actual solutions to these problems that are most important.

Actual Solutions: Preventing Recurrence

In most cases, we take only emergency measures when trouble occurs. Current conditions are masked until they recur, and visual control is not effective. At Toyota, the simple rule is that recurrence must be prevented. This rule is explained with the following analogy.

When you have an appendicitis, you can apply an icepack externally to alleviate the pain or remove the appendix surgically to prevent recurrence. Solutions will vary from one situation to the next, so Toyota makes the general recommendation that treatment in the nature of an appendectomy be chosen to prevent recurrence.

Superficial imitation, like putting up andon and so on, will not achieve significant results. Visual control is helpful, but taking thorough corrective measures in response to trouble is essential. Stop machines and processing lines now so they won't have to be stopped in the future!

A short anecdote will illustrate this point: Once, a visitor from A Electric was given an explanation of the Toyota production system.

He was impressed with the results achieved and was ready to return home when the presenter continued:

"Sir, you may be impressed by the success of the Toyota production system, but don't use it unless you really need it. At any rate, our inventories are very small, so whenever we go through our workplaces we are on the lookout for trouble: 'Do any machines sound abnormal?' 'Are workers using any odd motions?' We are thinking about improvements from eight in the morning until five in the evening."

Our visitor was most impressed with the following comment: "If top management will not commit itself to halt the machines or production lines when there is trouble, the Toyota production system should not be adopted and stockless production should not be attempted."

This is the sort of thinking that led to the development of Toyota's famous concept of autonomation — automation with a human touch.

7

Mechanics of the Toyota Production System

Improving Process —
Leveling and the Nagara System

In the past, process control had two important functions in production:

1. *Schedule control* — When will it be made (timing of production)?
2. *Balancing load* and *capacity control* — Can the work be performed? (Are load and capacity balanced?)

It is very important that load and capacity be balanced. They are defined as follows: *Load* is the volume of work that needs to be performed and *capacity* is the ability of machine and operator to complete the work. Toyota uses the term "leveling" to describe this balance.

WHAT IS LEVELING?

Production leveling is one of the pillars of the Toyota production system. It is aimed at producing the quantity taken by one process from the one that precedes it. In this system, the production processes are arranged to facilitate production of the required quantity at the required time, and workers, equipment, and all other factors are organized toward that end.

Thus, timing and volume are critical. If the later process takes the quantity it requires at irregular intervals, the preceding process will need extra equipment and labor. The greater this inconsistency, the more people and equipment the preceding process will require to meet its production requirements.

Moreover, Toyota employs the kanban to synchronize processes at its own plants and parts suppliers. Thus, the harmful effects of inconsistencies are transmitted from the preceding processes and on down to the parts suppliers.

The way to prevent creating vicious circles of this sort is to start at the chassis manufacturer — or to make it even clearer — go to the final process in which finished cars are assembled at Toyota Motors. There, make the flow as level as possible by rounding down peaks and filling in valleys.

Balancing Load and Capacity

Excess capacity, shown in the following formula, is determined by the relationship between load and capacity.

$$\text{excess capacity} = \frac{\text{capacity} - \text{load}}{\text{capacity}}$$

For example, if capacity equals 320 hours (8 hours × 20 days × 2 units) and load equals 280 hours, then

$$\text{excess capacity} = \frac{320 - 280}{320} = \frac{40}{320} \quad \text{or } 12.5\%$$

If capacity equals or exceeds load, the load can be processed, no matter how large it may be. On the other hand, no matter how small the load, if corresponding capacity is also small, the load probably cannot be processed. In such cases, some excess capacity must be available to balance load and capacity.

There are two time considerations regarding this balance of load and capacity: month to month over the course of a year (addressed earlier under "Flexibility of Capacity") and day to day within the month. Consider the example illustrated in Figure 31: During the first ten days, 300,000 sets of product A are produced at 50 percent capacity; during the next ten days, 600,000 sets of product B are produced at 100 percent capacity; during the last ten days, 900,000 sets of product C are produced at 150 percent capacity.

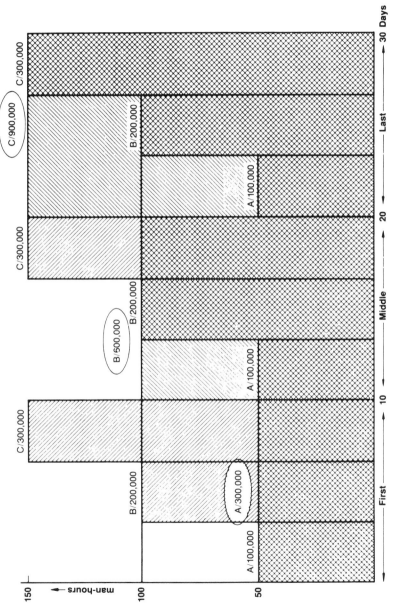

FIGURE 31. Load Adjustment and Leveling

If production is carried out according to this plan, there will be idle times during the first ten days because equipment is loaded at only 50 percent of capacity. The second ten-day period will be balanced, but capacity will have to be increased through overtime or temporary help to manage the 50 percent overload during the last period. In other words, load and capacity are balanced for the entire month but *not* within each ten-day period.

Obviously, this combination of idle time and overtime is unreasonable. Traditional control methods improve this situation by producing 50 percent of the product B load during the first ten days and 50 percent of product C load during the second ten days. This solution does equalize the ten-day periods, but it also results in the accumulation of stock. Since it effectively eliminates idle time and overtime, however, the resulting buildup of stock is considered reasonable, a "necessary evil."

Overproduction, however, is not tolerated at Toyota, so a different solution is required. We assumed that market demand for the month amounts to 300,000 units of product A, 600,000 of product B, and 900,000 of product C. As a practical matter, it would be difficult to produce 300,000 units of product A by the tenth of the month, 600,000 of product B by the twentieth, and 900,000 of product C by the thirtieth in three large lots — nor would this production pattern match consumer demand. Only a portion of the 300,000 of product A would be sold by the tenth of the month; the remainder would sit as excess inventory.

To avoid this, one third of the monthly production requirement for each product could be produced during each ten-day period — 100,000 A, 200,000 B, and 300,000 C — in other words, produce A during one-sixth of the production period of the first ten days, B during two-sixths, and C during three-sixths. In this way, inventory of products B and C produced during the first ten days can be reduced to one-third. If the time period were reduced even further, to five, three, or just one day, inventories would be still smaller.

Finally, if this pattern is replicated on the processing line so that one product A is followed by two of product B and three of product C, and so on, stock will be kept at a minimum.

This is "mixed production" as practiced at Toyota. Actual demand is determined through thorough market research; load and capacity are then balanced without resorting to overproduction. In the past, excess capacity adjustments and the existence of stock were considered mutually contradictory propositions. The genius of the Toyota production system is that it has transcended this conflict and led the way to an entirely new approach to regulating loads and capacities.

Segmented and Mixed Production

Characteristics of Load Plans

Under conventional process control systems, production was often planned in three stages:

- Master schedule — annual load plan
- Intermediate schedule — monthly load plan
- Detailed schedule — load plan for one to three days

These load plans might be for either *anticipatory* or *confirmed* production requirements and were determined by the relationship between the order-to-delivery period (D) and the production cycle (P).

Master schedule. Since the master schedule spans a lengthy period, it is generally a speculative plan based on demand forecasts.

Intermediate schedule. The intermediate schedule can be a confirmed plan if firm orders are determined before the production cycle; otherwise, it will be speculative. Typically, a one-month plan may be considered confirmed early in the month, but if actual demand differs, it will turn out to have been speculative. Confusion arises as more and more changes in production are required.

Detailed schedule. This schedule is generally confirmed because it is for only a short time period. When the production cycle or *lead time* (P) is longer than the period between order and required delivery (D), however, we must rely on a speculative plan.

Whether we produce to forecast or to demand is not actually related to the length of the period planned for. Rather, it is determined primarily by the relationship between how early orders are confirmed and production lead time.

Even if a factory is organized to produce to demand, when its order period is shorter than the production period, it is engaged in anticipatory production.

Reducing Inventories of Finished Goods

In anticipatory production, 100 percent accuracy of a forecast is unlikely. Finished goods inventory is inevitable along with the possibility of unnecessary stocks and losses. In the past, efforts were made to move up order decisions (that is, to lengthen the order-to-delivery period (D). But consumers have their own constraining circumstances and market demand is generally uncertain with respect to the amounts or types of product and when they will be needed. For these reasons, increasing the period between order and delivery is inappropriate. Anticipatory production appears to be the only solution. Toyota's policy, however, is one of production to orders received, or production to demand, which is based on significantly reducing the production cycle rather than pressuring customers to make ordering decisions earlier. This is accomplished by:

- Using the SMED system to implement small lot production
- Adopting production leveling, synchronization, and one-piece flow operations
- Using SMED to facilitate swift response to changes in orders

If we implement these innovations, we can begin production after an order has been placed. And, because forecasting is necessary only for very short periods, accuracy is improved. As a result, a significant reduction in finished goods inventories is achieved.

Segmented Production and Plan Units

The longer the period of production covered by a production plan, the more likely it is that production will deviate from actual orders. For example, when lead time is three days, a firm production schedule set on a monthly basis will become speculative later in the month, as time outruns the decisions to order.

A shortening of the production cycle must be accompanied by a shortening of the production segment adopted for the plan in order to avoid unnecessary inventory. A segmented production system (SPS) uses the following segments:

- H plan for *h*alf a month
- T plan for *t*en days
- W plan for one *w*eek
- D plan for one *d*ay

Under this system, monthly plans are also used for raw materials, machine capacities, and personnel requirements, etc. Once the monthly production plan is made, final or confirmed plans for units of half a month, ten days, one week, and one day are issued in advance at appropriate points. How much advance notice is given depends on the production cycle or lead time.

> Example 7.1 — Production planning — the T plan. At A Electric Company, production schedules are issued as follows:
>
> - The forecast for the next month on the 15th;
> - The confirmed plan for the first 10 days on the 25th;
> - The confirmed plan for the middle 10 days on the 5th;
> - The confirmed plan for the last 10 days on the 15th along with next month's forecast.
>
> Originally, all product A's were manufactured together once a month. Under the T plan:
>
> 1. The production of product A is divided among the three ten-day periods.
> 2. Regardless of the monthly schedule, production is revised in accordance with actual orders before a plan is finalized.
> 3. As a result, finished goods inventories at the plant and sales outlets have been cut in half.
> 4. Instead of the earlier one-month delay, changes in orders can now be reflected in the next ten-day period, reducing delivery shortfalls considerably and leading to increased capital turnover.

Like A Electric, Toyota has adopted a T plan. Since many of our ordinary living cycles are weekly, a W system is probably the next logical step. How then should we adjust the difference between the monthly and weekly allocations? We might also consider a daily planning unit, but if we do, planning flexibility and the efficiency of setup changing procedures must be dramatically improved.

Segmented Production Systems and
Small Lot Production Systems

So far, I have described segmented production as a system that divides up the period or cycle specified by an assured production plan. The significant feature of the next type of segmented production system we'll look at, however, is that it involves dividing up production lots.

Let's refer to the example we used in the section on load averaging, where the monthly production load was scheduled as follows: For the first ten days, 300,000 units of product A; for the middle ten days, 600,000 units of product B; and for the last ten days, 900,000 units of product C.

If production capacity for each ten-day period is 600,000 units, overcapacity during the first third of the month will result in idle time, and overloading during the last third of the month will necessitate overtime operations. Ordinarily, the advance creation of inventory makes it possible to average the load and avoid these scheduling problems. I came to the realization at one point, however, that the production of product C could be spread out over the entire month — there was nothing inherent in the nature of demand that required all 900,000 units of product C to be produced during the last ten-day period. The same thing was true for products A and B.

Thus, stocks could be cut significantly and loads adjusted by producing according to the schedule below:

	Product A	Product B	Product C
First ten days	100,000	200,000	300,000
Middle ten days	100,000	200,000	300,000
Last ten days	100,000	200,000	300,000

Additional inventory reductions and improved load adjustment could be obtained with a five-day production cycle of 50,000 units of A, 100,00 units of B and 150,000 units of C.

Benefits would multiply by going one step further, to a one-day production cycle of 10,000 units of A, 20,000 of B, and 30,000 of

C. The only step necessary would be to divide production into specific time periods and then carry out small lot production:

8:00 to 9:20 a.m.	10,000 units	product A
9:20 a.m. to noon	20,000 units	product B
1:00 to 5:00 p.m.	30,000 units	product C

As the production is subdivided and smaller and smaller lots are produced, however, setup changes become more frequent which makes a rationalized approach to setup changes — that is, the SMED system — an essential precondition.

Many plants have achieved striking results with a small lot segmented production system and I highly recommend the approach. To be most effective, however, suitable measures must be devised in advance, for example:

- Workers must be trained so they adapt easily to new operations
- Parts to be attached next must be brought to the line
- Jigs, tools, and machines must be prepared so that setup changes can be carried out using one-touch methods
- Assembly and operation errors must be prevented through the use of successive checks or self-checks and especially poka-yoke devices

With these methods, assembly lines at many plants have carried out setup changes so quickly that there were no empty pallets at the assembly lines.

No matter how fast changeovers take place, the differences in tact times between products will result in losses. Imagine the following example:

- Product A: Tact time = 30 seconds
- Product B: Tact time = 25 seconds

Here, we have to wait for the slower time of 30 seconds until a complete changeover can be performed. The more processes there are, the more time will be lost. This phenomenon exists whether you are moving from a fast tact time to a slow one or vice versa. In sum, time losses will increase as lot size falls and changeovers become more frequent.

The Toyota Complex Mixed Production System

To overcome this problem, the Toyota production system combines the production flow of products A and B. This *mixed production system* works as follows:

- Products A and B are combined in a single flow, with the result that total tact time is 55 seconds (30 + 25). No time is lost in the changeovers between products.
- At the same time, production of a product with a longer tact time requires workers to move a bit faster as they work.

The solution is further refined with the use of a *complex mixed production system* in which assembled vehicles move along the line in a variety of combinations (for example, A-A-A-B-B-C), that are subject to change. Changeover losses are significantly reduced with the use of extra workers to help out with operations that require longer tact times.

Advantages and Disadvantages of Mixed Production

Like any manufacturing methodology, mixed production has both advantages and disadvantages. Let us first consider the advantages:

- Load averaging, known as production leveling at Toyota, will smooth out the peaks and valleys of the production process
- Production leveling provides leveled loads both for parts fabrication processes and to parts suppliers
- Inventory can be cut substantially
- The *non-adjusted ratio* is improved as *double transport* is eliminated, making it unnecessary to store finished products in the plant and then ship them to sales outlets
- Overall efficiency increases as the division of labor is narrowed with production of two (or more) products by one small group of workers

The biggest disadvantage of mixed production is that it increases setup changes. From the operator's point of view, each switch from product A to product B involves a setup. Several countermeasures have been developed to compensate for this disadvantage:

- Training workers in multiple operations

- Providing multi-purpose jigs, tools, and machines to facilitate one-touch changeovers or designating multiple jigs and tools for use with specific products
- Incorporating successive checks, self-checks, and poka-yoke devices to prevent defects and guard against omission of parts
- Supplying parts to the assembly line in small lots and without error

Defects and inefficiencies will abound if measures such as these are not taken, and considerable losses will result despite the installation of new jigs, tools, and machines.

Choosing Between Segmented and Mixed Production Systems

As we have seen, the employment of small lot production in either segmented or mixed production systems can provide leveled loads to upstream parts fabrication processes and parts suppliers as well as reduce stocks of finished products. While their impact may vary, exactly the same kinds of results can be expected from both systems.

A mixed production system has the advantage of absorbing differences in production tact times. On the other hand, frequent operational and jig and tool changes as well as problems involving the proper use of tools and jigs are major disadvantages that can lead to significant losses unless workers are adequately prepared and trained before production begins.

Toyota uses a mixed production system because of the high costs of storing large, expensive finished products. In essence, the Toyota production system may be thought of as a very advanced segmented production system — it is quite effective but also very difficult to attain. Indeed, imitating it without adequate preparation is extremely risky. Those who believe that the Toyota production system is simply a matter of mixed production are laboring under serious misapprehensions.

Even without a mixed production system, most plants can achieve fairly satisfactory results by adopting a segmented production system.

Under both segmented and mixed production, it is essential to abandon the notion that all production has to be speculative and that market fluctuations create inventories of unwanted products. Rather, production must be viewed as something that naturally and faithfully conforms to firm orders. Management must seek cost reductions by shortening production cycles and overcoming all other difficulties.

It is the proper appreciation of small lot production and, at a deeper level, the drastic reduction of setup times, that lie at the core of this process.

Toyota, of course, is not the only corporation to employ a mixed production system. Consider the examples that follow.

Example 7.2 — Mixed production of refrigerators. The T Electric Company produces both large and small refrigerators. Using mixed production, the company succeeded in cutting warehoused finished product stocks to nearly zero. In the past, large refrigerators were built during the first half of the month and small ones during the second half. Since shipments to retail outlets were made up of both large and small models, a great deal of warehouse space was required for the large models.

Now, the company alternates between one large refrigerator and two small ones in a mixed production scheme and items are shipped as they are produced. Refrigerators are sent directly to retail outlets without passing through a warehouse. Another benefit is that inventories can be reduced considerably since it is now possible to respond to demand fluctuations by changing the production ratio of large and small refrigerators.

Example 7.3 — Segmented production of washing machines. A division of A Electric was quite successful in eliminating finished goods storage of its washing machines by using segmented production where export models with similar completion dates were assembled together. The percentage of other products sent directly to retailers was also increased with the help of segmented or mixed production. At A Electric, a one percent rise in the non-adjusted ratio amounts to a savings of $1,500 a month when machines are shipped directly to retail outlets instead of each day's output being stored in a warehouse and then reloaded for delivery to retailers.

Example 7.4 — Mixed production with three products. Finally, consider a situation where required labor per piece, or tact time, for three different products was as follows: 30 seconds for product X; 45 seconds for product Y; and 60 seconds for product Z. Changeover losses inevitably occurred because assembly changes made it necessary to perform changeovers in step with the longest tact time. Losses were ordinarily on the order of 10 to 20 percent when changeovers were frequent.

Mixed production, however, allowed the flow of products to adhere to a mean tact time, calculated as follows:

total tact time: $X + Y + Z = 30 + 45 + 60 = 135$ seconds

$$\text{mean tact time:} \quad \frac{135 \text{ seconds}}{3} = 45 \text{ seconds}$$

The total tact time could be constant when operations were carried out as follows:

- A short break is taken before working on product X
- Work on product Y proceeds normally
- The worker walks a little while working on product Z

Thus, each set of three products could be synchronized, cutting changeover losses to zero.

Leveling and Non-Stock

As a system that adjusts surplus capacities and rejects stock, mixed production is the key to a new conception of leveling.

While some argue that the most important benefit of the Toyota production system is that it prevents surplus capacity disparities from influencing upstream processes, its real superiority lies in its ability to minimize stocks of finished products.

The adjustment of surplus capacities has always been an important function of process management. In the past, however, it was nearly always carried out in an environment where the existence of stock was tolerated. By contrast, the Toyota production system views *non-stock* as a prerequisite and asks what can be done to adjust surplus capacities while satisfying this essential condition. Leveling to adjust surplus capacities via a mixed production system is the distinctive feature of Toyota's mixed production system.

The preceding discussion makes clear that leveled production offers the following advantages:

1. Stocks of finished products can be minimized
2. Leveled loads can be provided to upstream processes

As examples 7.2 to 7.4 show, mixed production is not without problems. At Toyota, these revolve around:

- Errors in work motions
- The attachment of incorrect parts or the failure to attach some parts

Since each changeover requires different motions on the part of the worker, the following issues should be considered carefully:

- In common processes, combining operations that require similar motions viding poka-yoke devices that make inappropriate work motions impossible

- Installing poka-yoke devices that prevent parts errors and missing parts
- Combining models involving processes that could use common jigs and tools
- Using multiple tools and finding one-touch methods to exchange tools and dies

The old saying "you have nothing to fear but fear itself" is appropriate, however, because surprisingly few problems crop up with mixed production when you keep the above issues in mind. Moreover, a 10 to 20 percent improvement in productivity and considerable reductions in finished product stocks are usually achieved from the very first trial.

THE NAGARA SYSTEM

Within the Toyota production system, considerable energy has recently been devoted to promoting something called the *nagara system*. The name *nagara* derives from a Japanese expression that indicates the simultaneity of two actions. The nagara system takes mixed production one step further by facilitating a one-piece flow that transcends shop divisions in fulfilling the production process.

> *Example 7.5 — Use of the nagara system in automobile assembly.* At the S Automobile Company, spot welding is being carried out to assemble automobile bodies, and a simple press is provided nearby. After finishing the spot welding, the worker inserts a sheared plate into the press and activates a switch. A hydraulic cylinder then slowly lowers the upper die of the press and blanks the plate. When the one-minute welding operation is finished and the next piece comes to the press, the previous piece is already done and the worker picks it up and welds it to the body.
>
> The press makes use of a hydraulic cylinder to move the die very slowly, a mechanism that cost no more than $500 to construct.

Observing this arrangement, I realized that the nagara system is characterized by three significant features:

- Even the briefest increment of time is utilized. In this example, the approximately two seconds the worker needed to insert the material and push the switch were taken from excess spot welding time.

- Synchronization, not speed, is the issue. If only one part is needed per minute, there is no reason to finish the work more quickly. Here, an inexpensive press with a slow hydraulic cylinder was all that was required.
- The system disproves the theory that pressed products must be manufactured in a press shop. Here, the coherent one-piece flow transcended shop divisions to follow the production process.

In the past, the forming would have been carried out rapidly on a regular press, parts would have been deposited on a pallet, and a forklift would then have been used for transport. Clearly, however, there was no need for such high-speed equipment.

Example 7.6 — The nagara system in a spray painting operation. At K Manufacturing, after machines perform the drilling and tapping on the line, parts are placed in a one-meter cubical box that is, in fact, a device for spray-painting parts. Closing the lid of the box trips a switch and sets the operation in motion. Small fittings and wires are attached to parts in a one-piece flow after they are removed from the box. More than 100 of these boxes have been integrated into processing and assembly lines. This has eliminated approximately 80 percent of the painting which earlier required moving parts to the painting shop.

This elimination of transport and storage not only led to a considerable decrease in labor costs; by significantly cutting lead times, it also facilitated dramatic reductions in stock. One might think that this new approach required more paint, yet paint costs actually decreased. Paint sprays now conform to the specific parts being painted, while, in the past, paint was sprayed indiscriminately over a wide area. Indeed, the people at the plant were correct when they told me they used to spray-paint the air inside the painting booth. In observing the new method, I realized that what had been achieved was a comprehensive and coherent one-piece flow — from machines, to painting, to assembly.

Some years ago, while touring Europe on a study mission, I visited a machine tool manufacturer in Milan. The president of the company told me it was the creation of the European Economic Community that made his business possible. He said that the absence of tariffs made raw materials cheaper and finished products easier to sell. "Without the EEC," he told me, "our business would not have survived." His remark left me deeply impressed with the power of the EEC.

Similarly, the critical significance of the nagara system is that we obliterate the boundaries between forging, casting, presswork, machining, painting, and assembly. In their place, we establish comprehensive and coherent one-piece flow processes which conform faithfully to the processes for the particular product.

Recently, I have observed nagara systems at plants that have implemented the Toyota production system, and I sometimes get the impression that people, perhaps because of an impressionistic understanding of the concept, pay attention only to one of its aspects — the effective utilization of time. This is a limited and ultimately ineffective perspective, however. We need to understand that the real significance of the nagara system lies in comprehensive and integrated one-piece flow operations unrestrained by divisions existing within a plant.

While the nagara system may be expected to continue as one of the directions in which the Toyota production system will develop, it has already been adopted by many organizations. Consequently, it is extremely important that the true significance and intent of the system be clearly understood.

Summary of Chapters 6 and 7

Processes are composed of four phenomena: processing, inspection, transport, and delays. Of these, only processing increases added value, the other three — inspection, transport and delay — do not; in fact, for the most part, they only increase costs.

The Toyota production system is focused on a relentless elimination of "waste." Everything except work that increases added value is regarded as waste, so every effort must be made to eliminate inspections, transport, and delays.

Various strategies have been adopted to accomplish this:

- Inspections: Inspections that don't permit defects and 100 percent inspections — including the active use of specific poka-yoke techniques — aim at eliminating all defects at a very low cost. Additionally, defects are prevented by making improvements in the conditions that generate them in the first place.
- Transport: Transport is eliminated or cut to an absolute minimum by improving layout to conform as much as possible to process flow. Efficient transport devices are used when transport is unavoidable.

There remains the problem of delays. By their very nature, delays compensate for shortcomings in processing, inspection, and transport. For example, a delay — the storage of stock — can avoid confusion in the production flow when machines break down, defects occur, or items are not transported in time. This is why production management tends to treat stock as a lubricant that assures the smooth flow of production. In reality, stock is like a narcotic — tolerate it once and you'll soon slide into a state of addiction and require larger and larger quantities in order to feel secure.

The Toyota production system utterly rejects this view of stock. Indeed, it takes a fundamentals-oriented approach to improvement, asking why stocks are necessary in the first place and then making improvements in the areas that create the need for stocks.

As one carries the Toyota production system philosophy further, one constantly encounters the fundamental notion of non-stock — the idea of doing away with delays and the waste of overproduction. Correctly understood, the Toyota production system is an innovative approach to production that is founded on the revolutionary insight that stock must be rejected utterly.

How did this come about?

- Market demand calls for high-diversity, low-volume production in response to customer orders.
- This requires relentless efforts to carry out production in small lots. Once this was understood, the need to drastically shorten setup and changeover times became apparent. The SMED system responded to this need.
- Production cycles had to be shortened as well. One-piece flows were used to accomplish this, working upstream from assembly processes to build coherent flows from parts processing to assembly.
- Attempts to develop such a system under stringent non-stock conditions were successful — this was the genius of the Toyota production system and the fundamental reason for the company's astonishingly high profits.

A clear understanding of these concepts is essential. If you merely imitate the superficial aspects of the Toyota production system and hastily apply what you see as a system for getting parts just-in-time, you will end up with the opposite of the desired result. This will not only create havoc in your own plant but also cause your suppliers a great deal of stress.

I have stressed repeatedly that the essential feature of the Toyota production system is the relentless elimination of stock. In fact, however, this is not itself the ultimate goal. The real aim is to lower costs, and the elimination of stock is nothing more than a means to this end.

The following story drives home this crucial point. Some years ago, I organized a reunion of about 50 alumni of the production engineering course I taught at Toyota Motors. Despite his busy schedule, Mr. Ohno kindly agreed to address the group.

At the gathering, various people talked about the good old days. About half-way through the meal, I overheard Mr. Ohno say to his neighbor, Mr. Takimura, president of Tsuda Ironworks and a graduate of the second training class:

"All right, Takimura! Go ahead and keep a little stock around. After all, the crucial thing is for the company to make money."

Knowing that Mr. Ohno viewed stock as his archenemy, I was shocked to hear him tell someone that it was all right to keep inventory on hand. My surprise, however, merely added to the impact of his true intentions as revealed in his next sentence:

"However, don't think that it is all right to keep stock around forever!"

All too often, we tolerate stock as long as we are making money and in no time at all, we come to accept inventory as a fact of life. What impressed me in Mr. Ohno's words, by contrast, was his aggressive attitude toward making fundamental improvements:

"Current conditions may make it necessary to keep stocks around right now; but keeping them is inherently wasteful, and you will have to find ways to make money without carrying inventory at some point."

This story illustrates that the elimination of stock is nothing more than a means to an end, and the end is cost reduction. In some circumstances, it may be permissible to keep inventories. One must not be lulled into complacency, however, and forget that stock is inherently wasteful. A major feature of the Toyota production system is that it continuously seeks out higher-order means to cut costs without accumulating stock. This is the line of thinking that leads to true understanding.

8

Mechanics of the
Toyota Production System

Improving Operations

Operations are the second pillar supporting production activities. As noted earlier, operations concern the flow of equipment and operators in time and space. Improvements in operations have long been emphasized in the Toyota production system.

In this section, we will discuss these topics: the components of operations, standard operations, the man-machine interaction and "human intelligence," and manpower cost reduction. Each is analyzed with reference to the Toyota production system.

COMPONENTS OF OPERATIONS

As explained earlier, operations have three basic components: preparation and after-adjustment, principal operations, and marginal allowances. Operational improvements must be developed for each of these categories.

Preparation and After-Adjustment

These are the so-called *setup change* operations that usually take place before and after production of each lot. They are considered useful operations. In the past, most production occurred in large lots because setup changeovers were very time-consuming. Under those conditions, producing in large lots resulted in lower labor costs but it also caused an undesirable increase in in-process stock. Economic lot sizes were calculated to balance out these two effects.

The basic assumption behind economic lot size, however, is that drastic reductions in changeover times are impossible. The development of SMED setups led to the collapse of this assumption, and the need for economic lots vanished.

Using SMED to cut setup times is often regarded merely as a way to improve the operating rates of machines, and there is no question that it does so. It should not be forgotten, however, that even greater business profits can be gained by applying SMED to process improvements, such as using small lot production to eliminate stocks or getting rid of finished product inventories through the use of quick changeovers for order-based production.

The adoption of SMED setups is a decisive element of the Toyota production system and is discussed in detail in Chapter 3.

Principal Operations

Principal operations are those useful operations that are repeated for each item. They can be subdivided into two categories:

Main operations. Operations that directly carry out actual cutting, forming, welding, etc. In terms of the process, they are the only tasks that actually fulfill these substantive functions:

- Processing — Operations directly carrying out cutting, forming, welding, etc.
- Inspection — Operations in which comparisons with standards are conducted, such as measuring an item with a gauge
- Transport — Operations that change the location of items
- Delay — Operations in which items are maintained in their current state

Incidental operations. Operations in which switches are operated or items are attached or removed for processing. These operations complement main operations.

Margin Allowances

These operations occur irregularly and are of two types, personal and non-personal.

Personal allowances. These allowances are related to human physiological and psychological needs and include:

- Fatigue allowances — Breaks that allow workers to recover from fatiguing work
- Personal hygiene allowances — Breaks that allow workers to use rest rooms, drink water, wipe away perspiration, etc.

Non-personal allowances. These allowances are related to the non-human aspects of tasks and include:

- Operational allowances — Allowances for the operation itself, including oiling, clearing away chips, etc.
- Workplace allowances — Allowances for late parts, machine breakdowns, etc.

STANDARD OPERATIONS

The second aspect of operational improvement lies in an understanding of the concept of standard operations. In this section, we fully explore this idea within the Toyota production system and its three temporal aspects.

Standard Operations and the Toyota Production System

Mr. Taiichi Ohno has provided an excellent summary of standard operations and the Toyota production system. In his book, he writes as follows:

> Standard work sheets and the information contained in them are important elements of the Toyota production system. For a production person to be able to write a standard work sheet that other workers can understand, he or she must be convinced of its importance.
>
> We have eliminated waste by examining available resources, rearranging machines, improving machining processes, installing autonomous systems, improving tools, analyzing transportation methods, and optimizing the amount of materials at hand for machining. High production efficiency has also been maintained by preventing the recurrence of defective products, operational mistakes, and accidents, and by incorporating workers' ideas. All of this is possible because of the inconspicuous standard work sheet.

The standard work sheet effectively combines materials, workers, and machines to produce efficiently. At Toyota, this procedure is called a work combination. The result is the standard work procedure.

The standard work sheet has changed little since I was first asked to prepare one 40 years ago at the textile plant. However, it is based thoroughly on principles and plays an important role in Toyota's visual control system. It clearly lists the three elements of the standard work procedure as:

1. Cycle time
2. Work sequence
3. Standard inventory

Cycle time is the time allotted to make one piece or unit. This is determined by production quantity; that is, the quantity required and the operating time. Quantity required per day is the quantity required per month divided by that month's number of operating days. Cycle time is computed by dividing operating hours by the quantity required per day. Even when cycle time is determined this way, individual times may differ.

In Japan, it is said that "time is the shadow of motion." In most cases, delay is generated by differences in operator motion and sequence. The job of the field supervisor, section chief, or group foreman is to train workers. I have always said that it should take only three days to train new workers in proper work procedures. When instruction in the sequence and key motions is clear, workers quickly learn to avoid redoing a job or producing defective parts.

To do this, however, the trainer must actually take the hands of the workers and teach them. This generates trust in the supervisor. At the same time, workers must be taught to help each other. Because people are doing the work, rather than machines, there will be individual differences in work times caused by physical conditions. These differences will be absorbed by the first worker in the process, just as in the baton touch zone in a track relay. Carrying out the standard work methods in the cycle time helps worker harmony grow.

The term "work sequence" means just what it says. It does not refer to the order of processes along which products flow. It refers rather to the sequence of operations, or the order of operations in which a worker processes items: transporting them, mounting them on machines, removing them from machines, and so on.

Standard inventory refers to the minimum intra-process work-in-process needed for operations to proceed. This includes items mounted on machines.

Even without changing machine layout, standard inventory between processes is generally unnecessary if work is carried out in the order of machining processes. All that is needed are the items mounted on the various machines. On the other hand, one item's worth (or two where two items are mounted on machines) of standard inventory will be required if work proceeds by machine function rather than by the process flow.

In the Toyota production system, the fact that parts have to arrive just-in-time means that standard inventories have to be met that much more rigorously.*

Three Temporal Aspects of Standard Operations

In the past, standard operation times were usually set either by observing current operations and excluding any abnormal elements or by using a shorter time than the observed one. I believe this approach to be faulty on two counts. First, differences in time will indicate fundamental differences in motion since time is merely a reflection of motion. Furthermore, it is possible for motions to differ even though times are the same; setting fixed times does not guarantee identical work motions. Second, even when all abnormal values are excluded, the times obtained by measuring the status quo are no more than mean values that hardly qualify as standards.

What then are standard times? And what are the standard operations on which they are based? To answer these questions, we must take into account what we might call the three temporal aspects of standard operations: past, present, and future.

The Past

As noted above, standard times are not the same as mean operating times with abnormal values excluded. Similarly, standard operations are not the same as average operations.

Clearly, differences in times are caused by underlying differences in motions. In turn, motions differ because work conditions vary considerably.

It follows, then, that a true standard operation is carried out in a setting where work conditions have been optimized through the relentless pursuit of the goals behind each of the questions below.

- What — the object of production. What product?
- Who — the subject of production. What people and machines?

---

* *Toyota*, pp. 21-23.

- How — the method. How to go about it?
- Where — the space. Where should items be put? By what method of transport?
- When — What time frame? What timing?

This is what is meant by the past, or pre-existing, aspect of standard operations. In the Toyota production system, the phrase "IE for profits" reflects this pursuit.

When I visited the Y Auto Body Company, Mr. Yamaguchi, a department head, told me the following story:

"We recently purchased a video camera and began filming operations on the shop floor. After each recording session, we'd invite the worker we had filmed, the improvement team concerned, and the worker's immediate supervisor and play the tape for them. The workers, after observing themselves perform the particular operation, usually came up with lots of suggestions for improvement, many of them quite good, and we'd implement the good ones immediately. As a result, the percentage of suggestions integrated into production increased tremendously. It used to be that people wouldn't go along with suggestions made by improvement teams; now, the workers were coming up with their own ideas and putting them into effect right away. After their initial ideas had been implemented, they continued to report even small problems promptly and make suggestions for further improvement. In the past, many problems had simply been ignored.

"As I watched the videos," Yamaguchi went on, "I was struck by the realization that people usually don't get the chance to see themselves from behind." This was an important observation; the fact is that we hardly ever get to see ourselves from the rear — to see ourselves objectively.

The Toyota production system insists that shop floor workers themselves write out standard operations because it is a form of objective viewing, a process that goes beyond mere observation of the tasks in question. Describing operations on paper in this fashion makes objective observations possible and facilitates operations improvement.

The Present

This is the phase of standard operation in which a standard operating chart is used to train new workers. Using a standard operating chart is more efficient and less subject to inadvertent omissions than having a supervisor teach directly from personal experience. It is particularly effective in teaching new workers the key tips and tricks involved in a task.

The Toyota production system trains new employees to work independently in three days; standard operating charts play a major role in making this possible. The approach also increases learning efficiency because the workers keep referring to the standard operating charts until they are familiar with the techniques.

The Future

Inspection is defined as comparison with a standard. Comparison of actual conditions with standards tells whether or not outcomes are acceptable and reveals any abnormalities.

The Toyota production system demands that all work be performed within standard times, and shop supervisors are charged with holding workers to those standards. The future aspect of standard operations lies in the constant improvement of these criteria. Shop supervisors are encouraged to feel embarrassed when the same standard operating charts are used for a long time because improvements in shop operations should be made continuously.

If a task is not carried out within the standard time established for it, it must be determined whether nonstandard motions are to blame. The standard operating chart is most significant here since it facilitates the collecting of information needed for improvements. In this way, the past aspect reappears and the three aspects of standard operation progress in an unending cycle.

Types of Standard Operating Charts

So far, I have limited myself to using the generic term "standard operating chart." There are several versions of the chart. Here are a few specific examples:

- *Capacity charts by part* record the order of processes, process names, machine numbers, basic times, tool-changing times, number of items and processing capacity.
- *Standard task combination sheets* determine the order in which individual workers' operations take place.

- *Task manuals* determine procedures for elements of the operations requiring special attention, for example, machine operation, tool changing, setup changes, parts processing, and assembly. Indications are provided for each process.
- *Task instruction manuals* for those engaged in training workers provide guidelines for correctly teaching standard operations. They outline the tasks of each worker with respect to the output of the line and indicate key safety and quality points according to the sequence of operations. They also diagram equipment layouts for operations performed by individual workers and indicate quality check methods, cycle times, operational procedures, and standard on-hand stock.
- *Standard operating sheets* are the equipment layout diagrams from the Task Instruction Manual enlarged for display at processing or assembly lines on the shop floor. They indicate cycle times, order of operations, standard on-hand stocks, net work times, and safety and quality checks.

FROM WORKER TO MACHINE

As we already discussed, the use of human labor in production developed through several stages:

1. Manual power was used to attach and remove workpieces, feed tools, and carry out cutting.
2. Cutting was mechanized but manual power was still used to attach and remove workpieces and to feed tools.
3. Cutting and tool feeding were mechanized and manual power was used only to attach and remove workpieces. At this point, processing became independent of workers. Because equipment was not 100 percent reliable, however, workers performed the job of monitoring machines.
4. The developers of the Toyota production system, realizing that humans were needed to monitor machine processing only because machines did not have the capacity to detect abnormalities in production, built "human intelligence" into the machine design. This eliminated the need for workers to monitor the machines.

At this stage, most plants needed to go through a long period in which:

- "Automation" meant the mechanization of processing as well as workpiece attachment and removal. Even so, "automated" machines were not endowed with functions of the human brain. This meant that workers had to remain close even to those machines that had been automated.
- True autonomation was reached when machines were provided with a human brain function, that is, the ability to detect abnormalities.

In sum, the shift from workers to machines encompasses two issues: how to transfer the work of human hands to machines, and how to transfer the work of the human brain to machines. The early success in making this important shift is a significant feature of the Toyota production system.

MANPOWER COST REDUCTION

To improve operations, the Toyota production system focuses on manpower cost reductions. By comparison, relatively little emphasis is placed on raising the operating rates even though they are, along with man, the primary agents of production.

The reason for this is straightforward: For a given period of time, the loss will be about five times greater for idle workers than for idle machines. Moreover, Toyota realized that no matter how low equipment operating rates might be, for the purposes of cost reduction, it was more effective to concentrate on human labor costs. Failure to grasp this point clearly and keep it in mind may well lead to a misunderstanding of the exact role manpower cost reduction plays in the Toyota production system.

Improving Methods of Operation

Nearly all of our current operations may be thought of as a combined effort of humans and machines. The improvement of methods of operation, therefore, takes the three forms described below.

Improvements in Human Motions

These are *motion study* improvements involving such factors as the arrangement of parts or operational procedures. In the typical case, we can cut operation times 10 to 20 percent by such means.

Boxes play a key role in improving human motions. Although people generally make use of boxes for transporting and storing large quantities of products, little attention has been paid to their usefulness for processing. Several conditions must be satisfied in this latter regard:

- Items must be arranged neatly
- Items must be uniformly aligned
- Items must be easily accessible at a fixed location

This subject matter will require considerable additional study.

Improvements in Machine Movements

These involve the development of superior machines and improved work methods to raise efficiency. Examples include raising output by increasing machine cutting speeds, reducing times through simultaneous cutting on multi-axis machines, and using multiple turret heads to shorten tool replacement times. Another approach might be to increase efficiency by milling instead of using a shaping process.

Mechanizing Human Motions

This involves the elimination of human motions and includes: mechanized (as opposed to manual) attachment and removal of workpieces and the adoption of automatic lubricating devices.

In the Toyota production system, mechanization is considered only after human motions have been thoroughly improved. Why? One might spend a mere $500 to mechanize existing human motions and achieve a 20 percent increase in efficiency. Suppose, however, that one could achieve the same 20 percent gain by examining the physical arrangement of items and changing operational procedures. One would have to say that the $500 investment was a waste.

There are many engineers who ignore the waste in motions right before their eyes because of their preoccupation with mechanizing everything in sight. For example, they will take delight in raising efficiency with a device to feed workpieces automatically into a process when it might have been possible to achieve the same increase manually by bringing the machines in the preceding process closer so that products could flow directly, thereby eliminating the need for a parts feeder.

Another example involving an automobile parts assembly process with numerous model types illustrates the point nicely. Here, the original idea was to place pallets on a mechanized turntable and bring the needed part to the front at the press of a button. Instead, parts were rearranged to conform to their frequency of use, making the more frequently used parts the most easily accessible. This increased ease of movements and achieved the required rise in efficiency.

There are two lessons here: First, make thorough improvements in work motions before considering mechanization. Second, don't confuse improving equipment with improving operations. Instead of lowering costs, improving equipment first will tend to raise them.

Saving Labor, Manpower Cuts, and Minimal Manpower

Taiichi Ohno's book contains the following discussion about saving labor:

> In our company, we use the term "worker saving" instead of "labor saving." The term "labor saving" is somehow easily misused in a manufacturing company. Labor-saving equipment such as the lift and bulldozer, used mainly in construction work, is directly connected to reducing manpower.
>
> In automobile plants, however, a more relevant problem is partial and localized automation. For example, in work involving several steps, an automatic device is installed only at the last stage. At other points in the operation, work continues to be done manually. I find this kind of labor saving all wrong. If automation is functioning well, that is fine. But if it is simply used to allow someone to take it easy, it is too costly.*

Mr. Ohno further explains the concept in terms of minimal manpower:

> The company newspaper reported on a talk I gave on worker saving. In the story, the term "labor saving" was printed in error as "using fewer workers." But when I saw it, I thought, "This is true." "Using fewer workers" gets at the heart of the problem far better than "labor saving."

---

* *Toyota*, p. 67.

When we say "labor saving," it sounds bad because it implies eliminating a worker. Labor saving means, for example, a job that took 10 workers in the past is now done by eight workers — eliminating two people.

"Using fewer workers" can mean using five or even three workers depending on the production quantity — there is no fixed number. "Labor saving" suggests that a manager hires a lot of workers to start with, reducing the number when they are not needed. "Using fewer workers," by contrast, can also mean working with fewer workers from the start.

In actual experience, Toyota had a labor dispute in 1950 as a result of reducing its workforce. Immediately after its settlement, the Korean War broke out and brought special demands. We met these demands with just enough people and still increased production. This experience was valuable and since then, we have been producing the same quantity as other companies but with 20 to 30 percent fewer workers.

How was this possible? In short, it was the effort, creativity, and power of its people that enabled Toyota to put into practice the methods that ultimately have become the Toyota production system.*

At first glance, the above seems to suggest that manpower should not be cut to make jobs easier. I don't think that is what is really being said.

Qualitative versus Quantitative Manpower Reduction

Consider some instances of qualitative manpower reduction:

- Mechanical power is used when items are too heavy for human beings to lift
- Mechanization is used where transporting loads over a long distance is difficult
- Mechanization is used where the need to apply force (however minimal) in an unnatural position can bring on occupation-related deformities such as kyphosis

The Toyota production system fully accepts cases like the above where mechanization is used to make work easier.

Now consider a case of quantitative manpower reduction where only a little force is needed but mechanization is used to get a time-consuming job done more quickly than it can be done by hand. The

---

* *Toyota*, pp. 67-68

production engineering department's theoretical calculations will show that manpower was reduced and that a 30 percent time savings was achieved. In many cases, however, the reduction in time will merely increase waiting time and have no effect on the number of people involved. The Toyota production system argues that such an exercise is pointless unless the number of people can actually be reduced — no matter how much emphasis is placed on calculated values — even if "labor" has been saved.

As seen below, mechanization has other pitfalls. The Toyota production system places high priority on active improvements because mechanization often involves the following scenario:

- There is a high probability that main operations (for example, cutting and forming) and other operations that contribute to added value are actively tied to profits.
- The mechanization of incidental operations (such as attaching and removing workpieces or operating switches) achieves only passive improvement since such operations raise costs but are not directly linked to increasing added value.

When we aim for improvement, we look for ways to make things easier, better, quicker, and cheaper; initial priority is generally given to making things easier. The reason for this is simple; work is a strain and its most obvious manifestation is fatigue. It is an instinctive human desire to make production easier, and there is nothing wrong with this desire.

A review of the long history of human progress shows that every improvement has been accompanied by labor savings. Just as the six-day work week was shortened to five days and the 45-hour week is now 40 hours, the work week will probably be shortened to 35 hours and even to 30 hours in the future. At any point in history, however, we will have to admit that time reductions referred to as *labor savings* are pointless if they simply result in increased waiting.

There is a much better approach. Rather than starting out with a wasteful excess of people and gradually cutting back, it is better to begin the job with minimal manpower and handle production increases not by adding people but through creative ideas for improvement and rationalization. It is more effective, in other words, to try to improve before you find yourself in an absolutely critical state.

Many companies hire large numbers of people. When work falls off, they continue to operate at full capacity because they don't want workers to be idle. This gives rise to the waste of overproduction which, in turn, causes other kinds of waste. As the Toyota production system demonstrates, this can be prevented by producing only required quantities and building a system in which tasks are always performed by the minimum number of workers. In this way, unneeded items simply are not produced.

The Toyota production system also makes liberal use of forklifts and belt and chain conveyors. In short, it argues that:

- Effective labor-saving measures must be employed.
- Starting out with a wasteful excess of workers must be avoided because it will later necessitate manpower cuts.
- Changes in production must be addressed by using minimal manpower to begin with.
- Manpower reductions based on abstract calculations must be avoided because they are meaningless. Costs will not fall unless manpower cuts are made.

Integrating Waiting and Margin Allowances

Obviously, waiting time is seen as wasteful in any production plant. In the Toyota production system, however, the roles of humans and machines are totally distinct. The term *waiting*, for example, is used in situations where humans monitor machines even though the machines do the work automatically.

Take the case of a machine once activated by one press of a button. For "safety" reasons, the button must now be manually depressed during the entire time the machine is running. At Toyota, this too is considered waiting. Their approach is to start the machine with a single push of the button and to deal with the safety problem as a separate issue.

The Toyota production system also makes every effort to free people from operational allowance tasks such as adding cutting oil or wiping away chips. In addition, fatigue allowances and workplace allowances (such as delays due to the late arrival of parts or machine breakdowns) are kept separate from regular cycle times as a matter of course.

Fatigue allowances are consolidated in the form of breaks in mid-morning and mid-afternoon, and there is a one-hour lunch break. When parts are delayed or a machine breaks down, the problem is attacked by stopping the line or the equipment and then taking fundamental steps to ensure that it doesn't recur.

Merely to remove waiting and marginal allowances from standard times is meaningless. These actions will not contribute to cost reduction unless linked to minimal manpower. This is why the Toyota production system stresses the need to avoid "isolated islands." Ohno explains the term as follows:

> If workers are isolated here and there, they cannot help each other. But if work combinations are studied and *work distribution*, or work positioning, done to enable workers to assist each other, the number of workers can be reduced. When work flow is properly laid out, small isolated islands do not form.*

Machine Layout and Worker Efficiency

Human beings and machines are completely separate from one another in the Toyota production system. Machine layout, therefore, follows the process flow of the product. The "flow of people," however, is entirely independent of machines and need not adhere to the product flow; indeed, it need only take varying automatic processing times into account and lay out operations to maximize operator efficiency and avoid isolated islands.

This means that comprehensive layouts, such as the V, L, or U-layout, are needed because they address themselves to the flow of both products and people. As much as possible, equipment should be laid out around the outside of the chosen pattern and workers stationed on the inside, both to reduce isolation and to facilitate mutual assistance.

We can say that one of the most important ways of increasing productivity in the Toyota production system is to consolidate the excess capacity generated by operational improvements and link it to the achievement of minimal manpower.

Similarly, when there is a certain variability in actual operations, for example with the joint operations involved in assembly tasks, this

---

* *Toyota*, p. 123.

approach encourages adjacent workers to assist one another. As discussed earlier, there are two models for passing the baton from one team member to another: the swimming model and the track-and-field model.

In the swimming model, the next swimmer — no matter how fast she may be — cannot start until the previous swimmer has touched the edge of the pool.

Track events, on the other hand, use a "relay zone" that allows runners to help each other out. If the first runner is the faster, he will hand over the baton at the end of the relay zone. Conversely, he can hand over the baton at the beginning of the relay zone if the second runner is faster.

Applying this concept in a manufacturing setting, we could say:

- If worker A finishes early, he begins work on surplus parts received from the preceding process.
- If worker A is slow, worker B takes up one of the parts between A and B, and no confusion arises in the flow.

Cushions of this sort mean that the number of items on the line is nearly always some multiple of the number of workers on the line. When you ask people to describe these items between processes, the most frequent response is that they are goods being assembled.

Since the Toyota production system does not permit items to accumulate between work stations, all goods not being handled are referred to as stock. And because stock is not tolerated, the system requires each worker to learn the operations performed at the two processes adjacent to her own. As in any good team, when one worker falls behind in her task the worker at the next process will assist her. Conversely, a worker who finishes early is generally asked to wait. It is the supervisor's job to reapportion tasks on the basis of these phenomena. This, in fact, constitutes one type of visual control.

These situations clearly reflect the Toyota production system's concepts of non-stock production and thorough waste elimination.

Use of Multiple Machine Handling Operations

When I first visited Toyota Motors in 1955, one of the things that surprised me most was their use of multiple machine handling operations. At the time, Toyota operated 3,500 machines with only

700 workers, a ratio of one worker to five machines. The accepted practice in most plants of that era was to have each worker in charge of one machine; it was not unusual, in fact, for machines to be run by two or even more workers.

Multiple machine handling operations put a single worker in charge of more than one machine. This worker inserts or removes workpieces on one machine while another one carries out automatic processing. With this kind of operation, it can happen that a machine has stopped processing by the time the operator reaches it. If this lowers the operating rate of the machine, the number of machines for which the operator is responsible could be reduced. Most likely, however, this would result in the operator having to wait. When faced with such decisions, the Toyota production system will nearly always opt for a drop in machine operating rates instead of an increase in operator waiting time. Capital equipment depreciation eventually gives a company free use of a machine, but humans must be paid wages indefinitely — wages that tend to rise over time. In addition, per-hour losses for humans are generally about five times higher than those for machines.

In recent years, the Toyota production system has been forcefully advocating what it calls "multi-process handling" which can be defined as the performance of multiple machine handling operations in accordance with the flow of operations. This is in contrast with multi-machine handling which refers to having a worker in charge of several machines without relation to the flow of operations. These two types of multiple machine handling operations can also be distinguished as follows:

- Vertical multiple machine handling operations equal multi-process handling
- Horizontal multiple machine handling operations equal multi-machine handling

The use of multi-process handling in which a worker handles several machines in accordance with the process flow has two advantages. First, it improves the flow of processes. Second, it raises worker productivity.

Figure 32 illustrates these principles. Here, actual equipment processing time per piece is as follows: process one, 30 seconds; process two, 40 seconds; process three, 25 seconds.

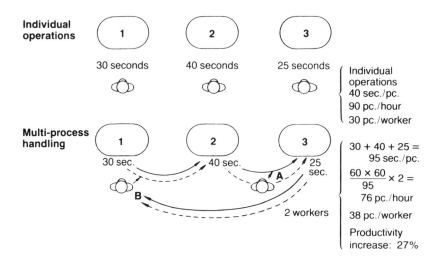

FIGURE 32. **Productivity Improvements through Multi-process Handling Operation**

When there is one worker at each process, the most that can be produced is one piece every 40 seconds, or 90 pieces per hour, for an average hourly output per worker of 30 pieces (90 pieces divided by three workers).

Suppose, however, that we use multi-process handling with two workers in parallel operations each handling all three processes: Each worker's output would be one piece per 95 seconds (30 + 40 + 25). With two workers, the time would be 47.5 seconds (95 ÷ 2). This is nearly the same time as when three workers were involved, representing a productivity improvement of 27 percent.

Thus, multi-process handling has the capacity to absorb disparities among processing times. Presswork, for example, may involve three processes: punching, drawing, and bending.

Multi-process handling can be extremely effective in cases where the times for individual processes inevitably differ from one another.

Example 8.1 — Multi-process handling. At San'ei Metal Industries, operations used to be carried out by four workers involved in four processes handling each press. Product stocks accumulated between processes because there was no way to equalize all the processing times. The worker would take up a product from these stocks and form it on the press. For safety reasons, he would hold down switches with both hands while this took place. When forming was completed, the product was sent to the next process via a nearby chute.

In the improved scheme, two workers carry out multi-process handling by moving successively from one machine to the next. Safety devices are provided so that each press is run by a single touch of a button. This change resulted in an 82 percent increase in productivity:

- Before improvement, four workers had a daily output of 550 units
- After improvement, two workers had a daily output of 500 units

More is involved here, of course, than the simple absorption of disparities in processing times among individual processes. The motions involved in picking up stored products and putting them aside again have been eliminated. The worker now already has the product in his left hand from the preceding process. He inserts it in the die as soon as he has removed the previous product with his right hand. The improvement, then, has eliminated both the wasteful motions involved in placing and retrieving items from storage and the waiting time used to hold down the safety buttons while the machine is running.

Multi-process handling can boost productivity significantly in two respects:

- It absorbs processing time disparities between processes
- It eliminates temporary storage between processes

"Counterflow" multi-process handling, in which operations are performed in the order opposite to that of the process flow, will in some instances make it even easier to eliminate temporary storage.

In such cases, temporary storage may occur if machines are not positioned closely together. While some maintain that counterflow operations increase waiting between processes, the problem doesn't lie in the direction of flow but in how closely together machines are arranged. Thus, while multi-process handling may reduce a given day's output in some cases, it will always raise productivity. Of course, one day's output is important in fulfilling orders. At the same time, the only way a company can increase profits is through absolute increases in productivity, and simply boosting output will not achieve that. Production figures may rise as more people are brought in, but this will not automatically lead to increased profits. If output needs to be maintained, merely adding on an hour of overtime may be sufficient. On the other hand, the plant will be able to raise absolute production output by assigning two excess workers to produce a different product on four presses with the use of multi-process handling. There is no doubt that this approach is effective in boosting plant profits.

Human Time, Machine Time

Consideration of human time and machine time elements provides further understanding of the role multi-process handling plays in operations improvement.

A typical operation can be divided as follows:

1. Remove processed product	human time
2. Place removed product on bench	"
3. Attach next product to machine	"
4. Operate switch	"
5. Processing proceeds automatically	machine time
6. Processing ends; brief wait	"

In procedures like the above, the number of machines one worker can handle increases to the extent that machine time is longer than human time. Consequently, if the required volume can be produced without running machines 100 percent of the time, the number of machines assigned to one worker can be increased by extending the machine waiting time (item 6 above). This is true, no matter how high the processing capacity.

Conversely, the number of machines handled by a single worker can be increased by shortening human time elements (1 through 5). In this context, safety considerations often lengthen the time of switch operation (item 4). This can be shortened by using switches that require only a single touch or by operating switches from a distance by remote control. In multiple machine handling operations, then, the number of machines handled by one worker is typically controlled by the ratio of human time to machine time. Multi-process handling, moreover, is more advantageous than multi-machine handling in the elimination of temporary storage. Consider this comparison:

- Multi-machine handling — Requires item 2 operations (placing removed product on bench)
- Multi-process handling — The fact that a worker removes products (item 1) one after another and then immediately attaches the next product to the machine (item 3) offers the possibility of doing away with elemental operation 2, (placing removed product on bench). This can be achieved by placing machines as closely together as possible.

As we have already seen, multiple machine handling operations are significantly influenced by the ratio of human time to machine time. Generally speaking, the expected advantages compared to having one worker in charge of one machine are on the following order:

- Multi-machine handling — 30-50 percent productivity improvement
- Multi-process handling — 50-100 percent productivity improvement

So far, I have emphasized the extreme effectiveness of vertical multiple machine handling operations, or multi-process handling. This is not meant to deny the importance of horizontal multiple machine handling operations or multi-machine handling. Even in an isolated operation involving no process flow, having a worker attach and remove products from one machine while another is running automatically remains an effective method for cutting costs.

We can conclude by saying that you should actively look for ways to use either multi-machine handling or multi-process handling, depending on the nature of the operations involved.

Table 8 compares the advantages and disadvantages of multi-machine handling and multi-process handling.

Autonomation: Automation with a Human Touch

It has often been argued that autonomation (or automation with a human touch) is one of the distinctive features of the Toyota production system, but I don't agree. The Toyota production system is supported by two characteristic notions:

- Non-stock production
- Labor cost reductions

Autonomation is one of many means available to achieve labor cost reductions. I think, however, that it should be viewed as the principal means to that end.

Mankind has succeeded in transferring many of the functions of the human hand to machines. We have seen a gradual evolution from the mechanization of main operations (processing or machining) to the mechanization of incidental operations (attaching and removing workpieces or operating switches). No matter how far this process is

Issues / Category	Advantages				Disadvantages		Productivity increase
	Can automatic processing time be used?	Can delays resulting from processing time variability be absorbed?	Temporary storage needed between processes?	Speed of flow between processes?	Machine operating rates drop?	Losses due to walking between processes?	
Multi-machine handling	yes	possibly yes	yes	normal	yes	yes	30 – 50%
Multi-process handling	yes	to a large extent	yes	increases	yes	yes	50 – 100%

TABLE 8. Pros and Cons of Multi-machine Handling and Multi-process Handling

carried, however, such efforts will never be more than mechanization of the functions of the human hand.

By comparison, the Toyota production system early on provided machines with human intelligence or the ability to detect abnormal situations. It is truly the first type of autonomation worthy of the name.

Toyota's move toward autonomation was, no doubt, promoted by Toyoda Sakichi, a man of great foresight, who had already invented an automatic loom that shut down whenever a thread broke.

Providing machines with human intelligence functions made possible the clear separation of worker and machine. This notion, in turn, evolved into multi-machine handling operations and helped improve human productivity.

When these advances are combined with the mechanization of incidental operations, machines become increasingly independent of humans. This is what has led to unprecedented reductions in labor costs through true autonomation.

Toward Pre-Automation

The idea of *pre-automation* dates from 1969, when Mr. Hachiya, the plant manager of Saga Iron Works, asked me the following question: "Why do people have to stand next to the machines if the machines are automated?" Why, indeed!

After some speculation, I answered: "The reason is that the machines do not have the intelligence necessary to detect abnormalities." We were able to achieve unsupervised operation by attaching various devices to the machines to detect abnormalities in the machines themselves as well as in the products. This, I understood, was the "autonomation" I had heard about in reference to the Toyota production system.

What distinguished mechanization from pre-automation, I realized, was whether or not machines and other apparatus had the capacity to detect abnormalities. Pre-automation provides this capacity across the full spectrum of operations:

- Main operations (automation of machining, processing, etc.)
- Incidental operations (automation of workpiece attachment and removal, switch operation, etc.)
- Operational allowances (automation of cutting oil supply, chip removal, etc.)

- Workshop allowances (automation of materials supply, product storage, etc.)

We can, moreover, distinguish two types of abnormality detection functions:

- S-type (which detects the causes of abnormalities)
- R-type (which detects the results of abnormalities)

Thus, pre-automation presents itself as a coherent system. Indeed, it may be justifiable to speak of pre-automation as having developed as a system based on the evolution and expansion of the idea of autonomation. In the near future we can expect to see the automation (including abnormality detection) of setup changes.

Using the SMED System

An explanation of the SMED system properly belongs in the section on the discussion of operational improvements (Chapter 3) because it raises the operating rates of workers and machines significantly.

Rather than concentrating on higher operating rates, however, the Toyota production system sees the two ways of reducing finished product and interprocess stocks — production in small lots and rapid response to changes in demand — as the greatest value of SMED. Accordingly, I have chosen to explain the SMED concept in the section on process improvements.

The aim of SMED is to bring setup changes down to the single-digit minute range. The next step is surely to cut setup changeovers down to seconds, through the use of one-touch setups. In fact, I could cite many examples where this stage has already been reached.

THE STRUCTURE OF PRODUCTION AND THE TOYOTA PRODUCTION SYSTEM

The following is an outline of the basic features of the Toyota production system based on the structure of production.

Basic Features of the Toyota Production System

- Targets cost reduction via the thorough elimination of waste
- Eliminates overproduction through the notion of non-stock and achieves labor cost reduction via minimal manpower — the two aspects of production in which the most waste occurs
- Reduces production cycles drastically through the use of the SMED system to achieve non-stock by carrying out small lot production, equalization, synchronization, and one-piece flows
- Thinks of demand in terms of order-based production. To attain this under non-stock conditions, looks at all problems from a fundamentals-oriented perspective
- Adheres consistently to the idea that the quantity produced should be the quantity ordered

Process Features

The Toyota production system views processing as follows:

1. Processing — Actively uses value engineering (VE) and value analysis (VA) and makes effective use of the division of labor
2. Inspection — Performs inspections to eliminate defects through the use of poka-yoke devices
3. Transport — Uses process flow machine layouts wherever possible to do away with transport
4. Delay — Relentlessly pursues the non-stock ideal
   - Eliminates *process delays* via equalization and synchronization; alternatively, makes use of full-work control systems
   - Eliminates *lot delays* with one-piece flows; this, too, calls for improved layouts
5. Nagara — Promotes the nagara system (Chapter 7)

Operation Features

1. Preparation and after-adjustment (setup change operations)
   - Uses SMED setups or one-touch setups
2. Principal operations (main and incidental operations)

- Uses multiple machine handling operations, especially multi-process handling
- Uses autonomation

3. Marginal allowances — Implements minimal manpower by such means as eliminating isolated islands
4. Actively pursues minimal manpower rather than labor savings because the main goal is to reduce labor costs

While developing these ideas, the Toyota production system made two crucial leaps in thinking about the nature of production.

First, Toyota abandoned the cost principle adhered to by many plants in favor of a subtracted-cost principle. With cost reduction as the cornerstone of management, it proceeded to get rid of waste relentlessly.

Second, Toyota reconsidered the old assumption that the ideal form of production is American-style large lot mass production based on estimated demand. Considering the peculiar characteristics of the Japanese market, it realized that demand would best be satisfied through the use of order-based production. Focusing on the notion of *non-stock*, the company tackled the issue of small lot production and solved a succession of previously intractable problems as it created a new production system.

Considering the above, then, it is fair to say that the Toyota production system represents a revolution in production philosophy.

9

The Evolution of
the Kanban System

The kanban system is a method of control designed to maximize the potential of the Toyota production system as well as a system with its own independent functions.

In his book, *Toyota Production System*, Taiichi Ohno states:

> The two pillars of the Toyota production system are just-in-time and automation with a human touch, or autonomation. The tool used to operate the system is kanban.*

Ohno further argues against a simplistic understanding of the Toyota production system as merely a kanban system.

MY FIRST ENCOUNTER WITH
THE KANBAN SYSTEM

Around 1960, I visited Toyota because I had some business in the office at the machine plant. There, I happened to run into Mr. Ohno who was the plant manager at the time. He told me he had something to discuss, that he was considering putting a "kanban system" into effect. I had never heard the term before, so I said only that I thought the idea sounded most interesting. I told him that my training was in the railway business and that what he was describing sounded like the so-called "tablet system" we had used there.

When a train is operated on a line that has only a single track for part of it, the engineer hands the stationmaster a "tablet" with a special pattern of holes in it. The stationmaster fits this tablet over the track switches which allows him to operate only those switches that open the correct section of the track. The stationmaster then hands the engineer the tablet for the next section of track. In this way, only one train can be operated on that particular section of track at one time.

---

* *Toyota*, p. 25

I told Mr. Ohno that the kanban system he had described seemed to serve the same function as these tablets. I felt it was a good concept and urged him to give it a try.

As Mr. Ohno and I parted, he commented that his shop floor workers inevitably produced too much. His remark has stayed with me; even today I believe the true significance of the kanban system is that it addresses that very problem.

DEVELOPMENT OF THE ORDER POINT METHOD

The Relationship Between Order Point and Inventory

Among the control techniques available to carry out repetitive production is the order point, *O.P.*, method. In this section, the *O.P.* method is explained in detail with reference to Table 9. Please refer to that table as you work through the calculations.

$$ⓐ = \text{the daily quantity consumed}$$

$$P = \text{the production cycle for parts to be supplied}$$

$$\alpha = \text{the minimum quantity in storage}$$

$$Q = \text{the size of one production lot of parts to be supplied}$$

The order point, that is, the quantity at which parts must be ordered, is determined by the formula:

$$O.P. = ⓐ \times P + \alpha$$

The elements of the order point formula are defined as follows:

1. ⓐ = daily quantity consumed. This value is determined by trends in demand and ideally is leveled as much as possible.
2. P = production cycle for parts to be ordered. This is not merely the time it takes to process the parts, it includes delays and transport as well. Transport must be recognized as an important factor when parts are shipped in from remote suppliers.
    Significant variation can also be due to the processing method:

- Are individual processing lots large or small?
- How long do process delays last?
- How well are processes synchronized?
- What size transport lots are used between processes? Are one-piece flows used?
- How much time is used up in transport?

3. α = minimum quantity in storage. This stock functions as a safety valve in the event of unforeseen disruptions to production.
   - It cushions against fluctuations in parts consumption — especially against running out of parts when consumption rises
   - It functions as a cushion when deliveries are late due to worker absence, machine breakdowns, defects, or other unforeseen problems at the supplier's plant

4. Q = size of one production lot of parts to be supplied. The length of time needed for setup changes is usually the biggest controlling factor here. Longer setups will probably necessitate larger lots; conversely, shorter setup times make smaller lots possible.

Order frequency diminishes as lot size increases; similarly, small lots mean more frequent orders. The size of production lots exerts a tremendous influence on the size of inventories.

From another viewpoint, since the supply lot quantity must be greater than or equal to the order point quantity, shortening the production cycle or reducing minimum quantities in storage can make it possible to decrease the lower limit of supply lot size. (If $Q \geq O.P.$, then lowering P or α will decrease Q.)

It is the interrelationships between order point, maximum inventory, and number of pallets (in a supply lot) that determine the degree of production efficiency. These are discussed in the following seven cases, each of which represents an improvement in the use of the *O.P.* method (Table 9 and Figure 33).

First Case

In this case, ordinary production control is carried out. The relationship between the three elements is shown below:

Order point	2,000 pieces
Maximum inventory	5,500 pieces
Number of pallets	110 (50 per pallet)

Stage	Production system	Daily consumption* @	Production cycle for supplied parts (P)	@ × P	Minimum storage	Order point @ × P + α	Supply lot size** (Q)	Maximum storage Q + α	Number of pallets @ 50 pieces/ pallet (n)
1	Conventional system	100	15	1,500	500	2,000	5,000	5,500	110
2	Improvements in eliminating process delays shorten production cycle (synchronization)	100	12	1,200	500	1,700	5,000	5,500	110
3	Setup change improvements cut supply lot sizes (and shorten production cycles)	100	6	600	500	1,100	1,000	1,500	30
4	Improvements in eliminating lot delays shorten production cycle (one-piece flows)	100	3	300	500	800	1,000	1,500	30

Stage	Production system	Daily consumption* $@$	Production cycle for supplied parts (P)	$@ \times P$	Minimum storage	Order point $@ \times P + \alpha$	Supply lot size** (Q)	Maximum storage $Q + \alpha$	Number of pallets @ 50 pieces/pallet (n)
5	Minimize inventories by analyzing production instabilities	100	3	300	200	500	1,000	1,200	24
6	Thorough secondary setup change improvements further reduce supply lot sizes	100	2	200	200	400	400	600	12
7	Abolish minimum inventory figures	100	1	100	0	100	200	200	4

* To give a clear illustration of improvements achieved, I have assumed a standard daily consumption figure of 100 pieces for each stage.

** Because the different sizes of supply lots change the length of the production cycle but transport and storage between processes would not necessarily conform to the reduction ratio of quantity per lot, the figures used were taken from actual cases.

TABLE 9. Evolution of an Order Point System

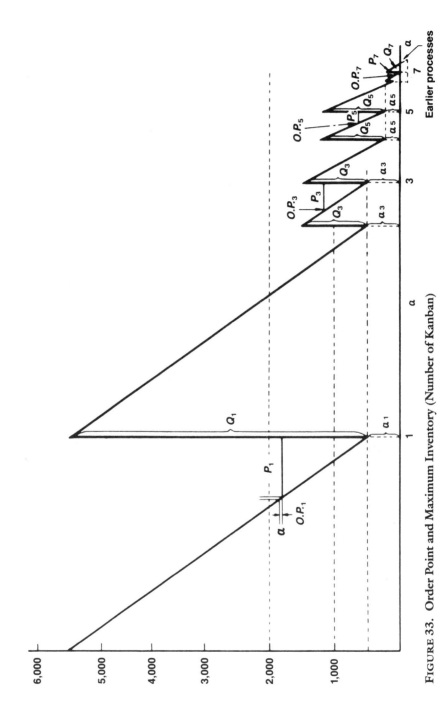

FIGURE 33. Order Point and Maximum Inventory (Number of Kanban)

Second Case

The method used in the first case is improved on here by synchronizing processes somewhat. As a result, the production cycle (*P*) is cut to 12 days.

Order point	1,700 pieces
Maximum inventory	5,500 pieces
Number of pallets	110

The only change, then, is that the order point has been lowered. Maximum inventory and the number of pallets remain the same as in the first case.

Third Case

Setup change improvements cut the size of supplied parts lots to one-fifth their previous value, reducing the supply production cycle.

Order point	1,100 pieces
Maximum inventory	1,500 pieces
Number of pallets	30

The reduction of individual supply lots through setup change improvements has had a striking impact on stock quantities. The order point drops somewhat, but the effect there is not as dramatic.

Fourth Case

Layout improvements allow the adoption of one-piece flows and reduce lot delays. As a result, the production cycle shrinks dramatically and the order point drops.

Order point	800 pieces
Maximum inventory	1,500 pieces
Number of pallets	30

Thus, the order point drops but there is no change in the size of stocks.

Fifth Case

Minimum inventory is set by easing production instability, that is, instability in production itself (caused by worker absences, machine breakdowns, product defects, etc.) and demand-side fluctuations. Various studies have shown that there is no need to carry large inventories, so stock quantities are cut to the minimum necessary for the current control situation. Supply lot sizes, however, remain the same as in the fourth case.

Order point	500	pieces
Maximum inventory	1,200	pieces
Number of pallets	24	

This action lowers inventory somewhat and, at the same time, cuts the order point proportionately.

Sixth Case

A second round of setup change improvements reduces setup times considerably and cuts supply lot sizes substantially. This results in a significant reduction in maximum inventory. In addition, small lot production shortens production cycles and the order point drops in proportion.

Order point	400	pieces
Maximum inventory	600	pieces
Number of pallets	12	

Here, although it may be possible to cut supply lot sizes even further, the extent of the reduction is limited because supply lot sizes cannot drop below the order point.

Seventh Case

Inventory **a** is eliminated and production instabilities are dealt with by rigid adherence to preventive measures. This leads to a major reduction in machine breakdowns and product defects. A lower order point minimizes the size of supply lots in general. This, in turn, makes it possible to reduce individual supply lots even further.

Order point	100	pieces
Maximum inventory	200	pieces
Number of pallets	4	

As we have seen, then, supply lot size must be greater than order point. Reducing supply lot sizes shortens the production cycle and that necessarily lowers the order point. The cycle of interrelationships begins again because these factors make it possible to cut supply lot sizes still further. Thus, the process is:

- Setup change improvements reduce supply lot sizes
- A shortened production cycle results
- This causes the order point to drop
- Which makes it possible to reduce supply lots even more

Thus, what first triggers this developmental cycle is the improvement of setup changes.

Lowering minimum inventories, furthermore, both reduces the size of supply lots and affects overall stock quantities drastically.

Small lot production, on the other hand, is problematic because it increases the frequency of transport. Appropriate strategies (such as layout improvements) must be developed to deal with the issue.

It seems to be generally believed that shortening the production cycle (lead time) is an effective measure for reducing maximum inventory. In fact, although it does result in lowering the order point, it has no direct relation to reductions in maximum inventory. Since it determines the lower limit for supply lot sizes and allows reductions to that limit, however, it can have an indirect effect in lowering inventories to minimum values. Thus, we must be clear that there are two factors that directly affect maximum stock levels:

- Reductions in lot size resulting from setup change improvements
- Reductions in minimum inventory maintained to deal with production instability

The Impact of Changes in Consumption

In order to make the discussion in these seven cases easier to follow, I have kept the daily quantity consumed (ⓐ) constant. Under actual manufacturing conditions, of course, this value fluctuates as well. We need to consider two types of cases:

Fluctuations before the Order Point Is Reached

When consumption rises. Here, the order point is arrived at earlier than forecast. Were the situation to persist, the time between two order points would become shorter. In such a situation, minimum inventory (α) serves as a cushion, and although the size of has some effect, increases of up to about 30 percent can be handled by increasing the order frequency. Of course, capacity would have to be raised through overtime and other devices should demand rise during this period.

When consumption falls. In this instance, the order point is arrived at later than forecast. If the situation persisted, the time between two orders would become longer. This means keeping stocks for a long time. Stock increases obviate the cushion effect of minimum inventory (α).

This situation involves a slight capacity surplus, so it will be problematic to make effective use of minimal manpower and labor hours.

Fluctuations Arising after the Order Point

Here, fluctuations in consumption can exert considerable influence.

When consumption rises. One way to deal with fluctuations that occur after orders have been placed is to shorten the production cycle. If this is possible, fine; but there is a much greater potential for problems when production cycles are their usual length or even longer. In such cases, it may be possible for a large minimum inventory (α) to absorb these fluctuations. As pointed out earlier, however, this would result in increased stocks and the generation of more waste.

On the other hand, the effects of higher consumption are felt very rapidly when the order point is low, so shortening the production cycle would increase flexibility and mitigate such effects to some extent.

In this sense, shortening the production cycle, or shortening lead time, can be extremely effective in countering production fluctuations.

When consumption falls. Here, inventory storage time will increase, but losses can be held down by shortening lead times.

As already explained, however, an effective way to reduce maximum stock is to cut:

- Supply lot size (Q)
- Minimum inventory (α)

With respect to minimum inventory, what is needed is a policy preventing drops in capacity because of:

- Worker absence and machine failure
- The appearance of defects

Another approach considers supply and demand factors separately: *supply-side* problems are handled by shutting down the demand-side line and taking measures to prevent any recurrence of instability on the supply side.

The following techniques can be used to reduce supply lot sizes:

- SMED setup changes to drastically cut setup times and facilitate small lot production.
- Small lot production, equalization, synchronization, and one-piece flow operations to effect dramatic reductions in the production cycle. Once this is done, lowering the order point becomes a matter of lowering the lower limit of supply lot sizes.

Shortening lead times merely lowers the lower limit of supply lot sizes through a drop in the order point; therefore, every effort must be made to actively improve production by reducing setup changeover times. Until that happens, there is always the threat of lowered operating rates and delivery delays, among other problems. This means that adopting the SMED system is the most fundamental step toward a non-stock production system.

The Toyota production system employs the *O.P.* method to take production as far as the seventh case above and thoroughly improves each element of production in order to minimize stocks. Kanban is essentially a means of visual control used to keep the system going.

SUPERMARKETS AND THE KANBAN SYSTEM

The kanban system is said to have been inspired by the supermarket system. Supermarkets have several distinctive characteristics that are also evident in the kanban system:

1. Consumers choose goods directly and buy their favorites.
2. Consumers decrease the work of store personnel by carrying their purchases to the cash register themselves.
3. Instead of using a system of estimated replenishment, the store restocks only what has been sold, thereby reducing defective inventories.
4. 2 and 3 above make it possible to lower prices; sales go up and profits rise.

The principal feature adopted by the kanban system is 3: Instead of using a system of estimated replenishment, the store restocks only what has been sold, thereby reducing defective inventories.

This can also be called a "substitution order format." Only those items that have sold are replenished. Yet, is there any guarantee that things that sold today will also sell tomorrow? What we have, in my opinion, is no more than a high probability that items that were popular and sold today will also sell tomorrow.

Ultimately, it is our hope to do away with inventories of finished goods by moving toward production to order, where the only items made are those that will sell. The best method, then, would be to go around taking orders in advance and selling only what was ordered. Since this would be very expensive, the supermarket system's substitution order format has been adopted instead. The problem was seen as one of the relationship between the order period, (D), and the production cycle, (P).

Again only what the consumer has purchased is replenished; orders work their way back in a chain from one process to the next: "(customer) → primary producer (customer) → secondary producer (customer) → third producer." As a matter of course, this results in a "pull" production system. But rather than quibbling over the trivial question of "push" versus "pull" production systems, the Toyota production system can be better understood when its fundamental concepts are explained and one realizes that a pull system is the more appropriate one.

As we saw in the example of Celica production presented in Chapter 6, the most desirable situation for manufacturers would be to have customers who tolerate a fairly long delay from order date through production, shipping, and sales in which to carry out production. This is not realistic, however — people want their desires satisfied quickly.

KANBAN AND THE KANBAN SYSTEM

The functions of kanban and the kanban system are often confused with one another. A closer look at the two will make the distinctions clear.

General Functions of Kanban

In ordinary process control, three tags fulfill the main functions of the system:

- Identification tag — indicates what the product is
- Job instruction tag — indicates what should be made, for how long, and in what quantities
- Transfer tag — indicates from where and to where the item should be transported

The kanban used in the Toyota production system are similar to those shown in Figure 34, and the functions they serve are precisely those enumerated above. Two tags are used:

- Work-in-process kanban — serve as identification and job instruction tags
- Withdrawal kanban — serve as identification and transfer tags

The repetitive nature of automobile production has produced two distinctive features — features, really, of a kanban system:

- Kanban are used repeatedly
- The number of kanban are restricted to limit product flows, eliminate waste, and hold stock to a minimum

The kanban itself retains the function of a job instruction tag, so that in nonrepetitive production, it serves simply to provide job and

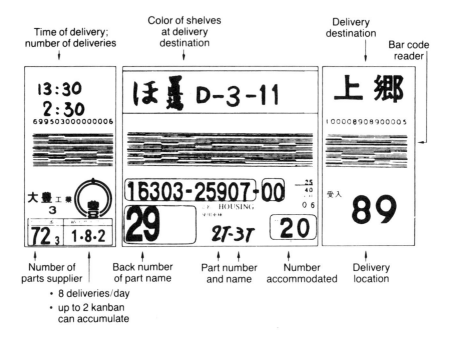

FIGURE 34. Kanban (for Parts Supplier)

transfer instructions. In the latter type of production, however, the kanban must be withdrawn from the work site after production is completed.

How Many Kanban?

The question of how many kanban to use is a basic issue in running a kanban system. The answer corresponds to the number of pallets in the *O.P.* system described earlier. Thus, the number of kanban can be calculated as follows:

$$\text{number of kanban } (N) = \frac{\text{maximum stock } (Q + \alpha)}{\text{capacity of 1 pallet } (n)}$$

In the Toyota production system, how to determine N is not nearly as important as how to improve the production system to *minimize N*. In other words:

- Carry out production in extremely small lots and minimize the size of each production lot (Q) by thorough reduction of setup times
- Use these measures to cut lead times to the minimum
- Eliminate the minimum stocks (α) that are kept as insurance against production instability

The significance of this process is twofold. First, it lies in using the above measures to lower the order point and cut the lower limit of Q; second, it lies in reducing the number of kanban (N) by using shortened setup times to lower the absolute value of Q.

Short setup changeover times make it possible to respond rapidly to change. Moreover, a short production cycle allows one to get by with a minimum of kanban since reliable information about changes is easily accessible and the system can respond promptly.

In this respect, the process of improvement described in the seven cases in the section on the order point method must be fully understood.

Furthermore, while a low order point would determine the lower boundary of supply lot size (Q), the order point is significantly affected by the production cycle (P).

The relationship between D (order-to-delivery period) and P (production cycle) is also relevant to the kanban system.

1. Order-to-delivery period — How much do assembly processes consume and in what amount of time?
2. Production cycle — The production cycle must be understood to include:
   - The time it takes to send withdrawal kanban to the previous process after removing the kanban
   - The time that elapses after exchanging withdrawal kanban for work-in-process kanban until processing is begun
   - The time it takes to produce supply lots
   - The time it takes to store the lot to be processed
   - The time it takes to transport processed items to the assembly line

The small lot transport of both kanban and products tends to take a considerable portion of overall processing time, and measures are needed to deal with this problem. This is especially important when processing is conducted outside the company.

In this regard, Toyota Motors has an advantage in that its own and its suppliers' plants are all located in the region surrounding Toyota City.

The following questions must be answered when it comes to determining the number of kanban to be used:

- How many products can be carried on a pallet?
- How many transport lots are needed given the relative frequency of transport?
- Will transport be dedicated to a single product or will mixed transport be used?

How Kanban Are Circulated

In order to minimize stocks of finished goods, the basic orientation of the Toyota production system is toward order-based production. This is why a pull system is used, in which the later processes go in succession to earlier ones to take the items they need. Thus the flow of kanban is as shown in Figure 35.

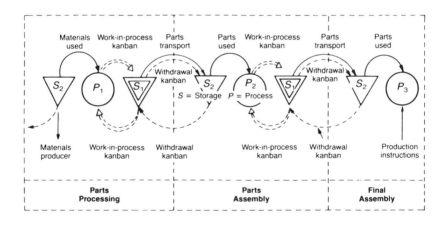

FIGURE 35. How Kanban Are Circulated

1. When the parts next to the assembly line are first used, a withdrawal kanban is removed and put in a specified place.
2. A worker takes this withdrawal kanban to the previous process to get processed items. He removes a work-in-process

kanban from the pallet and puts it in a specified place. The withdrawal kanban is placed on the pallet and the pallet is transported to the line.

3. The work-in-process kanban removed from the pallet at the previous process serves as a job instruction tag to prompt the processing of semiprocessed items fed from the next preceding process.

4. When this happens, the work-in-process tag from the process before the previous one is removed and replaced by a withdrawal kanban.

Thus, a chain reaction of exchanges of withdrawal for work-in-process kanban works its way backwards up the processing sequence. With this system, it is only at the final assembly line that a change of plans need be indicated. Notice of this change will travel automatically, simply, and reliably to upstream processes.

This arrangement has the added benefit of simplifying paperwork. When order-based production encounters fluctuations in demand, instructions are given only at the final process and travel to upstream processes easily and clearly. Conversely, when production is carried out by giving instructions at each process, some of it may be delayed, or speculative production may generate unneeded inventory. The kanban system prevents such waste.

The Toyota production system aims at minimizing inventories of work-in-process stocks as well as finished goods. For this reason, it requires small lot production, with numerous deliveries and frequent transport. The job instruction and transfer tags of conventional process control are not used. Instead, the times and places of deliveries are specified in detail. The system is set up as follows:

- Deliveries take place several times each day.
- Physical delivery points are specified in detail to avoid placing parts in storage and then having to retrieve them for transfer to the line.
- The space available for storing delivered items is limited to make it impossible to accumulate excess stock.

The movement of kanban regulates the movement of products. At the same time, the number of kanban constrains the number of products in circulation. Thus, a critically important condition of the system is expressed in the phrase "kanban must always move with the products." The considerable concern devoted to the problem of lost kanban must be understood in this context.

When processing several different types of parts, it is extremely important for maintaining stock at a minimum to start processing with parts whose kanban have circulated rapidly and then to proceed in order.

Kanban Circulation and the Order Point

The circulation of kanban from downstream to upstream processes will be determined, in turn, by the relationship between order point and size of the supply production lots. Consider the following two situations (Figure 35):

When the order point and supply lot size are equal. In this case, the order point has already been reached when the kanban comes around, so production must be started right away. In the Toyota production system, where so-called "minimum inventory" (α) has been eliminated, shortages may show up at the assembly line unless production begins without delay.

When supply lot size exceeds order point. Suppose a single pallet contains 50 parts and the following conditions hold:

- Order point — 300 parts (6 kanban)
- Supply lot size — 400 parts (8 kanban)

We then get the following:

- If *one* kanban comes to rest at the upstream process, there are still 7 kanban (8 − 1) and 350 parts (50 × 7) at the downstream process. This is greater than the order point of 300, so there is no particular need to begin production immediately.
- If *two* kanban accumulate at the upstream process, there are 6 kanban (8 − 2) and 300 parts (50 × 6) at the downstream process. This means there are only as many parts as the order point, so production must begin immediately.
- If *three* kanban accumulate at the upstream process, there are 5 kanban (8 − 3) and only 250 parts (50 × 5) — less than the 300 of the order point — at the downstream process. In a

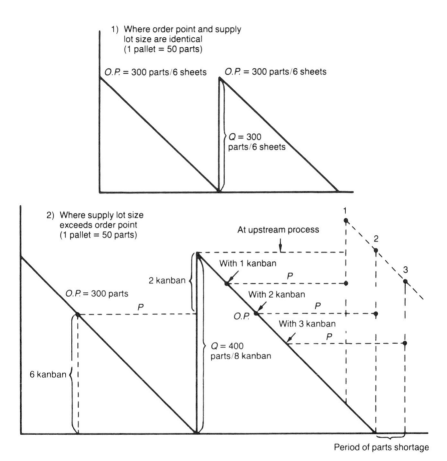

1. Suppose one kanban signals the production of 800 parts *(Q)*. When production stops at the upstream process, one kanban will remain at the assembly line and the overall frequency of flows increases. The situation does not change if only the 50 parts corresponding to a single kanban are produced.
2. Suppose two kanban signal the production of 800 parts *(Q)*. Parts would be delivered just as stock runs out at the assembly line.
3. Suppose production of 800 parts *(Q)* does not begin at the upstream process until three kanban accumulate. Shortages will show up at the assembly line when production adheres to the usual production cycle *P.*
4. In actually implementing a kanban system, it is vitally important to consider the appropriate relationship between order point *(O.P.)* and the supply lot size *(Q)*.

FIGURE 36. **Cases Where Kanban Accumulate at Upstream Processes**

conventional system, the start of production would already be delayed and shortages may already have shown up at the downstream process, so special operations must be carried out immediately.

We see, then, that setting the number of kanban indirectly determines the order point of the downstream process according to the number of kanban accumulated at the upstream process which, in turn, makes it possible to know the deadline for starting production. It follows that the number of kanban allowed to accumulate at an upstream process must be indicated clearly. In the above example, the indication "1, 8, 2" would show that each day (1), there will be 8 deliveries and up to 2 kanban can accumulate.

We should remember, however, that:

- Long setup times will inevitably mean larger lots if the SMED system has not yet been applied.
- There is a high probability that delays or other events will interfere with the timely transport of parts from suppliers.

Thus, it seems reasonable to regard keeping the supply lot size greater than the order point as compensating for setup changeover times and insuring against unstable elements in production, a function fulfilled by the minimum inventory value set by the *O.P.* system.

Regulatory Functions of the Kanban System

A kanban system assists with the fine-tuning of daily fluctuations in load.

When Loads Do Not Fluctuate Daily

Here, all that is needed is the periodic substitution of new car models, new delivery dates, and new quantities. Giving production instructions at the final assembly line allows the kanban system to make necessary corrections automatically and easily by providing job instructions to upstream processes. In this sense, the kanban system is truly convenient.

It is important to remember, however, that all the kanban system does is make the transmittal of information easy and prompt. It is nearly meaningless unless the production system itself has been improved through the adoption of the SMED system or one-piece flows. Thus, the claim that a kanban system can make fine-tuning adjustments needs to be understood in two contexts: that of the kanban system itself and that of the overall Toyota production system. A mere superficial view will lead to misunderstanding.

When Loads Fluctuate Daily

Although loads may remain the same from month to month, they can fluctuate over the shorter term. This situation can be dealt with, to some extent, by increasing the frequency of order points. A kanban system possesses the same capability: Increasing the number of times kanban circulate may not mean changing the number of kanban. Even so, such local load fluctuations may give rise to delays or stock increases.

In ordinary order point systems, minimum inventory (α) serves to absorb these fluctuations. A kanban system, however, lacks this cushion because the inventory has been eliminated. In the kanban system, semiprocessed parts waiting between processes may take the place of minimum inventory in providing a cushioning effect. Fluctuations beyond a certain magnitude, however, cannot be absorbed in this fashion, and leveled production becomes necessary.

Next, if the monthly load exceeds predictions, or if production increases from one month to the next, the number of kanban may have to be increased. Other measures to be considered include raising capacity through overtime and bringing in temporary workers.

In the opposite case, when the load is smaller than expected, it may be sufficient to decrease the frequency with which kanban circulate, and altering the number of kanban may not be necessary. Suitable measures will have to be devised, however, when surplus capacity is generated. When the load decrease is substantial, a reduction in the number of kanban will also have to be considered.

Experience teaches us that fluctuations in the order of 10 to 30 percent can be handled without altering the number of kanban in circulation. Actual implementation is the most reliable guide, and these figures will vary according to the nature of the plant. Obviously, thorough consideration should be given to leveling production so that such fluctuations can be prevented.

Improvement Functions of the Kanban System

A kanban system promotes improvement in two respects:

- Kanban spotlight abnormal situations when they are halted by machine failures and product defects.
- A gradual decrease in the number of kanban leads to decreases in stock, which terminates the role of stock as a cushion

against production instability. This highlights undercapacity processes and those generating abnormalities and simplifies discovery of the major points needing improvement. Overall efficiency is increased by concentrating on the weakest elements.

As shown in Figure 37, the metaphor of a pond nicely illustrates the role of kanban in reducing stock: When the water level (stock) of the pond is lowered, it brings the highest point on the bottom to light. When the high point is removed, the pond deepens, and by continually lowering the water, the whole leveled bottom will be exposed.

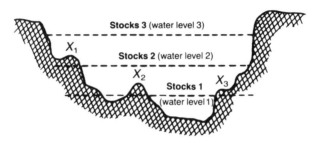

FIGURE 37. The Improvement (Kaizen) Function of Kanban

Thus, reducing the number of kanban is significant not merely in itself, but in making it possible to produce with reduced stock.

The essence of this approach lies in reducing stock by reducing the number of kanban. They are nothing more than a means toward an end.

Summary

Kanban and kanban systems are nothing more than a *means* and their essence lies in the thoroughgoing improvement of production systems.

Kanban and kanban systems do have considerable value: setting the number of kanban to regulate the flow of items overall and hold stock to a minimum, and providing visual control to carry out these functions accurately.

Kanban systems are extremely effective in simplifying office work and giving autonomy to the production floor which makes it possible to handle changes with greater flexibility. One of the advantages of kanban systems is that, by giving instructions at the final process, they allow information to be transmitted organically and swiftly.

Basically, kanban systems can be applied only in plants involved in repetitive production. The repetitive nature of the production may not exert much influence, however, if there are temporal or quantitative instabilities.

Kanban systems *are not* applicable in one-of-a-kind production based on infrequent and unpredictable orders.

The type of production most likely to benefit from kanban is one that deals with parts using common processes.

If it were to be used only for its own characteristics, the kanban system could be applied tomorrow. But substantial delays, waiting, and other losses will result if a kanban system is simply copied or if the number of kanban is reduced when no thorough improvements have been made in the production system itself.

When looking at the kanban system, we must differentiate between its effects in improving the Toyota production system, on the one hand, and its own inherent functions, on the other.

10

Some Peripheral But Important Issues

THE TOYOTA PRODUCTION SYSTEM: AN EXPLANATION

Elimination of the Seven Kinds of Waste

This chapter addresses three issues that, although appearing peripheral, are essential to a full understanding of the Toyota production system: waste, extending the system to parts suppliers, and materials requirement planning (MRP).

The Toyota production system identifies seven kinds of waste:

1. Overproduction
2. Delay
3. Transport
4. Processing
5. Inventory
6. Wasted motions
7. The waste of making defective products

These different wastes are not equal in status or effect. We will discuss them with reference to the structure of production.

Processes

Processing. Here, value engineering and value analysis improvements must be carried out first. Instead of trying to make increases in cutting speed more rational, for example, we should be asking why we make a given product and use a given processing method (4, processing waste).

Inspection. Inspections should eliminate rather than discover defects. Simple 100 percent inspections are therefore more effective than sampling inspections. Source control, self-inspection, and successive checks are extremely effective here, as are poka-yoke devices (7, the waste of making defective products).

Transport. Transport actions never increase added value. We must, therefore, begin by reducing the need for transport by improving plant layout. The next step is to make the means of transport more rational (3, transport waste).

Delay. In the past, stock was seen as useful because the emphasis was placed on its role in cushioning against production instabilities. It was tolerated because setup changes took a long time. Adoption of the SMED system certainly eliminates this problem. Since the development of the SMED system, the excuse for holding stock because setup changes take a long time no longer holds. Inventories are clearly wasteful, and losses due to stock and related waste are substantial. We must, therefore, eliminate stock by eliminating unstable conditions.

Equalization and synchronization between processes can reduce or eliminate process delays, and one-piece flow operations can do away with lot delays. Since these measures increase the frequency of transport, however, the improvement of layout is a basic precondition for their use.

This is how we can attain the number one objective of the Toyota production system (1, elimination of overproduction waste).

Product inventory. The relationship between order-to-delivery period (D) and production cycle (P) exerts considerable influence on product inventories. If D is substantially longer than P, production must be guided by speculation, which makes growth in product stocks inevitable.

Order-based production does not tolerate a long order-to-delivery period, however, so the production cycle must be shortened drastically through equalization, synchronization, and one-piece flows. Small lot production is another very effective measure, but it can be achieved only through the use of the SMED system. This sequence of actions can reduce product inventories substantially (5, inventory waste).

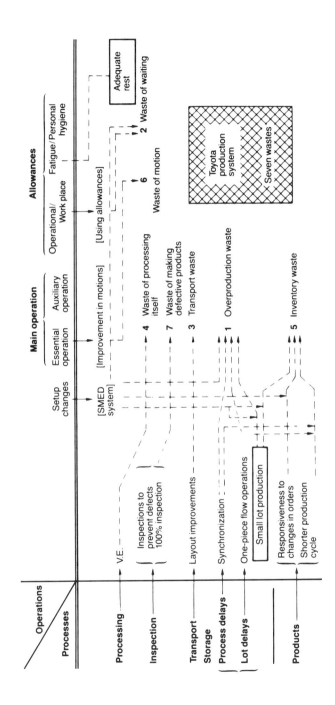

FIGURE 38. The Toyota Production System and the Seven Kinds of Waste

Operations

Preparation, after-adjustment (setup change operations). Long setup times lower work rates of workers and machines. Unfortunately, the need to lower labor costs necessitates large lot production which, in turn, generates unneeded inventory. Here, too, the improvement of setup changes can have a tremendous impact on eliminating both unnecessary delays and the need for large lot production (1, overproduction waste; 2, delay waste; 5, inventory waste).

Main operations. Worker motions need to be improved thoroughly and more effective standard operations determined. We tend to look only at the superficial temporal aspects of operations. Since time, however, is merely a reflection of motion, our efforts at improvement should be directed first of all at the underlying motions of operations, rather than hastily considered equipment improvements. When the latter are carried out before basic operational improvements have been made, what often results is merely the mechanization of wasteful operations.

Parts boxes also have an important role in main operations and we need to focus more on their function as convenient tools for processing. We need to be more concerned with:

- Clearly separating and arranging parts
- Aligning parts uniformly
- Allowing parts to come into reach one at a time

We should also consider using parts boxes on turntables to bring the needed parts into position. Moving parts boxes, which deliver the needed parts when needed, one part at a time, are especially effective. In general, we should give serious consideration to this principle of delivering needed parts only when needed, one at a time (6, wasted motions).

Integration of the Kanban and Toyota Production Systems

Taiichi Ohno has stated clearly that the Toyota production system is a manufacturing method, while the kanban system is only a means for applying that method. Actual applications, however, integrate the Toyota production system and the kanban system, and many explanations do not distinguish between the two.

The integration of the two systems extends to the six kanban rules listed below. For the sake of clarity, we will now explain each rule in turn, differentiating between kanban system rules and Toyota production system rules. This, it is hoped, will give the reader a clearer understanding of the interdependence of the two systems.

Rule One

A process withdraws parts from the preceding process when kanban are removed. (Kanban provide withdrawal or transport instruction.)

This rule is composed of two elements:

- Withdraw only as many parts as specified by removed kanban
- Go from one process to withdraw parts from the preceding one

Of course, if the later process collects parts from the preceding process without removing the kanban, unnecessary stocks will appear.

Since the Toyota production system is oriented toward order-based and not speculative production, the idea behind having later processes withdraw parts from earlier processes is to make only what has already been sold. Consequently, the rule presented above is not a kanban rule, but a Toyota production system rule.

Rule Two

The earlier process makes parts in the quantities and order dictated by the removed kanban. (Kanban provide production instruction.)

Kanban prevent overproduction waste by constraining the total flow of parts. Therefore, no part should be made without reference to kanban. Kanban also hold inter-process stock to a minimum, so making parts in any order other than that specified by the kanban risks shortages. Thus, this too is a Toyota production system rule that stipulates the use of kanban as a means of visual control. When considerable stock exists between processes, this rule becomes unnecessary.

Rule Three

Nothing is transported and nothing is made without kanban. (Kanban prevent overproduction and excessive transport.)

Since kanban prevent overproduction, the Toyota production system would collapse if Rule Three were not obeyed. In this respect, this is doubtless the most important kanban system rule for carrying out non-stock production through the Toyota production system.

Rule Four

Kanban always accompany the parts themselves. (Kanban are identification tags certifying the need for parts.)

The system could not function if kanban strayed from parts. Consequently, this is a crucial kanban system rule.

Rule Five

Every part must be of acceptable quality. (The system prevents defects by ensuring that any defect-generating process suffers the consequences.)

Circulating many kanban will not cause a process to suffer significantly. This is because the Toyota production system compresses stock to a minimum and prescribes only a corresponding number of kanban. Rather than a kanban rule, then, this is a Toyota production system rule.

Rule Six

The number of kanban decreases over time. (Kanban are tools for spotlighting problems and for inventory control.)

In the sense that the use of kanban can limit inventories to appropriate quantities by controlling what should and should not be made, this is certainly a kanban system rule. On the other hand, Rule Six captures a kanban application that actively sets improvement activities in motion by reducing stock in the production system. In a real sense, it makes it impossible to neglect improvement which means that this principle is more appropriately considered a Toyota production system rule.

In this discussion, we have made a clear distinction between the kanban system and the Toyota production system although, in actual practice, the two are often thought of as nearly synonymous. If these rigorous distinctions are not maintained, however, efforts to improve the above principles can lead to misguided policies or superficial measures.

EXTENDING THE SYSTEM TO PARTS SUPPLIERS

The Toyota production system was once criticized as being the "devil's system." Why? Many thought that its primary conceptual approach lay in the notion of just-in-time. Just-in-time, in turn, was superficially understood as a stock minimization system in which desired items were taken at the desired time and in the desired quantities. With this conception, parts and raw materials suppliers thought they were expected to provide Toyota with the desired items at the desired time and in the desired quantities, all at Toyota's convenience. In addition, they thought they would be forced to keep large inventories on hand, since they could not possible know what, when, and how much they would be required to provide.

If this were indeed the way things were supposed to work in the Toyota production system, the "devil's system" appellation would have been well deserved. In reality, Toyota's monthly production plans are announced in advance and the company draws leveled quantities of parts and materials from suppliers. At the same time, extremely small lots and the demand for frequent deliveries combined with unavoidable changes mean that affiliates and materials suppliers must improve their own production systems in order to respond quickly to Toyota's needs. This explains why, after 20 years of actual implementation in its own plants, it still took Toyota nearly 10 years to create a comprehensive system that encompassed both Toyota Motors and its suppliers. Suppliers and affiliates have experienced substantially higher profits because of improvements to their own production systems. Clearly, the charge that the Toyota production system is the work of the devil is completely unfounded.

In any event, it is faulty expansion of the system beyond Toyota that is responsible for this problem, not the Toyota production system itself.

Still, some people are satisfied with a superficial understanding of the Toyota production system. They suggest that Toyota's insistence on receiving what it wants when it wants it and in the quantities it wants simply passes responsibility for one company's bungling to its suppliers. If examined carefully, this view is revealed as completely lacking in a correct understanding of the Toyota production system.

THE TOYOTA PRODUCTION SYSTEM AND MRP

In recent years, materials requirement planning (MRP) has been embraced enthusiastically as the latest innovation in managerial techniques by American firms. Several Japanese companies are also using it.

The purported objective of the MRP system is the "effective use of limited production resources — people, materials and money." To that extent, the stated goal of MRP is no different from that of any other management or control method.

The distinctive feature of MRP is its extensive use of computers to improve production by searching out the optimal conditions among many competitors.

Because this system appeared in Japan and the United States at about the same time as the Toyota production system, it is often contrasted with the latter. But are the two systems, in fact, mutually incompatible?

I have not studied the MRP system in detail and may not have a firm grasp of its essence. I cannot avoid the impression, however, that MRP is a *management system* for finding previously unknowable optimal conditions by applying computer processing to conventional production control systems. As far as it goes, I think it is a truly innovative technique.

By the same token, I do not believe that MRP addresses itself to improving the basic production system in the same way as the Toyota production system, which makes fundamental improvements in the system of control and management by:

- Drastically shortening setup changeover times
- Using those shortened setups in the relentless pursuit of small lot production
- Carrying out coherent one-piece flow operations from parts processing to the assembly process
- Aiming to achieve order-based production through a pull system

I doubt MRP is as committed to such fundamental improvements.

It seems to me, then, that MRP and the Toyota production system are not comparable. Organizations may apply systematic MRP methods in addition to a fundamental and revolutionary production system such as the Toyota production system.

MRP is not the only new form of computerized process control. Another concept we have mentioned in this book is the economic lot, which claims that long setup times can be handled by using larger lots. Since doing so would increase stocks, a balance must be struck between lot size and inventory size. Yet, a fundamental assumption with economic lots is that setup times are long. In any case, the development of the SMED system has rendered the economic lot concept meaningless.

Consider another issue: the basic conceptual approach of statistical quality control was truly excellent; in practice, however, over-infatuation with computers and statistical science, both only means to an end, prevented the total elimination of defects.

In each of these examples, computers — which are only a means — have been relied on excessively and true innovation in conventional production systems has been neglected. I sincerely hope this trend can be reversed.

11

The Future Course of the Toyota Production System

The future of the Toyota production system involves thoroughly eliminating waste in the pursuit of maximum cost reductions.

MOVING TOWARD JUST-IN-TIME

I have been told that just-in-time means simply *timely* whereas, to convey the sense of "exactly at a given time," one should say just *on* time. Whatever the distinction between the two, it is clearly the aim of the Toyota production system to deliver items precisely at a given time, with the underlying purpose of eliminating stock.

This objective is controlled largely by the relationship between the order-to-delivery period (D) and the production cycle (P). As noted previously, if the order-to-delivery period is longer than the production cycle ($D > P$), production begun after a firm order is received will be on time, without generating inventory.

While market research can improve the accuracy of demand forecasts, we also need policies to extend the order-to-delivery period. Below, some methods for extending this period are explained. They can be used not only in the manufacture of automobiles but also with ordinary consumer goods, such as household electrical appliances:

- Solicit repeat orders from your customers based on the life expectancy of items purchased in the past
- Approach those who are learning to drive or have just obtained their driver's license
- Suggest electrical appliance purchases to people building new homes
- Read wedding and engagement announcements to identify people who might be interested in ordering appliances

There are other strategies besides these. The point is to key into events that precede actual demand as a way of lengthening the order-to-delivery period.

Of course, we should be striving, at the same time, to shorten the production cycle. This could be accomplished, for example, by:

- Exploiting small lot production to the utmost
- Cutting setup changeover times drastically (in addition to making it possible to conduct small lot production, this would improve flexibility in responding to change)
- Extending equalization, synchronization, and one-piece flows to the entire process to achieve extremely short-term production

FROM SMED TO ONE-TOUCH SETUPS

The Toyota production system repeatedly emphasizes the need to eliminate overproduction waste. Only small lot production can deal with high-diversity, low-volume demand, and the adoption of SMED setups is an essential prerequisite of it. SMED setups are doubly effective because they also facilitate rapid response to changes in demand.

It follows from this that setup times need to be reduced even more. Setup changeovers which, with SMED, are in the range of minutes, will have to be reduced to a few seconds with one-touch methods. Below, two approaches leading in this direction are discussed.

Automatic Changeovers

Automatic changeovers are best achieved with the use of the least common multiple method described in Chapter 3. Three examples of automated changeovers follow.

First case. Guide widths had to be changed to accommodate products of different sizes on a conveyor feed. One-touch changes were achieved for several positions by retracting the guides on one side with springs, inserting 4-step, wedge-shaped spacers, and using electromagnets to move the spacers up and down.

Second case. The positions of limit switches had to be changed to accommodate different length strokes for movable forming dies. Previously, the dies actually had to be moved which required repeated adjustments to pinpoint the correct position for the switches. The solution was to install limit switches at five fixed positions and provide other switches to send current to each of the limit switches. One-touch changeover could be accomplished by simply turning the appropriate limit switches on or off. This also eliminated the need for switch position adjustments.

Third case. At a washing machine plant, forming dies for two models had to be changed completely, despite identical exterior dimensions, because:

- The holes for attaching ornamental trim at the corners were in different positions for the two models (Standard and Deluxe)
- Hole positions were also different for right- and left-handed models

To improve the operation, all functions were assembled in one die, and the insertion of a "fitting plate" between the ram and die allowed holes to be blanked on the two models. When the plate was removed, the ram would strike without blanking holes. One-touch hole position changes could be carried out by activating a switch to insert the fitting plate, and machine bodies could be produced continuously, at a ratio of two standard models to one deluxe model.

Thus, one very effective method for one-touch setup changes is to distinguish which parts of the dies involved are identical and which are different and then devising a simple method to switch only the differing parts.

No-Touch Methods

There is a saying that "the easiest way to change something is to change nothing at all." This is a way of describing no-touch methods for improving setup times. The most effective method is the "set" method, where changeovers are eliminated by producing parts in sets of two or more.

First case. It took four different types of styrofoam cushioning blocks to package washing machines. In the past, molds had to be switched four times, but this approach was improved. All the molds needed for products A, B, C, and D are now fitted into one large mold so that one set of blocks can be molded with a single die. This eliminates the setup changes for the four blocks.

Second case. Two very similar television knobs, A and B, were produced on a plastic forming machine. Dies had to be switched because different resins were used for the two types of knobs. In the improved version, A and B molds are cut into a single die at right angles to one another. Now, the resin channels can be rotated 90 degrees which obviates the need for removal and attachment of dies (Figure 39).

Third case. Molds for parts A and B used on the same product model are provided on a single press die, so that sets of parts can be produced continuously and separated after the press operation. This makes changing dies unnecessary.

These examples show that the production of parts in sets can eliminate changeovers completely if common elements are identified and skillfully combined. Important questions to consider include:

- Are the parts in question common to the same product or similar products?
- Are the materials the same?

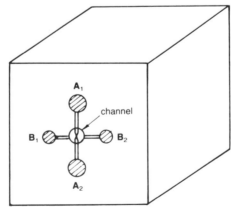

In this example, the flow of resin is directed into A1 and A2

FIGURE 39. **No-touch Setup Change for Knob Production**

Instead of assuming that changeovers are inevitable, look for ways to produce multiple parts without changeovers. Such efforts will, with surprising frequency, result in a no-touch system that requires no changeovers at all.

If changeovers are absolutely unavoidable, efforts should be focused on developing automatic one-touch pushbutton changeovers.

THE DEVELOPMENT OF A COMPREHENSIVE FLOW SYSTEM

The task of reducing overproduction waste involves the elimination of finished product stocks and work-in-process stocks.

The use of production equalization, synchronization, and one-piece flows to do away with interprocess delays (process and lot delays) represents a tremendous advance of the Toyota production system over the Ford system. The Ford system was a method in which only the assembly process used a synchronized "one-car" flow. The Toyota production system, by comparison, links the assembly process to upstream machine and painting processes by applying equalization, synchronization, and one-piece flow operations. This advance has shortened the production cycle dramatically and made it possible to respond swiftly to orders requiring quick delivery and to fluctuations in demand.

The next task for the Toyota production system is to link together and carry out equalization, synchronization, and one-piece flow operations for processes even further upstream, such as sheet metal, press, welding, forging, and casting processes. These can then be joined to existing machine, painting, and assembly processes to form a complex integrated flow system.

The outlines of such a system may be seen in nagara operations. Here are three examples:

First case. It involves having punching and tapping operations flow to a small painting box where parts are painted. From there, they are immediately sent to the next parts assembly operation. This eliminates the need to transport parts to a painting shop.

Second case. Small-scale plating equipment is provided between parts machining processes so that plating can be carried out in the course of the production flow. This makes it possible for parts to be sent immediately to the next parts assembly process.

Third case. A simple press equipped with a hydraulic cylinder is provided near a spot-welding body assembly process. This allows the worker performing the welding to carry out the press operation and then immediately weld the part to the body.

Such nagara operations disprove the conventional, unconscious assumption that forging must be done in a forge, painting in a painting shop, and plating in a plating shop. We do not necessarily need high-capacity unit machines. On the contrary, in some cases overall synchronization calls for machines of lower capacity than those now in use. This approach represents a great leap forward achieved by faithfully linking the disposition of equipment to the sequence of parts processes.

I believe that extending the domain of one-piece flow operations further and further upstream will be a major theme in the development of the Toyota production system.

EXPANDING AND EXTENDING MIXED PRODUCTION

The Toyota production system stresses small lot production. Its lower limit is mixed production which is quite effective for two reasons:

- Product inventories can be cut to a minimum
- Leveled loads can be provided to upstream processes

Mixed production of this type will find increasingly more application in the Toyota production system, not just to assembly lines but to upstream processes, such as machine processes, presswork, welding, forging, and casting. It is already being used on painting lines linked to the assembly process, and its expansion to other upstream processes is scheduled to follow soon.

Currently, most production is repetitive, based on relatively fixed daily production ratios of various car models. I am certain that mixed production will allow these combinations to be extremely fluid in the future. The adoption of no-touch changeovers, leveling, an effective system of inspections to obviate defects, and the adoption of poka-yoke devices will be key issues in this evolution.

KANBAN SYSTEM DEVELOPMENTS

The kanban system, too, will evolve to keep pace with the production system improvements mentioned above. I anticipate the following developments:

- There will be a dramatic decrease in the number of kanban between processes.
- The existing system in which withdrawal, or pull, kanban are taken to the *immediately preceding* process could be changed into one in which withdrawal kanban are taken to processes farther upstream. This would be possible only if the production cycle were shortened considerably and the coherent system of comprehensive flow operations between processes were enlarged to include upstream processes. Put another way, if upstream processes are making the needed parts while assembly, or other downstream processes, are emptying their pallets, *and* if the flow of parts is rapid, it will not be necessary to take withdrawal kanban to the immediately preceding process. Such an improvement would cut the number of kanban substantially and cause a dramatic decrease in stock between processes.

CUTTING LABOR COSTS

The Toyota production system emphasizes that motions should be improved before equipment. Even if low-cost mechanization increases efficiency by 20 percent, those expenditures are still wasted if improved work motions could have raised efficiency by the same amount. Elimination of waste in motion is therefore the first priority.

The next step is to mechanize human work, and not merely to mechanize it but to provide machines with functions of human intelligence, to carry out autonomation or pre-automation by providing machines with the capacity to detect abnormalities and by shifting more and more of man's work to machines.

Complete automation, where machines are equipped with devices to detect and respond to abnormal situations will follow.

Labor costs will fall as we move through these stages:

1. Human work motions are improved
2. Marginal allowances are integrated

3. Human work shifts to machines
4. Machines can detect abnormal situations
5. Machines can both detect and respond to abnormalities

Imagination and innovation will be needed at each stage to accomplish mechanization and automation at low cost.

DEVELOPING MULTIPLE MACHINE HANDLING OPERATIONS

As discussed earlier, multiple machine handling operations may be of two kinds:

- Multi-machine handling (horizontal multiple machine handling operations)
- Multi-process handling (vertical multiple machine handling operations)

Every effort should be made to implement multi-process handling operations since they result in the greatest savings. Human tasks should be improved and work actively shifted from workers to machines in order to maximize the number of processes an individual can handle.

Since loss per unit time is five times greater for workers than for machines, every effort should be made to keep people from waiting, even if lower machine operating rates result.

The notion of multiple machine handling operations is based on the understanding that machine operating rates need not be high. At the same time, one should design and build one's own inexpensive machines that have specific performance characteristics. These dedicated machines should be versatile so that, with simple modifications, they can be used for the next product that comes along.

It should not be forgotten that all these efforts are rooted in the idea of making machines independent of workers.

ELIMINATING BREAKDOWNS AND DEFECTS

Machine failures demand that we be committed to detecting abnormal situations, halting machines instantly when they occur, and preventing similar abnormalities.

The approach to defects is similar. The goal of zero defects can be achieved only through inspections that *prevent* defects — inspection to *detect* defects is inadequate. Consequently, it must be the function of a poka-yoke device to make it impossible for defects to occur within a given process; simply preventing a part from fitting a jig at the process following the one where the defect occurred is not enough.

Finally, it is a mistake to think that inspecting the first and last of 100 items in a high-speed press chute is a kind of 100 percent inspection. A high-speed 100 percent inspection device that can keep up with the press is needed to actually prevent defects.

INCREASING THE FLEXIBILITY
OF PRODUCTION CAPACITY

The Toyota production system takes it as axiomatic that demand fluctuations should be handled without increasing personnel if at all possible. Mixed leveled production was developed in response to the load fluctuations that occur over the course of a month. When this method fails to absorb the fluctuations, personnel is kept at minimum load requirements and load increases are taken care of by overtime and the assistance of indirect personnel.

When demand remains high for an extended period of time, it may become necessary to hire temporary workers or seek assistance from subcontractors. When this happens, the improved and simplified jobs allow newly arrived workers to pull their weight within three days. In the ordinary course of events, there is also some leeway in equipment operating rates. When the load rises, the number of machines overseen by a single operator is cut and machine operating rates are improved to increase daily production output.

Decreases in load create more serious problems. At present, several countermeasures are available:

- Decreasing the number of people in proportion to the decrease in load
- Increasing the number of machines overseen by an individual worker
- Taking extra workers off the line for such tasks as performing unscheduled machine maintenance, practicing setup changes, and constructing jigs, tools, and other devices for improvement projects

• If there is still no work for them, it is better to have them idle

In the future, better methods will no doubt be developed to deal with this problem. The most effective way to handle this situation would be to use pre-automation. Extending hours of unsupervised operation to deal with increased loads and shortening the hours of unsupervised operation when loads decrease would constitute the most effective use of labor hours.

EXPANDING TO SUPPLIER PLANTS

Because the automobile industry is a comprehensive, integrated industry that relies on suppliers, there is a limit to what can be achieved merely by rationalizing production at the parent plant.

In the future, it will become more common to help suppliers improve their production systems. Efforts will be made to spread the Toyota production system to the entire Toyota group of enterprises so that the parent company and its suppliers can develop as an integrated whole.

12

Implementing the Toyota Production System

This chapter discusses the introduction and development of the Toyota production system at American production facilities, specifically those of the readers of this book. The chapter answers two questions.

First, what should be taken into account when considering the introduction of the Toyota production system in the average company?

Second, what considerations and procedures should be adopted when bringing the Toyota production system into your company?

In answering these questions, the chapter first reiterates basic principles of the Toyota production system and then makes specific recommendations and comments on their implementation.

I believe that it would be a mistake merely to imitate the external features of the Toyota production system. The system cannot be applied properly without a thorough understanding of the principles on which it is based. In addition, it is important to embark on its application only after a clear understanding of how individual techniques fit into the overall picture has been attained. These cautions apply equally for the kanban system.

If the Toyota production system and the kanban system are adopted without adherence to these precepts, not only will results fall short of expectations but the side effects may induce a kind of addiction that will confuse production and invite undesirable consequences.

SETTING THE STAGE

The Toyota production system makes a subtracted-cost principle rather than the traditional cost principle the keynote of its management style. This subtracted-cost principle holds that *the consumer* sets the selling price and that the company will make no profit unless it lowers costs by eliminating waste. Thorough elimination of waste calls for a revolution in accepted production thinking.

In pursuit of this goal, the Toyota production system rejects conventional ideas about speculative and large lot production in favor of order-based and small lot production. Moreover, it demands strict adherence to the principles of non-stock production.

Adopting the Toyota production system thus requires a true revolution in production. Everyone, from top executive to shop floor worker, must have a clear understanding of the following issues, divided here between *process* and *operation*:

Process

The Toyota production system insists on the elimination of stock, that is, the waste of overproduction. In the past, stock was considered useful for relieving some of the uncertainty of production. It is important to understand that the Toyota production system focuses principally on scheduled overproduction (making goods too soon) instead of numerical overproduction (making too many goods).

The Toyota production system is revolutionary in that it looks at the various causes underlying the need for stock. Previously, machine failures and defects had resulted in uncertainty and instability in the production process. In addition to seeking to keep these phenomena from occurring in the first place, the Toyota production system alleviates their basic causes. Here are some examples:

- Where the production cycle (P) is longer than the order-to-delivery period (D), the Toyota production system seeks to shorten P drastically by linking processes through equalization, synchronization, and one-piece flow operations.
- Adoption of the SMED system made it possible to cut setup times drastically, to use small lot production, and to respond swiftly to changes in orders.

Operations

In its drive to cut costs generally, the Toyota production system carries out thorough manpower reductions which promote the drive toward automation. It pursues this aim without necessarily raising machine operating rates. Indeed, low rates are tolerated so long as labor cost reductions are achieved. Without this strategy, multiple machine handling operations (multi-machine and multi-process handling) could not be used.

Regarding breakdowns and defects, we need fundamental measures designed to prevent recurrence. To accomplish this, the Toyota production system cannot be used without top management commitment to shut down machines and production lines if necessary. In the past, inventories were kept as a cushion to prevent delays, but the Toyota production system refuses to tolerate inventory, which it calls overproduction waste, for any reason.

The above is a brief outline of the Toyota production system; its individual features have been discussed in great detail throughout this book. There are three other books I'd like to recommend to the serious reader:

1. Ohno's *Toyota Seisan Hōshiki* (*Toyota Production System*)
2. My own *Kōjō Kaizen no Gententeki Shikō* (*A Fundamentals-Oriented Approach to Plant Management*) [not available in English]
3. Ohno's *Toyota no Genba Kanri* (*Workplace Management*, Cambridge, MA: Productivity Press, 1988)

Before applying the principles of the Toyota production system in your own company, a visit to a plant that has already implemented the system would also be helpful.

PRODUCTION SYSTEM IMPROVEMENT

In addition to an appreciation of the techniques of the Toyota production system, an understanding of the concepts that lie behind those techniques is crucial. If it is missing, errors in application are unavoidable.

A Cushion Stock System

The aim of the Toyota production system is to create a non-stock system, that is, a system that eliminates the waste of overproduction. In actual working conditions, however, stock provides a cushion against production instability by absorbing the impact of machine failures, defects, altered delivery schedules, and other irregularities. An abrupt change to non-stock production would, therefore, probably result in considerable confusion on the shop floor. Some of it might be due to real irregularities in production, but it would be amplified by the uneasiness of supervisors and workers.

Thus, it would be wise to use what I call a *cushion stock system* during the early stages of transition to the Toyota production system:

1. Designate current stock as cushion stock and seal it.
2. Without relying on this stock, run a trial in which, every day, needed parts from parts processes or suppliers are supplied in small lots directly to the assembly line.
3. "Borrow" items from the cushion stock only when defects occur or when equipment breaks down.
4. Replace borrowed quantities the following day.

With this approach, you can discover exactly how much cushion stock is needed to serve as a cushion at current control levels. In addition, you can feel secure because you know that there is a cushion of stock to protect against unforeseen problems.

Earlier, we noted the case of Asahi National Electric, which used this cushion stock system for two months in the production of washstands. Here are some of the results of that experiment:

- Of the 60 parts used in the washstands, 24 (40 percent) were untouched. Stocks of these were eliminated.
- Of the remaining 36 parts, on average, no more than one-third of previous stocks had to be kept.
- One of these parts was damaged because of errors in mirror assembly, and the line had to be shut down twice because parts needed could not be supplied on time.

Investigation revealed that the breakage rate was unexpectedly high because a temporary worker was substituting for the expert who usually assembled the mirrors. A closer examination of the task itself led to the development of a new cam method that made it easy for even an unskilled worker to fit mirrors into frames correctly. This completely eliminated mirror breakage.

As this case demonstrates, holding stock down to low levels hastens improvement because it reveals problems previously hidden in the shadow of inventory.

The above example shows that assembly line shutdowns may become necessary when a cushion stock system is used. Unless top management agrees from the start that shutdowns are permissible, however, this system cannot succeed. After two months of experimentation, shop supervisors and workers have a better understanding of how much stock is really needed at current control levels. They will then relax and not object to holding stock down as much as necessary. The cushion stock system is an ideal intermediate step in the transition to a Toyota production system. The change can be made easily and smoothly and undesirable side effects are avoided.

Toward SMED Setups

The Toyota production system aims at achieving order-based production, but without SMED, it would not be possible to respond promptly to changes in orders. Indeed, no transition to a Toyota production system can occur without drastic reductions in setup times.

Furthermore, the system stresses the elimination of overproduction waste, and small lot production is an extremely important strategy for eliminating finished product stocks. Small lot production, in turn, requires adoption of the SMED system which should evolve into one-touch and no touch setups.

That is why a visit to a plant that has successfully adopted the SMED system is important. The first step, the first important precondition, is to believe unequivocally that SMED setups are feasible. If you tell the average shop floor people that two-hour setup changes can be completed in, for example, six minutes, 99 out of 100 will not believe you; and even the one who does believe you will think that such dramatic improvements would require more sophisticated equipment or would increase costs.

When these people can observe an actual SMED setup and examine the equipment, they will be astounded at what simple measures can produce such dramatic setup changeover time reductions. Understanding will be instantaneous and their thinking will be revolutionized.

After this demonstration, you should begin by implementing SMED on two dies in your own plant and convince the rest of your workers by giving them a demonstration of a changeover.

Shortening the Production Cycle

Since the Toyota production system is oriented toward achieving non-stock and order-based production, being able to fulfill demands for quick delivery is essential. This requires a dramatic shortening of the production cycles. Again, several approaches must be used to achieve this:

- Carry out small lot production
- Carry out equalization, synchronization, and one-piece flow operations for each process, including assembly, machine processing, presswork, forging, and casting
- Link all plants in a system of comprehensive integrated flow operations

Beginning Integrated Flow Production

Until recently, most people believed that flow operations could be used only on assembly lines, but the same approach can be applied equally well to machine, press, and all other processes. It all boils down to some simple measures:

- Equalize consecutive processes and synchronize
- Since one-piece flows increase the frequency of transport, improve layout, and then, where necessary, provide conveyors or other supplementary means of transport

These layout improvements will have three major benefits:

- Savings on interprocess transport costs
- Elimination of interprocess delays and reductions in labor costs for handling those delays
- Reduction of finished product stocks

Tokai Iron Works, for example, improved the layout in its press shop and adopted one-piece flow operations with the following results:

- Productivity doubled in the space of three months
- Delivery deadlines were no longer missed
- The plant's space requirements were halved

Thus, layout improvement is a fundamental precondition for the setting up the *flow* so crucial to the Toyota production system. It is on that basis that equalization, synchronization, and one-piece flow operations must be carried out.

At this stage, it is very helpful to combine common and similar processes using "the law of determining machine placement based on the coefficient of transport difficulty" explained in my book, *Kikai Haichi Kaizen no Gihō* (*Techniques of Machine Layout Improvement*, Nikkan Kōgyō Shimbun, 1965).

Using Nagara as a Building Block

As noted later in this chapter, trying to achieve multi-plant integrated flow production is a tremendous challenge. The average plant has a much better chance of implementing it successfully by using a nagara system for a single crucial product. One would begin by transcending the traditional division of labor among plants and then align processes according to the parts process flow. For example, one could integrate the flow of operations from machine processing to painting to parts attachment.

Use of this step approach will gradually lead to the development of a broad fabric of integrated flow operations. The success rate with this approach is very high.

Furthermore, this approach makes sense since traditional plant layout has led people to assume that painting should be carried out in painting shops and presswork in press shops. Once this conceptual barrier is overcome, the line can follow the specific process sequence of the product in an integrated flow. Although this has long been a blind spot of production management, reexamination of these old assumptions will bring about a revolution in thinking and facilitate the discovery and implementation of many powerful new ideas.

Toward Comprehensive Integrated Flow Production

To date, there are only a few examples of companies where comprehensive integrated flow operations encompassing all plants in a coherent system have been attempted. An example of efforts that might be made in this direction is linking a machine shop or a painting shop to an assembly plant with the use of equalization, synchronization, and one-piece flow operations.

This kind of comprehensive integrated flow production would shorten the production cycle dramatically and create very favorable conditions for achieving production-to-order. At the same time, it would greatly contribute to improving productivity by slashing labor costs for transport and storage. As noted above, improvements in plant layout are a precondition here.

Toward a Segmented Production System

The fact that production plans at most plants are determined on a monthly basis often causes considerable confusion on the shop floor since increases in demand are either satisfied in the following month or squeezed in as rush jobs.

Therefore, only surplus capacity plans and materials plans should be determined once a month; actual production plans should be set up on a ten-day or weekly basis. Thus, segmented production can be carried out where, for example, a month's quota of 30,000 cars is produced in quantities of 10,000 units during each ten-day period.

This approach avoids much of the confusion on the production floor. Rush production may become unnecessary because the changes in demand that occur can be handled by extending production into the next ten-day period.

The segmented approach, of course, ties production more closely to demand. Since production begins with the next ten-day period, inventories can be reduced considerably because finished product stocks no longer have to be kept as a safety buffer against unexpected demand.

Leveling and the Mixed Production System

The Toyota production system makes a strong argument for leveling. Leveling has two aims:

- To provide upstream processes with balanced loads
- To reduce finished product inventories

In the past, the expression "load adjustment" has been used to refer to the provision of balanced loads to upstream processes, so the idea itself is nothing new. The big break with conventional thinking was to combine this idea with small lot production and make load adjustments compatible with the notion of non-stock in the form of mixed production.

With mixed production, multiple products are produced in parallel. This often results in significant cuts in finished product stocks. Major improvement is also experienced in the area of changeover losses when switching from one product to another.

On the other hand, mixed production results in a marked increase in the frequency of setup changes. Use of one-touch or no-touch changeovers is therefore mandated. Successive assembly of multiple products also makes it imperative that appropriate measures, such as poka-yoke devices, be taken in order to prevent defects arising from missing or incorrect parts.

Recent experience with mixed production indicates that, despite various concerns, few serious problems develop. Implementation is simpler than expected and results are often impressive. As the old saying goes, you have nothing to fear but fear itself.

I hope many companies will take up the challenge of putting mixed production to work.

Toward Multiple Machine Handling Operations

Multiple machine handling is a major component of the Toyota production system.

As we have already seen, there are two types of such operations: multi-machine handling and multi-process handling. For purposes of implementation, each type has several advantages.

Multi-machine handling. With multi-machine handling, machines A and B have no process relationship. This has two advantages:

- The task can be carried out effectively because the machines are running automatically. While machine A is engaged in automatic processing, the worker can remove and attach products on machine B, and vice versa.
- The worker does not have to hold down safety switches because the machines are activated at one push of a button from remote locations.

This approach usually increases human productivity by 30 to 50 percent.

With multi-machine handling, the number of machines assigned to a single operator is determined by how much time automatic processing takes and by how quickly attachment, removal, and switch activation can be performed. Machines must shut down automatically once processing is complete.

Multi-process handling. In multi-process handling, machines A and B are linked by process sequence. This has the advantage of eliminating the motions executed for temporary rack storage in multi-machine handling. The worker first removes a finished item from machine A with one hand and inserts unprocessed material in the die with the other. She then starts machine B by activating a switch near A. Finally, she removes a finished item from machine B with one hand and inserts a new piece already processed by machine A into the B die with the other.

Consequently, multi-process handling usually increases human productivity by 50 to 100 percent.

With multi-process handling, it is sometimes helpful to reverse the order of processes once the last one in the sequence has been reached. Thus, a sequence of A $\rightarrow$ B $\rightarrow$ C would immediately be followed by C $\rightarrow$ B $\rightarrow$ A.

A second advantage of multi-process handling is that it can absorb line imbalances when per-piece processing times differ from one process to another. Finally, it simplifies dealing with demand fluctuations: all that needs to be done is to increase or decrease the number of machines for which a single worker is responsible.

There are two key arguments for carrying out multiple machine handling operations.

- While depreciation eventually makes machine use free of charge, workers must always be paid salaries — and it is in the nature of salaries to rise over time.
- Human losses per unit time are roughly five times higher than machine losses.

From this, it follows that the elimination of human idle time should be the highest priority, even at the expense of a drop in machine operating rates. At any rate, until recently, multiple machine handling operations were out of the question because manufacturers focused exclusively on high machine operating rates. Here, too, a cost-cutting perspective should prevail.

Toward Pre-Automation

Pre-automation, or autonomation, results when functions of the human mind, in addition to functions of the human hand, are transferred to machines. It may be said to be the systemized form of this transfer. Dramatically lower labor costs can result when pre-automation can be adopted. The reason for this is that under normal conditions there is no need to have an operator stand by the machine. The only time a human worker is needed is when the machine transmits notice of an irregularity. The frequency of irregularities can be reduced and their impact mitigated if each irregularity receives prompt attention, analysis, and corrective action. In the long term, this approach contributes to reducing labor costs.

By increasing or decreasing the period of unsupervised operations, plants can respond swiftly to load fluctuations. This is especially advantageous when the load diminishes because shutting down machines does not lead to enormous losses.

The Challenge of Zero Defects

Defects generate waste in and of themselves and because they cause confusion in the production process. When implementing the Toyota production system, therefore, we must challenge ourselves to achieve zero defects. There are three components to this effort:

Inspections. The focus of inspections must shift from *detection* to *prevention* of defects. This requires a move from sampling to 100 percent inspection, the ultimate means of achieving quality assurance.

Quality control. Quality control methods must be based on the above approach, using such methods as source inspection, self-inspection, and successive checks.

Poka-yoke devices. Develop and install these devices as a practical means of fulfilling the above conditions.

TOWARD A KANBAN SYSTEM

As explained earlier, the kanban system is no more than a means for putting the Toyota production system into practice, and thorough rationalization of production cannot be achieved merely by applying it. Full implementation of the Toyota production system will definitely include the kanban system. The proper procedure, however, is to first carry out thorough improvement of the production system itself. The use of kanban will flow naturally if one stresses the elimination of overproduction waste and moves toward order-based production.

A kanban system, however, can be applied only to repetitive processes, not to one-of-a-kind production — unless it functions merely as identification, job instruction, and transport tags.

If the number of kanban is gradually reduced, the following benefits can be expected:

- The limit for stock reduction at the current control level can be identified.
- Further reduction of kanban will spotlight bottleneck processes which can then be improved.
- Inventories cannot exceed the fixed number of kanban.

The Sailor Pen Company has created a system where only goods that have been sold are produced. Plant inventories are reduced to one-quarter of previous levels, and sales office inventory to one-half. A kanban accompanies each carton shipped from the plant to the sales office. The kanban is sent back to the plant when the accompanying carton is shipped to retailers and the plant produces only what has been sold.

Half a year after setting up this system, the company had succeeded in cutting overall inventories by 60 percent. Stocks at the sales office could be cut because the plant committed itself to respond positively even to unexpected demands from that source.

That the plant had already made considerable headway in implementing SMED setups and shortened its production cycle by means of one-piece flow operations was a major factor in the success of the kanban system.

Of course, it would be possible to implement the kanban system even before adopting the SMED system by increasing the number of kanban. One should, however, expect only lukewarm results.

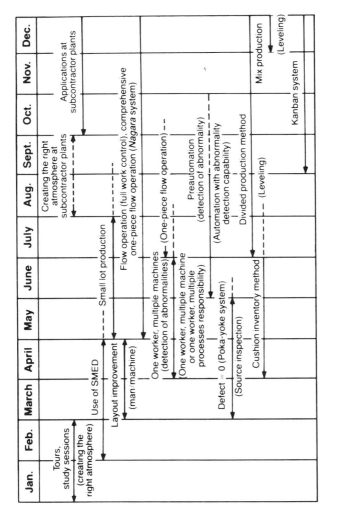

FIGURE 40. **Plan for Introducing the Toyota Production System**

A SCHEDULE FOR INTRODUCING THE TOYOTA PRODUCTION SYSTEM AND KANBAN SYSTEM

Procedures for introducing the Toyota Production System and the kanban system are shown in Figure 40. The figure gives a schedule for a hypothetical average plant. Times may be adjusted to reflect the control levels and capacities of individual plants. Or, introduction of the systems might begin in the middle of the process where certain improvements have already been implemented.

In general, however, I think the overall order of implementation given in Figure 40 is the appropriate one to follow.

It has taken the Toyota production system 20 years to get where it is today. Obviously, plants that wish to learn the system will not need another 20 years to do so. The critical point — and the one that takes the most time to ensure — is that top management must have both a clear understanding of the issues and the zeal needed to carry through to the end. More important than anything else is securing the understanding and consent of everyone in the plant, especially of the people on the production floor. Indeed, that is the key point that will determine ultimate success or failure.

13

The Toyota Production System in Summary

The Toyota production system developed to its present state after repeated trial and error. This chapter summarizes the basic principles upon which it was built and presents the philosophy, methodology, and outlook of this revolutionary approach to modern production in the order of its development.

1. The Minus-Cost Principle

The first concept developed as a basis for production management is the minus-cost principle. It offers a totally different view of the source of profits: Instead of subscribing to the facile formula

$$cost + profit = selling\ price$$

producers must let the market determine price, using the formula

$$price - cost = profit$$

With this approach, the only means of increasing profit is to reduce costs. In turn, the only method for cutting costs is thorough waste elimination. This is the foundation on which all other principles are developed.

2. Non-Stock: The First Cornerstone of Waste Elimination

What waste should be eliminated? Production management has long had a blind spot with regard to inventory, considering it a necessary evil. Asking *why* it was necessary revealed that keeping stock was, in fact, tremendously wasteful. This resulted in the determination to eliminate stock and the birth of the just-in-time concept. Elimination of the waste of overproduction became a distinct possibility.

Similarly, the waste of untimely production was reexamined. In the past, large lot production systems generated enormous inventories of finished products. Doubts about this approach led to the development of production to order as the best way to respond to demand.

Two things are clearly required to achieve production to order: small lot production and dramatically shortened production cycles.

3. Toward Flow Operations

The demands of production to order produced solutions to a number of problems. The first of these is flow operations. Once they were implemented on the assembly line, another question surfaced: Why not use this approach at upstream processes as well?

Since then, the concept has been applied successfully to machine processing, presswork, and other processes. At that point, it became clear that flow operations would be even more effective if upstream processes were linked directly to the assembly line, and the system evolved toward comprehensive integrated flow operations.

4. Shortening Setup Changeover Times

As noted above, production to order is inherently high-diversity, low-volume (small lot) production. Shortened setup changeover times are an indispensable prerequisite for production to order.

In response to this keenly felt need, I proposed my SMED system and its adoption resulted in significant progress.

5. The Elimination of Breakdowns and Defects

The instability of production (created by breakdowns and defects) results in the need for stock. In a non-stock system, therefore, high priority is placed on eliminating these factors. A firm policy to shut down a machine or line whenever an abnormal situation arises must be adopted. The andon system is used as a form of visual control to promptly transmit information about irregularities in an easily understandable form.

6. Fusing Leveling and Non-Stock Production

In non-stock production, the emphasis on the elimination of inventories means that load fluctuations have an immediate impact on the shop floor, and waiting and extended operating times become more frequent.

Because of the purpose ascribed to stock, it was considered impossible to eliminate inventories while absorbing load fluctuations effectively. This apparent contradiction was reconciled by the use of leveling and mixed production.

7. Toward Comprehensive Integrated Flow Operations

Comprehensive integrated flow operations were achieved by further expansion of the flow operations concept (3 above). The traditional barriers created by the division of labor by plants and shops were transcended by this step.

The nagara system was a pioneering experiment in this area that I think will enjoy further development and expansion in the future.

8. Labor Cost Reduction: The Second Cornerstone of Waste Elimination

The reduction of labor costs became the next focus in the fight to eliminate waste. This was carried out by three means:

- Improving human work motions
- Combining marginal allowances
- Transferring human motions to machines

Measures such as the elimination of isolated islands were implemented based on the conviction that minimal manpower, not mere labor savings, is essential for truly effective cost reduction. In addition, the shift from manual processing to machines could not make machines totally independent unless they shut off automatically when processing was completed. The creation of automatic shut-off devices led to the adoption of multiple machine handling operations. This development is based on the recognition that, from the point of view of cost reduction, losses per unit time are far greater for humans than for machines.

9. From Mechanization to Autonomation

The next step was to transfer manual attachment, removal, and switch activation functions to machines. Even when this was done, however, human operators still had to stand near their machines because mechanization — in which the work of human hands is transferred to machines — was not enough. What was needed was a higher-level transfer of human mental functions to machines, referred to as autonomation. Here, machines were equipped with devices that not only detected abnormal situations but shut the machine down whenever irregularities occurred. This systematized form of autonomation is called pre-automation.

10. Maintaining and Developing Standard Operations

Gradually, operations were improved and standard operations were determined at each step. Deviations from a particular standard were checked in order to maintain the level of operations. At the same time, standard operations were printed up as "standard operation sheets" for everyone to see. This step facilitated continuous improvement and further boosted progress.

11. Toward a Kanban System

The basic production system took shape as described above. It was out of a need to maintain the level of improvement that the kanban system was devised. Kanban became an effective tool to support the running of the production system as a whole.

Kanban is a simplified self-regulating visual control system that focuses on the production floor and makes it possible to respond to changes in production quickly and simply. In addition, it proved to be an excellent way for promoting improvements because restricting the number of kanban in circulation highlighted problem areas.

The kanban system has the effect of gradually enhancing the precision of a production system since adjusting the number of kanban elevates the level of the production system itself. By analogy, if a standard surface plate is brought into contact with a plane surface covered with red ink, any protrusions that leave ink on the surface plate can then be scraped away. Repeating this procedure will gradually improve the precision of the plate surface.

The above clarifies why the Toyota production system can be applied effectively only when the development of the system and its relationship to kanban are correctly understood.

Conclusions

The Toyota production system has the following main features:

- The minus-cost principle is a basic concept underlying the Toyota production system. The survival of a company depends, therefore, on cost reduction. This calls for the thorough elimination of waste.
- The ultimate response to demand is production to order. Under this system, conventional large lot production must be abandoned. The requirements of production to order (high-diversity, low-quantity production; quick delivery, and load fluctuation handling) can be met only by the relentless elimination of overproduction waste.
- It takes on the challenge of labor cost reduction and recognizes the advantage of using machines that are independent of workers. Labor cost reduction is an ongoing commitment of the Toyota production system, symbolized by the phrase *minimal manpower.*
- Accompanying the construction of this revolutionary production system, the development of the kanban system provides a powerful, simple, and highly flexible control technique. These two systems have a synergistic relationship.
- Toyota transformed a traditionally passive, conciliatory production system by tracing conventional production back to its roots and exploding commonly accepted beliefs to build a new system on concepts that had never before been used.

Figure 41 shows the systematic components of the Toyota production system from the industrial engineering viewpoint described so far. It provides a perspective different from that of Figure 42, which was taken from Mr. Ohno's *Toyota Production System.*

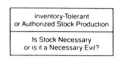

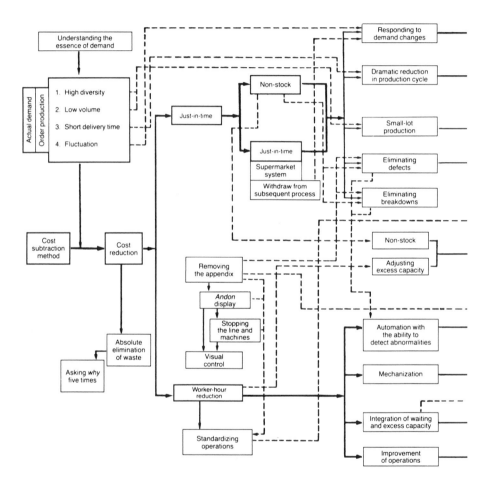

Figure B-1. An IE-Based Analysis of the Toyota Production Method
(Shigeo Shingo)

FIGURE 41. IE-based Observations of the Toyota Production Method

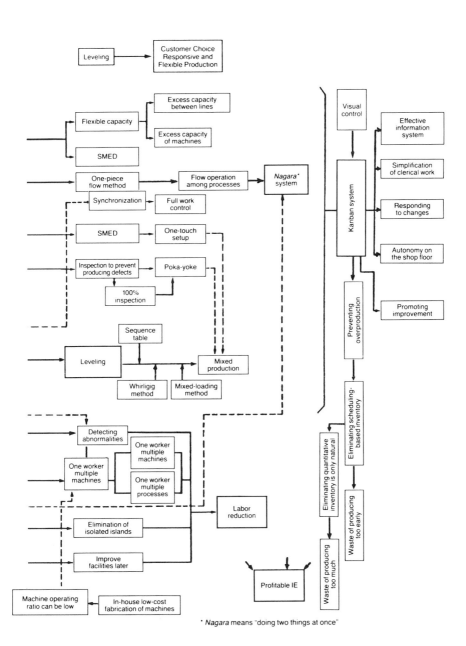

* *Nagara* means "doing two things at once"

1945

JUST-IN-TIME

1949 ▶   **1958 ▶**
Intermediate warehouses abolished   Warehouse
withdrawal slips
abolished

1950 ▶   **1955 ▶**
Machining and assembly   Assembly and body
lines synchronized   plants linked

1948 ▶   **1953 ▶**
Withdrawal by subsequent   Supermarket system
processes ("upstream" transport)   in machine shop

1955 ▶
Required number system adopted
for supplied parts

1953 ▶
Call system for
the machine shop

1955 ▶
Whirligig water system
(small load/mixed transportation)

HISTORY
OF THE
TOYOTA
PRODUCTION
SYSTEM

1945-55 ▶
Setups (2 to 3 hours)

1957 ▶
Procedural chart
(*andon*) adopted

1947 ▶   **1949-50 ▶**
2-machine handling   3- or 4-machine handling (horseshoe)
(parallel or in   or rectangular layout)
L-shaped layout)

Separation of machine work and worker's work begins

1950 ▶   **1955 ▶**
Visual control, *andon*   Main plant assembly line production system
system adopted in   (*andon*, line stop, mixed load)
engine assembly   (automation ⟶ autonomation)

FIGURE 42. History of the Toyota Production System

1953 ▶   **P**   **R**

AUTONOMATION

1945

── **1975**

1961 ▶ ───── (Ended in failure)
Pallet kanban

1962 ▶
Kanban adopted company-wide
(machining, forging, body assembly, etc.)

1961 ▶ ───── **1965** ▶
Red and blue card system   Kanban adopted for ordering
for ordering outside parts   outside parts, 100% supply system;
                               began teaching Toyota system to affiliates

1959 ▶ ───── **1973** ▶
Transfer system (in ⟶ in or in ⟶ out)   Transfer system
                                             (out ⟶ in)

1962 ▶ ───── **1971** ▶
Main plant setups (15 minutes)   Main office and
                                     Motomachi setups
                                     (3 minutes)

1963 ▶ ───── **1971** ▶
Use of inter-writer; system   Body indication system
of autonomated selection of   (Motomachi Crown line)
parts adopted; information
indicator system adopted

1963 ▶
Multi-process operation

1962 ▶ ───── **1966** ▶
Full-work control of machines,   First autonomated line,
machine *baka-yoke*   Kamigō plant

1961 ▶ ───── **1971** ▶
Andon installed, Motomachi assembly plant   Fixed-position stopping
                                                  system in assembly

O D U C T I O N   L E V E L I N G

14

Afterword

In dialectics, you start off with an idea called a *thesis*. Opposed to this is an *antithesis*. In ordinary thinking, the antagonism between thesis and antithesis is usually resolved with a compromise.

However, this problem of contradiction and opposition can be viewed from a different perspective. Through *sublation*, a higher-level *synthesis* is reached. The opposition vanishes and both sides are satisfied. This method of reasoning is called the dialectic process.

Let us now use dialectics in thinking about the Toyota production system: Let's suppose, for example, that an argument (thesis) for the reduction of stocks is proposed in the form of the desire to have deliveries take place four times a day. The opposing argument (antithesis) is that more frequent deliveries will reduce truck-loading efficiency. Debating these arguments within the same framework of assumptions will lead only to contradiction and opposition — no conclusion can result.

In a situation like this, the discussion would probably end with some halfway measure, perhaps a compromise to reduce the disadvantages for both sides by delivering twice a day.

From a broader perspective, however, the advantages of both proposals can be combined in a synthesis achieved by sublating the two arguments. For example, trucks could carry four mixed loads a day, making the rounds of several companies and picking up a partial load at each. This arrangement would both preserve truck-loading efficiency and make it possible to cut inventories.

Initially, both sides had been operating on the untested assumption that Company A's products had to be transported by Company A's trucks. Transcending this limitation allowed for the formulation of synthesis, a higher-level plan involving a totally new method — frequent mixed-load deliveries.

Here's a second example: A thesis is advanced that processing costs could be reduced by increasing lot sizes in operations requiring long setup changeover times. In opposition to this, the antithetical argument is that larger lot sizes result in losses due to increased stock.

As they stand, the two propositions are irreconcilable. The typical solution is to determine an economic lot size as a compromise point between the two arguments. As we have learned, however, economic lot sizes are not a solution to the problem. They are, at best, a compromise.

So what is the real problem? The unarticulated belief both sides are clinging to is that setup time cannot be reduced dramatically. Yet, with the SMED system, it is possible to carry out four-hour setups in three minutes. This completely eliminates any contradiction between the two arguments. It represents a higher-level solution, a synthesis.

The Toyota production system comes into clearer focus once it is understood that this dialectic is applied throughout.

The primary features of the Toyota production system are:

- Elimination of waste (based on the belief that a company's only legitimate source of profits is cost reduction
- Demand inherently calls for order-based, not speculative, production

The Toyota production system has been compared to squeezing water from a dry towel. What this means is that it is a system for thoroughgoing waste elimination. Here, waste refers to everything not serving to advance the process, everything that does not increase added value. Many people settle for eliminating the waste that everyone recognizes as waste. But much remains that simply has not yet been recognized as waste or that people are willing to tolerate.

People had resigned themselves to certain problems, had become hostage to routine and abandoned the practice of problem-solving. This going back to the basics, exposing the real significance of problems and then making fundamental improvements, can be witnessed throughout the Toyota production system.

The Toyota production system is therefore correctly understood as follows: Thorough waste elimination is the core around which the system is built which, in turn, is supported by the kanban system.

Anyone undertaking the study of the Toyota production system comes face to face with the SMED concept. It is essential for carrying out small lot production and for dealing with changes in demand. Indeed, it lies at the heart of the Toyota production system.

As explained in this book and elsewhere, the SMED concept is a product of my own thinking and practical experience with setup changes and Toyota's demand that a 1,000-ton press setup that had already been cut from four hours to one hour be slashed to three minutes.

Some people argue that thorough preventive maintenance leads naturally to SMED. Others, partisans of skill engineering, reportedly argue that it took Toyota 30 years to cut a three-hour setup changeover to three minutes and that the roughly 340,000 times the operation was carried out during that period accounts for this reduction.

When people invite me to talk about SMED, I cannot get them to believe me just by telling them that one-hour setup changes have been cut to three minutes, I have to give them a demonstration. So I ask for an hour's time, go into the production shop, and do a number of things:

- I ask to have two 100-ton press dies brought out.
- I measure the die heights and add plates or blocks to the shorter one to make die height uniform.
- To set the die center, I measure their width and install a suitable block at the back.
- I measure the height of clamping sites and use blocks to match them.
- I get two workers to carry out parallel operations.
- I have the new die put on a forklift and brought to the side of the machine. Another forklift is readied to take away the old die immediately.

I then claim that these simple changes will make it possible to perform the changeover in less than three minutes and we immediately try a setup with the new arrangement. Once, we slashed a one-hour setup to 2 minutes and 26 seconds with the very first try. Clearly, the success of the SMED concept has nothing to do with skill but results from improvements in theory and technique.

As the creator of SMED, I enjoy the fact that the SMED system is used in hundreds of Japanese companies and has achieved considerable success in Switzerland and the in United States. I am, however, somewhat dismayed that articles about SMED often don't even mention me. Surely, common courtesy demands at least that much. Only Taiichi Ohno consistently gives me credit when referring to the SMED system.

Since it is a production management system, the Toyota production system cannot be said to be entirely different from ordinary production management methods. This is why I call it an *extrapolation* of a production management system. It must be understood, though, that one of its prime features is that it is permeated with its own advanced concepts and accompanying special techniques. This does not necessarily mean, however, that one can simply copy the distinctive external techniques of the Toyota production system in another manufacturing environment.

For example, it would be dangerous to take one of the distinctive techniques of the Toyota production system — such as mixed production — and use it without fulfilling the requisite preconditions. Defects and lower productivity would result. The proper approach is to begin with measures like SMED, proceed to a cushion stock system, to segmented production and, finally, to a mixed production system. In short, there is no need to rush into techniques as long as costs are being reduced.

Similarly, satisfactory results should not be expected if one simply treats the Toyota production system as synonymous with a kanban system and rushes into the implementation of a kanban system without first rationalizing the production system itself.

About the Author

CAREER: 50 YEARS IN FACTORY IMPROVEMENT

First Period: Private Enterprise

1909 Born in Saga City, Saga-Pref., Japan, on January 8.

1924 While studying at Saga Technical High School, reads and is deeply impressed by Toshiro Ikeda's *The Secret of Eliminating Unprofitable Efforts,* said to be a translation of Taylor's thesis.

1930 Graduates from Yamanashi Technical College with a degree in mechanical engineering; goes to work for the Taipei Railway Factory.

1931 While a technician in the casting shop at the Taipei Railway Factory, observes worker operations and feels the need for improvement. Reads accounts of the streamlining of operations at Japan National Railways plants and awakens to the need for rational plant management.

Reads Taylor's *The Principles of Scientific Management* and, greatly impressed, decides to make the study and practice of scientific management his life's work.

Reads and studies many books, including the works of Yoichi Ueno and texts published by the Japan Industrial Association.

1937 For two months beginning September 1, attends the First Long-Term Industrial Engineering Training Course, sponsored by the Japan Industrial Association, the precursor of the Japan Management Association. Is thoroughly instructed in the "motion mind" concept by Ken'ichi Horikome.

239

1943   Transfers to the Amano Manufacturing Plant (Yokohama) on orders from the Ministry of Munitions. As Manufacturing Section Chief, applies flow operations to the processing of depth mechanisms for air-launched torpedoes and raises productivity by 100%.

Second Period: The Japan Management Association

1945   On orders from the Ministry of Munitions, transfers to Ishii Precision Mfg. (Niigata), a maker of similar air-launched torpedo depth mechanisms, for the purpose of improving factory operations.

With the end of the war in August, accepts a post at Yasui Kogyo (Kita Kyushu) starting in April 1946 and moves to Takanabe-cho in Miyazaki Prefecture. Stops by Tokyo at this time and visits Isamu Fukuda at the Japan Management Association, where he is introduced to Chairman of the Board Morikawa. Is asked to participate temporarily in a plant survey to improve operations at Hitachi, Ltd.'s vehicle manufacturing facility at Kasado. Afterwards enters the service of the Japan Management Association.

1946   When asked by a survey team member during process analysis at the Hitachi plant how to treat times when goods are delayed while waiting for cranes, realizes that "processes" and "operations," which had previously been thought to be separate and parallel entities, form a "network of processes and operations" — a systematic, synthetic whole. Reports this finding at a Japan Management Association technical conference.

Invents a method of classifying like operations by counting non-interventions while studying the layout of a Hitachi, Ltd. woodworking plant.

1948   Elucidates the "true nature of skill" in *A Study of 'Peko' Can Operations* at Toyo Steel's Shitamatsu plant.

Between 1948 and 1954, takes charge of Production Technology Courses. Also runs production technology classes at companies.

At a production technology course held at Hitachi, Ltd.'s Fujita plant, begins to question the nature of plant layout. Studies and reflects on the problem.

1950 Perfects and implements a method for determining equipment layout based on a coefficient of ease of transport at Furukawa Electric's Copper Refinery in Nikko.

Analyzes work at a press at Tōyō Kōgyō and realizes that a setup operation is composed of "internal setup" (IED) and "external setup" (OED). This concept will become the first stage of SMED.

1954 Morita Masanobu from Toyota Motor Co., Ltd. participates in a production technology course at Toyoda Automatic Loom and achieves striking results when he returns to his company. This occasions a series of productivity technology courses inaugurated in 1955. By 1982, eighty-seven sessions of the course had been held, with approximately 2,000 participants.

1955 Observes multiple machine operations at the first production technology training course at Toyota Motor Corp. and is impressed by the separation of workers and machines.

1956 From 1956 to 1958 takes charge of a three-year study of Mitsubishi Shipbuilding's Nagasaki shipyards. Invents a new system for cutting supertanker assembly from four months to three and then to two. This system spreads to Japanese shipbuilding circles and contributes to the development of the shipbuilding industry.

1957 To raise the machining efficiency of an engine bed planer at Mitsubishi Shipbuilding's Hiroshima shipyards, constructs a spare table, conducts advance setup operations on it and changes workpiece and table together. This doubles the work rate and foreshadows a crucially decisive conceptual element of SMED, that of shifting IED to EOD.

Third Period: The Institute for Management Improvement (Domestic)

1959   Leaves the Japan Management Association to found the Institute of Management Improvement.

1960   Originates the "successive inspection system" for reducing defects and implements the system at Matsushita Electric's Moriguchi plant.

1964   From Matsushita Electric's insistence that no level of defects is tolerable, realizes that although selective inspection may be a rational procedure, it is not a rational means of assuring quality.

1965   Stimulated by Toyota Motor's "foolproof" production measures, eagerly seeks to eliminate defects entirely by systematically combining the concepts of successive inspection, independent inspection, and source inspection with "foolproof" techniques.

1966   Works as a business consultant to various Taiwanese firms, including Formosa Plastic Co., Matsushita Electric (Taiwan), and China Grinding Wheel Co. Consulted annually until 1981.

1969   Improves setup change for a 1,000-ton press at Toyota Motor's main plant from four hours to one and a half. Is soon afterward asked by management to cut setup time to three minutes and in a flash of insight thinks to shift IED to OED. With this, a systematic technique for achieving SMED is born.

Notices the difference between mechanization and automation when asked by Saga Ironworks' plant manager Yaya why automatic machines needed to be manned. This observation evolves into the concept of "pre-automation" which, Shingo later realizes, is identical to Toyota Motor's "autonomation."

1970   Is awarded the Yellow Ribbon Medal for contributions to streamlining operations in the shipbuilding industry, etc.

Fourth Period: The Institute for Management Improvement (International Expansion)

1971   Participates in observation tour of the European machine industry.

1973   Participates in observation tours of the machine industries in Europe and the United States.

1974   Lectures on SMED at die-cast industry associations in West Germany and Switzerland.

On this visit, observes vacuum die-casting methods at Daimler Benz in West Germany and Buehler in Switzerland and grows eager to implement vacuum molding in die-casting and plastic molding.

1975   Grows more enthusiastic about the "zero defects" concept on the basis of the achievement of zero defects in one month at the Shizuoka plant of Matsushita Electric's Washing Machine Operations Division.

Works for improvement based on fundamental approaches including high-speed plating, instantaneous drying, and the elimination of layout marking.

1976   Consults and lectures widely to promote SMED in Europe and the United States.

1977   Treats Toyota Motor's *kanban* system as essentially a scheme of "non-stock" production and develops systematic techniques for the system.

1978   Visits America's Federal-Mogul Corporation to provide on-site advice on SMED.

The sale by the Japan Management Association of an audio-visual set of slides on SMED and pre-automation meets with considerable success.

1979   Further success is attained by the Japan Management Association's sale of "zero defects" slides.

       Visits Federal-Mogul to give follow-up guidance on SMED.

       The collected results of Shingo's experiences and ideas concerning improvement are published.

1981   Makes two trips, in the spring and fall, to provide plant guidance to the French automobile manufacturers Peugeot and Citroen.

       Travels to Australia to observe Toyota (Australia) and Borg-Warner.

1982   Makes follow-up consulting visits to Peugeot and Citroen in France and is impressed by the considerable results achieved through the application of SMED and nonstock production.

       Consults and lectures at the Siemens company in Germany.

       Lectures on "The Toyota Production System — An Industrial Engineering Study" in Munich.

       Gives lectures at Chalmers University in Sweden.

       Lectures at the University of Chicago.

CONSULTING

Below is a list of companies where Shigeo Shingo has given a training course or lecture, or has consulted for productivity improvement.

Industry	Name of Company	
JAPAN		
Automobiles and Suppliers	Toyota Motor Car Co., Ltd. Toyota Auto Body Co., Ltd. Toyo Motor Car Co., Ltd. Honda Motor Co., Ltd. Mitsubishi Heavy Industries Co., Ltd. Daihatsu Motor Car Co., Ltd. Bridgestone Cycle Kogyo Co., Ltd.	Yamaha Motor Co., Ltd. Kanto Auto Works, Co., Ltd. Central Motor Car Co., Ltd. Arakawa Auto Body Co., Ltd. Koito Manufacturing Co., Ltd. (Car parts) Aishin Seiki Co., Ltd. (Parts of motor car, diecast) Hosei Brake Co., Ltd.
Electric apparatus	Matsushita Electric Industrial Co., Ltd. Tokyo Shibaura Electric Co., Ltd. Sharp Electric Co., Ltd. Fuji Electric Co., Ltd. Nippon Columbia Co., Ltd. (Stereo Disk) Stanley Electric Co., Ltd. Matsushita Electric Works Co., Ltd. Matsushita Jutaku Setsubi Kiki Co., Ltd. (House equipment) Matsushita Denchi Kogyo Co., Ltd. (Lighting parts)	Hitachi Co., Ltd. Sony Electric Co., Ltd. Mitsubishi Electric Co., Ltd. Yasukawa Electric Mfg. Co., Ltd. Kyushu Matsushita Electric Co., Ltd. Asahi National Lighting Co., Ltd. Matsushita Denshi Buhin Co., Ltd. (Electric parts) Sabsga Denki Co., Ltd. (Rectifier)
Precision machine	Nippon Optical Co., Ltd. Sankyo Seiki Mfg. Co., Ltd. (Music box)	Olympus Optical Co., Ltd.
Steel, Non-ferrous Metals and Metal Products	Nippon Steel Co., Ltd. Toyo Steel Plate Co., Ltd. Mitsui Mining and Smelting Co., Ltd. Sumitomo Electric Industries, Ltd. Toyo Can Industry Co., Ltd. Nippon Spring Co., Ltd. Togo Seisakusho Co., Ltd. (Spring)	Nisshin Steel Co., Ltd. The Furukawa Electric Co., Ltd. The Fujikura Cable Works, Ltd. Hokkai Can Industry Co., Ltd. Chuo Spring Co., Ltd.
Machine	Amada Co., Ltd. (Metallic Press Machine) Iseki Agricultural Machinery Mfg. Co., Ltd.	Aida Engineering, Co., Ltd. (Metallic press machine) Toyota Automatic Loom Works, Ltd.

Industry	Name of Company	
	Kanzaki Kokyu Koki Co., Ltd. (Machine tools) Nippon Seiko Co., Ltd. (Bearings) Taiho Industry Co., Ltd. (Bearings) Asian Industry Co., Ltd. (Carburetor)	Kubota Ltd. (Engine and farming machinery) Daikin Kogyo Co., Ltd. (Coolers) Nach-Fujikoshi, Co., Ltd. (Bearings, cutters, etc.)
Rubber	Bridgestone Tire Co., Ltd. Nippon Rubber Co., Ltd.	Toyota Gosei Co., Ltd. Tsuki-Boshi Shoemaking Co., Ltd.
Glass	Asahi Glass Co., Ltd. Yamamura Glass Bottle Co., Ltd. Noritake China Co., Ltd.	Nippon Sheet Glass Co., Ltd. Onoda Cement Co., Ltd.
Marine products	Taiyo Fishery Co., Ltd.	
Mining	Mitsui Mining Co., Ltd. Dowa Mining Co., Ltd.	Nippon Mining Co., Ltd.
Food	Morinage & Co., Ltd. (Confectionery) Hayashikane Sangyo Co., Ltd.	Snow Brand Milk Products Co., Ltd.
Textile	Katakura Industries Co., Ltd. Kanebo Co., Ltd. Daiwa Spinning Co., Ltd. Teikoku Jinken Co., Ltd.	Gunze Co., Ltd. Fuji Spinning Co., Ltd. Daido Worsted Mills Co., Ltd. Asahi Chemical Industry Co., Ltd.
Pulp and Paper	Jujyo Paper Co., Ltd. Rengo Co., Ltd.	Oji Paper Co., Ltd.
Chemicals	Showa Denko Co., Ltd. Tokuyame Soda Co., Ltd. Hitachi Chemical Co., Ltd. Shionogi Pharmaceutical Co., Ltd. Shiseido Cosmetics Co., Ltd.	Nippon Soda Co., Ltd. Ube Industries Co., Ltd. Nippon Kayaku Co., Ltd. Fujisawa Pharmaceutical Co., Ltd.
Others	Nippon Gakki Co., Ltd. (Yamaha Piano) Saga Tekkosho Co.,Ltd. Zojirushi Mahobin Co., Ltd. Iwao Jiki Kogyo Co., Ltd. Koga Kinzoku Kogyo Co., Ltd. (Metallic press) Sanei Metallic Col., Ltd. (Metallic press)	The Sailor Pen Co., Ltd. Nippon Baruka Kogyo Co., Ltd. Gihu Dai & Mold Engineering Co., Ltd. Dia Plastics Co., Ltd. Yasutaki Industrial Co., Ltd. (Metallic press)

Industry	Name of Company	
U.S.A.	Federal-Mogul Corp. Omark Industries Storage Technology Corporation (Industrial products)	Livernois Automation Co., Ltd. Hewlett-Packard
FRANCE	Automobiles Peugeot	Automobiles Citrœn
WEST GERMANY	Daimler Benz Co., Ltd. **Bayrisches Druckgusswerk** Thurner KG Co., Ltd.	Verband Deutscher Druckgiessereien Co., Ltd. Beguform-Werke
SWITZERLAND	Gebr Buhler Co., Ltd. H-Weidmann Co., Ltd.	Bucher-guyer AC Co., Ltd.
TAIWAN	Formosa Plastic Co., Ltd. Co., Ltd. Formosa Chemicals and Fiber Co.,Ltd. China Grinding Wheel Co., Ltd. Matsushita Electric (Taiwan) Co.,Ltd. Chin Fong Machine Industrial Co., Ltd. (**Metallic press**)	Nanya Plastic Fabrication Plywood and Lumber Co., Ltd. Sunrise Plywood Co., Ltd. Taiwan Fusungta Electric Co., Ltd. (Speakers) Super Metal Industry Co., Ltd.
NETHERLANDS	Philips	

Publications

Mr. Shingo's books have sold more than **40,000** copies worldwide in English translation. For convenience, all titles are given in English, although most have not yet been translated into English.

The improvement examples presented in *Shingo Sayings* were drawn from Mr. Shingo's broad experience as a consultant. Many appear in three of his earlier works (in Japanese):

Technology for Plant Improvement. Japan Management Association, 1955.

Views and Thoughts on Plant Improvement and *Plant Improvement Embodiments and Examples*. Nikkan Kōgyō Shimbun, Ltd., 1957 (2 volumes).

A Systematic Philosophy of Plant Improvement. Nikkan Kōgyō Shimbun, Ltd., 1980.

Mr. Shingo's other works include:

"Ten Strategies for Smashing Counterarguments," *Practice and Cooperation*, (*Sakken to Kyoryoku*) 1938.

A General Introduction to Industrial Engineering. Japan Management Association, 1949.

Improving Production Control. Nihon Keizai Shimbun, 1950.

Production Control Handbook (Process Control). Kawade Shobō, 1953.

Don't Discard New Ideas. Hakuto Shobō, 1959.

Key Issues in Process Control Improvement. Nikkan Kōgyō Shimbun, Ltd., 1962.

Issues in Plant Improvement. Nikkan Kōgyō Shimbun, Ltd., 1964.

Techniques of Machine Layout Improvement. Nikkan Kōgyō Shimbun Ltd., 1965.

Fundamental Approaches to Plant Improvement. Nikkan Kōgyō Shimbun, Ltd., 1976.

"The Toyota Production System — An Industrial Engineering Study," published serially in *Factory Management* Nikkan Kōgyō Shimbun, Ltd., 1979.

A Revolution in Manufacturing: The SMED System. Japan Management Association, 1983 (English edition by Productivity Press, 1985).

Zero Quality Control: Source Inspection and the Poka-yoke System. Japan Management Association, 1985 (English edition by Productivity Press, 1986).

The Sayings of Shigeo Shingo: Key Strategies for Plant Improvement. Nikkan Kōgyō Shimbun, Ltd., 1986 (English edition by Productivity Press, 1987).

Non-Stock Production: The Shingo System for Continuous Improvement. Japan Management Association, 1987 (English edition by Productivity Press, 1988).

Index

OTHER BOOKS ON
MANUFACTURING IMPROVEMENT

Productivity Press publishes and distributes materials on continuous improvement in productivity, quality, customer service, and the creative involvement of all employees. Many of our products are direct source materials from Japan that have been translated into English for the first time and are available exclusively from Productivity. Supplemental products and services include newsletters, conferences, seminars, in-house training and consulting, audio-visual training programs, and industrial study missions. Call 1-800-274-9911 for our free book catalog.

Non-Stock Production
The Shingo System for Continuous Improvement

Shigeo Shingo

Shingo, whose work at Toyota provided the foundation for JIT, teaches how to implement non-stock production in your JIT manufacturing operations. The culmination of his extensive writings on efficient production management and continuous improvement, this book is an essential companion volume to his other landmark books on key elements of JIT, including SMED and Poka-Yoke.
ISBN 0-915299-30-5 / 480 pages / $75.00 / Order code NON-BK

A Revolution in Manufacturing
The SMED System

Shigeo Shingo, translated by Andrew P. Dillon

SMED (Single-Minute Exchange of Die), or quick changeover techniques, is the single most powerful tool for Just-In-Time production. Written by the industrial engineer who developed SMED for Toyota, the book contains hundreds of illustrations and photographs, as well as twelve chapter-length case studies. Here are the most complete and detailed instructions available anywhere for transforming a manufacturing environment to speed up production (Shingo's average setup time reduction is an astounding 98 percent) and make small-lot inventories feasible.
ISBN 0-915299-03-8 / 383 pages / $70.00 / Order code SMED-BK

Productivity Press, Inc., Dept. BK, P.O. Box 3007, Cambridge, MA 02140 1-800-274-9911

The Sayings of Shigeo Shingo
Key Strategies for Plant Improvement

Shigeo Shingo, translated by Andrew P. Dillon

Quality Digest calls Shigeo Shingo "an unquestioned genius — the Thomas Edison of Japan." The author, a world-renowned expert on manufacturing, "offers new ways to discover the root causes of manufacturing problems. These discoveries can set in motion the chain of cause and effect, leading to greatly increased productivity." By means of hundreds of fascinating real-life examples, Shingo describes many simple ways to identify, analyze, and solve problems in the workplace. This is an accessible, readable, and helpful book for anyone who wants to improve productivity.

ISBN 0-915299-15-1 / 208 pages / $39.95 / Order code SAY-BK

The Shingo Production Management System
Improving Process Functions

Shigeo Shingo

Shigeo Shingo sparked a revolution in the manufacturing industry with tools such as the Single-Minute Exchange of Die, Non-Stock Production, and Zero Quality Control. Here, in his long-awaited and final book, he ties it all together to give us a comprehensive system for the improvement of production functions. This powerful book's broad scope encompasses such diverse topics as Value Engineering, CAD/CAM techniques, and information management. If you've never read Shingo, this book will give you an overview of his brilliant concepts and how they interrelate. If you are familiar with his genius, you'll find in this book a much-needed network of his ideas.

ISBN 0-915299-52-6 / 272 pages / $45.00 / Order code SHPMS-BK

Zero Quality Control
Source Inspection and the Poka-yoke System

Shigeo Shingo, translated by Andrew P. Dillon

A remarkable combination of source inspection (to detect errors before they become defects) and mistake-proofing devices (to weed out defects before they can be passed down the production line) eliminates the need for statistical quality control. Shingo shows how this proven system for reducing defects to zero turns out the highest quality products in the shortest period of time. With over 100 specific examples illustrated. (Audio-visual training program also available.)

ISBN 0-915299-07-0 / 328 pages / $70.00 / Order code ZQC-BK

Productivity Press, Inc., Dept. BK, P.O. Box 3007, Cambridge, MA 02140 1-800-274-9911

Kanban and Just-In-Time at Toyota
Management Begins at the Workplace (rev.)
Japan Management Association (ed.), David J. Lu (translator)

Based on seminars developed by Taiichi Ohno and others at Toyota for their major suppliers, this book is the best practical introduction to Just-In-Time available. Now in a newly expanded edition, it explains every aspect of a "pull" system in clear and simple terms — the underlying rationale, how to set up the system and get everyone involved, and how to refine it once it's in place. A groundbreaking and essential tool for companies beginning JIT implementation.
ISBN 0-915299-48-8 / 224 pages / $36.50 / Order code KAN-BK

Canon Production System
Creative Involvement of the Total Workforce
compiled by the Japan Management Association

A fantastic success story! Canon set a goal to increase productivity by three percent per month — and achieved it! The first book-length case study to show how to combine the most effective Japanese management principles and quality improvement techniques into one overall strategy that improves every area of the company on a continual basis. Shows how the major QC tools are applied in a matrix management model.
ISBN 0-915299-06-2 / 256 pages / $36.95 / Order code CAN-BK

20 Keys to Workplace Improvement
Iwao Kobayashi

This easy-to-read introduction to the "20 keys" system presents an integrated approach to assessing and improving your company's competitive level. The book focuses on systematic improvement through five levels of achievement in such primary areas as industrial housekeeping, small group activities, quick changeover techniques, equipment maintenance, and computerization. A scoring guide is included, along with information to help plan a strategy for your company's world class improvement effort.
ISBN 0-915299-61-5 / 264 pages / $34.95 / Order code 20KEYS-BK

Productivity Press, Inc., Dept. BK, P.O. Box 3007, Cambridge, MA 02140 1-800-274-9911

Co-makership
The New Supply Strategy for Manufacturers
Giorgio Merli

A cornerstone in the foundation of any world-class operation is strong supplier relations. A company that establishes partnerships with its suppliers opens the door to competitive advantage in terms of cost, service, quality, innovation, and time. International consultant Giorgio Merli describes the cultural evolution and the practical techniques necessary for a co-makership relationship to thrive. This approach is a prerequisite for product-planning systems, QFD, concurrent engineering, and other practices of world-class manufacturing.
ISBN 0-915299-84-4 / 224 pages / $39.95 / Order code COMAKE-BK

Total Manufacturing Management
Production Organization for the 1990s
Giorgio Merli

One of Italy's leading consultants discusses the implementation of Just-In-Time and related methods (including QFD and TPM) in Western corporations. The author does not approach JIT from a mechanistic orientation aimed simply at production efficiency. Rather, he discusses JIT from the perspective of industrial strategy and as an overall organizational model. Here's a sophisticated program for organizational reform that shows how JIT can be applied even in types of production that have often been neglected in the West, including custom work.
ISBN 0-915299-58-5 / 344 pages / $39.95 / Order code TMM-BK

Continuous Improvement in Operations
A Systematic Approach to Waste Reduction
Alan Robinson (ed.)

Now one handy book brings you the world's most advanced thinking on Just-In-Time, *kaizen*, Total Employee Involvement, and Total Productive Maintenance. Here in one volume is a compendium of materials from our best-selling classics by world-famous manufacturing experts. A lengthy introduction integrates the developments of these manufacturing gurus within a twofold theme the elimination of invisible waste and the creation of a work environment that welcomes and institutes employee's ideas. It's a perfect book for your study groups and improvement teams.
ISBN 0-915299-51-8 / 416 pages / $34.95 / Order ROB2C-BK

One-Piece Flow
Cell Design for Transforming the Production Process
Kenichi Sekine

By reconfiguring your traditional assembly lines into production cells based on one-piece flow, you can drastically reduce your lead time, manpower requirements, and number of defects. Kenichi Sekine examines the basic principles of process flow building, then offers detailed case studies of how various industries designed unique one-piece flow systems (parallel, L-shaped, and U-shaped floor plans) to meet their particular needs.
ISBN 0-915299-33-X / 392 pages / $75.00 / Order code 1PIECE-BK

ALSO FROM PRODUCTIVITY

Achieving One-Piece Flow through Cell Design
Kenichi Sekine

Visit a factory using one-piece flow production and you'll see its advantages in time, quality, and manpower. This video training series uses live action footage, graphics, and case examples to bring you into companies for a first-hand look at cell design implementation. It is a powerful, efficient, and low-cost way to enlighten your entire workforce in the techniques of cell design. Video set comes with three videotapes, one facilitator's reference guide, one application workbook, and one copy of One-Piece Flow: Cell Design for Transforming the Production Process.
ISBN 1-56327-001-3 / $1,495.00 / Order code VAPF1/2-BK

The Poka-Yoke System
Shigeo Shingo, translated by Andrew P. Dillon

Shingo shows how to implement Zero Quality Control (ZQC) on the production line with a combination of source inspection and mistake-proofing devices in this two-part program. Part I explains the theory and concepts and Part II shows practical applications. Package includes facilitator's guides with worksheets, and is available in either slide or video format (please specify when ordering). Each part is approximately 25 minutes long.
235 Slides / ISBN 0-915299-13-5 / $749.00 / Order code S6-BK
2 Videos / ISBN 0-915299-28-3 / $749.00 / Order code V6-BK

Productivity Press, Inc., Dept. BK, P.O. Box 3007, Cambridge, MA 02140 1-800-274-9911

The SMED System

Shigeo Shingo, translated by Andrew P. Dillon

In this two-part program, for line workers, Shingo shows exactly how the Single-Minute Exchange of Die (SMED) system works. Part I explains the theory and conceptual stages of SMED. Part II shows practical applications of this major change in the way setups are performed. Package contains facilitator's guides with worksheets, and is available in either slide or video format (please specify when ordering). Each part is approximately 20 minutes long.

181 Slides / ISBN 0-915299-11-9 / $749.00 / Order code S5-BK
2 Videos / ISBN 0-915299-27-5 / $749.00 / Order code V5-BK

Quick Changeover

Users Group Quick changeover, developed by Shigeo Shingo at Toyota, is the heart of JIT. Whether you're a novice or veteran of quick changeover techniques, you'll gain more information, more tools for implementation, and more applications of this powerful productivity booster by joining the Quick Changeover User Group. Benefits of membership include a monthly , special rates on conferences and seminars, and discounts on selected books. Annual fee is $357. For more information about membership and benefits, call 1-800-899-5009.

Productivity Press, Inc., Dept. BK, P.O. Box 3007, Cambridge, MA 02140 1-800-274-9911

COMPLETE LIST OF TITLES FROM PRODUCTIVITY PRESS

Akao, Yoji (ed.). **Quality Function Deployment: Integrating Customer Requirements into Product Design**
ISBN 0-915299-41-0 / 1990 / 387 pages / $ 75.00 / order code QFD

Akiyama, Kaneo. **Function Analysis: Systematic Improvement of Quality and Performance**
ISBN 0-915299-81-X / 1991 / 288 pages / $59.95 / order code FA

Asaka, Tetsuichi and Kazuo Ozeki (eds.). **Handbook of Quality Tools: The Japanese Approach**
ISBN 0-915299-45 3 / 1990 / 336 pages / $59.95 / order code HQT

Belohlav, James A. **Championship Management: An Action Model for High Performance**
ISBN 0-915299-76-3 / 1990 / 265 pages / $29.95 / order code CHAMPS

Birkholz, Charles and Jim Villella. **The Battle to Stay Competitive: Changing the Traditional Workplace**
ISBN 0-915299-96-8 / 1991 / 110 pages paper / $9.95 /order code BATTLE

Christopher, William F. **Productivity Measurement Handbook**
ISBN 0-915299-05-4 / 1985 / 680 pages / $137.95 / order code PMH

D'Egidio, Franco. **The Service Era: Leadership in a Global Environment**
ISBN 0-915299-68-2 / 1990 / 165 pages / $29.95 / order code SERA

Ford, Henry. **Today and Tomorrow**
ISBN 0-915299-36-4 / 1988 / 286 pages / $24.95 / order code FORD

Fukuda, Ryuji. **CEDAC: A Tool for Continuous Systematic Improvement**
ISBN 0-915299-26-7 / 1990 / 144 pages / $49.95 / order code CEDAC

Fukuda, Ryuji. **Managerial Engineering: Techniques for Improving Quality and Productivity in the Workplace** (rev.)
ISBN 0-915299-09-7 / 1986 / 208 pages / $39.95 / order code ME

Gotoh, Fumio. **Equipment Planning for TPM: Maintenance Prevention Design**
ISBN 0-915299-77-1 / 1991 / 320 pages / $75.00 / order code ETPM

Greif, Michel. **The Visual Factory: Building Participation Through Shared Information**
ISBN 0-915299-67-4 / 1991 / 320 pages / $49.95 / order code VFAC

Hatakeyama, Yoshio. **Manager Revolution! A Guide to Survival in Today's Changing Workplace**
ISBN 0-915299-10-0 / 1986 / 208 pages / $24.95 / order code MREV

Hirano, Hiroyuki. **JIT Factory Revolution: A Pictorial Guide to Factory Design of the Future**
ISBN 0-915299-44-5 / 1989 / 227 pages / $49.95 / order code JITFAC

Hirano, Hiroyuki. **JIT Implementation Manual: The Complete Guide to Just-In-Time Manufacturing**
ISBN 0-915299-66-6 / 1990 / 1006 pages / $2500.00 / order code HIRJIT

Horovitz, Jacques. **Winning Ways: Achieving Zero-Defect Service**
ISBN 0-915299-78-X / 1990 / 165 pages / $24.95 / order code WWAYS

Ishiwata, Junichi. **IE for the Shop Floor: Productivity Through Process Analysis**
ISBN 0-915299-82-8 / 1991 / 208 pages / $39.95 / order code SHOPF1

Productivity Press, Inc., Dept. BK, P.O. Box 3007, Cambridge, MA 02140 1-800-274-9911

Japan Human Relations Association (ed.). **The Idea Book: Improvement Through TEI (Total Employee Involvement)**
ISBN 0-915299-22-4 / 1988 / 232 pages / $49.95 / order code IDEA

Japan Human Relations Association (ed.). **The Service Industry Idea Book: Employee Involvement in Retail and Office Improvement**
ISBN 0-915299-65-8 / 1991 / 294 pages / $49.95 / order code SIDEA

Japan Management Association (ed.). **Kanban and Just-In-Time at Toyota: Management Begins at the Workplace** (rev.), Translated by David J. Lu
ISBN 0-915299-48-8 / 1989 / 224 pages / $36.50 / order code KAN

Japan Management Association and Constance E. Dyer. **The Canon Production System: Creative Involvement of the Total Workforce**
ISBN 0-915299-06-2 / 1987 / 251 pages / $36.95 / order code CAN

Jones, Karen (ed.). **The Best of TEI: Current Perspectives on Total Employee Involvement**
ISBN 0-915299-63-1 / 1989 / 502 pages / $175.00 / order code TEI

JUSE. **TQC Solutions: The 14-Step Process**
ISBN 0-915299-79-8 / 1991 / 416 pages / 2 volumes / $120.00 / order code TQCS

Kanatsu, Takashi. **TQC for Accounting: A New Role in Companywide Improvement**
ISBN 0-915299-73-9 / 1991 / 244 pages / $45.00 / order code TQCA

Karatsu, Hajime. **Tough Words For American Industry**
ISBN 0-915299-25-9 / 1988 / 178 pages / $24.95 / order code TOUGH

Karatsu, Hajime. **TQC Wisdom of Japan: Managing for Total Quality Control**, Translated by David J. Lu
ISBN 0-915299-18-6 / 1988 / 136 pages / $34.95 / order code WISD

Kato, Kenichiro. **I.E. for the Shop Floor: Productivity Through Motion Study**
ISBN 1-56327-000-5 / 1991 / 224 pages / $39.95 / order code SHOPF2

Kaydos, Will. **Measuring, Managing, and Maximizing Performance**
ISBN 0-915299- 98-4 / 1991 / 304 pages / $34.95 / order code MMMP

Kobayashi, Iwao. **20 Keys to Workplace Improvement**
ISBN 0-915299-61-5 / 1990 / 264 pages / $34.95 / order code 20KEYS

Lu, David J. **Inside Corporate Japan: The Art of Fumble-Free Management**
ISBN 0-915299-16-X / 1987 / 278 pages / $24.95 / order code ICJ

Maskell, Brian H. **Performance Measurement for World Class Manufacturing: A Model for American Companies**
ISBN 0-915299-99-2 / 1991 / 448 pages / $49.95 / order code PERFM

Merli, Giorgio. **Co-makership: The New Supply Strategy for Manufacturers**
ISBN 0915299-84-4 / 1991 / 224 pages / $39.95 / order code COMAKE

Merli, Giorgio. **Total Manufacturing Management: Production Organization for the 1990s**
ISBN 0-915299-58-5 / 1990 / 224 pages / $39.95 / order code TMM

Mizuno, Shigeru (ed.). **Management for Quality Improvement: The 7 New QC Tools**
ISBN 0-915299-29-1 / 1988 / 324 pages / $59.95 / order code 7QC

Monden, Yasuhiro and Michiharu Sakurai (eds.). **Japanese Management Accounting: A World Class Approach to Profit Management**
ISBN 0-915299-50-X / 1990 / 568 pages / $59.95 / order code JMACT

Nachi-Fujikoshi (ed.). **Training for TPM: A Manufacturing Success Story**
ISBN 0-915299-34-8 / 1990 / 272 pages / $59.95 / order code CTPM

Nakajima, Seiichi. **Introduction to TPM: Total Productive Maintenance**
ISBN 0-915299-23-2 / 1988 / 149 pages / $45.00 / order code ITPM

Nakajima, Seiichi. **TPM Development Program: Implementing Total Productive Maintenance**
ISBN 0-915299-37-2 / 1989 / 428 pages / $85.00 / order code DTPM

Nikkan Kogyo Shimbun, Ltd./Factory Magazine (ed.). **Poka-yoke: Improving Product Quality by Preventing Defects**
ISBN 0-915299-31-3 / 1989 / 288 pages / $59.95 / order code IPOKA

Nikkan Kogyo Shimbun/Esme McTighe (ed.). **Factory Management Notebook Series: Mixed Model Production**
ISBN 0-915299-97-6 / 1991 / 184 / $125.00 / order code N1-MM

Nikkan Kogyo Shimbun/Esme McTighe (ed.). **Factory Management Notebook Series: Visual Control Systems**
ISBN 0-915299-54-2 / 1991 / 194 pages / $125.00 / order code N1-VCS

Nikkan Kogyo Shimbun/Esme McTighe (ed.). **Factory Management Notebook Series: Autonomation/Automation**
ISBN 0-0-56327-002-1 / 1991 / 200 pages / $125.00 / order code N1-AA

Ohno, Taiichi. **Toyota Production System: Beyond Large-Scale Production**
ISBN 0-915299-14-3 / 1988 / 162 pages / $39.95 / order code OTPS

Ohno, Taiichi. **Workplace Management**
ISBN 0-915299-19-4 / 1988 / 165 pages / $34.95 / order code WPM

Ohno, Taiichi and Setsuo Mito. **Just-In-Time for Today and Tomorrow**
ISBN 0-915299-20-8 / 1988 / 208 pages / $34.95 / order code OMJIT

Perigord, Michel. **Achieving Total Quality Management: A Program for Action**
ISBN 0-915299-60-7 / 1991 / 384 pages / $45.00 / order code ACHTQM

Psarouthakis, John. **Better Makes Us Best**
ISBN 0-915299-56-9 / 1989 / 112 pages / $16.95 / order code BMUB

Robinson, Alan. **Continuous Improvement in Operations: A Systematic Approach to Waste Reduction**
ISBN 0-915299-51-8 / 1991 / 416 pages / $34.95 / order code ROB2-C

Robson, Ross (ed.). **The Quality and Productivity Equation: American Corporate Strategies for the 1990s**
ISBN 0-915299-71-2 / 1990 / 558 pages / $29.95 / order code QPE

Shetty, Y.K and Vernon M. Buehler (eds.). **Competing Through Productivity and Quality**
ISBN 0-915299-43-7 / 1989 / 576 pages / $39.95 / order code COMP

Shingo, Shigeo. **Non-Stock Production: The Shingo System for Continuous Improvement**
ISBN 0-915299-30-5 / 1988 / 480 pages / $75.00 / order code NON

Shingo, Shigeo. **A Revolution In Manufacturing: The SMED System**,
Translated by Andrew P. Dillon
ISBN 0-915299-03-8 / 1985 / 383 pages / $70.00 / order code SMED

Shingo, Shigeo. **The Sayings of Shigeo Shingo: Key Strategies for Plant Improvement**, Translated by Andrew P. Dillon
ISBN 0-915299-15-1 / 1987 / 208 pages / $39.95 / order code SAY

Productivity Press, Inc., Dept. BK, P.O. Box 3007, Cambridge, MA 02140 1-800-274-9911

Shingo, Shigeo. **A Study of the Toyota Production System from an Industrial Engineering Viewpoint**
ISBN 0-915299-17-8 / 1989 / 293 pages / $39.95 / order code STREV

Shingo, Shigeo. **Zero Quality Control: Source Inspection and the Poka-yoke System**,Translated by Andrew P. Dillon
ISBN 0-915299-07-0 / 1986 / 328 pages / $70.00 / order code ZQC

Shinohara, Isao (ed.). **New Production System: JIT Crossing Industry Boundaries**
ISBN 0-915299-21-6 / 1988 / 224 pages / $34.95 / order code NPS

Sugiyama, Tomo. **The Improvement Book: Creating the Problem-Free Workplace**
ISBN 0-915299-47-X / 1989 / 236 pages / $49.95 / order code IB

Suzue, Toshio and Akira Kohdate. **Variety Reduction Program (VRP): A Production Strategy for Product Diversification**
ISBN 0-915299-32-1 / 1990 / 164 pages / $59.95 / order code VRP

Tateisi, Kazuma. **The Eternal Venture Spirit: An Executive's Practical Philosophy**
ISBN 0-915299-55-0 / 1989 / 208 pages/ $19.95 / order code EVS

Yasuda, Yuzo. **40 Years, 20 Million Ideas: The Toyota Suggestion System**
ISBN 0-915299-74-7 / 1991 / 210 pages / $39.95 / order code 4020

Audio-Visual Programs

Japan Management Association. **Total Productive Maintenance: Maximizing Productivity and Quality**
ISBN 0-915299-46-1 / 167 slides / 1989 / $749.00 / order code STPM
ISBN 0-915299-49-6 / 2 videos / 1989 / $749.00 / order code VTPM

Shingo, Shigeo. **The SMED System**, Translated by Andrew P. Dillon
ISBN 0-915299-11-9 / 181 slides / 1986 / $749.00 / order code S5
ISBN 0-915299-27-5 / 2 videos / 1987 / $749.00 / order code V5

Shingo, Shigeo. **The Poka-yoke System**, Translated by Andrew P. Dillon
ISBN 0-915299-13-5 / 235 slides / 1987 / $749.00 / order code S6
ISBN 0-915299-28-3 / 2 videos / 1987 / $749.00 / order code V6

Returns of AV programs willl be accepted for incorrect or damaged shipments only.

TO ORDER: Write, phone, or fax Productivity Press, Dept. BK, P.O. Box 3007, Cambridge, MA 02140, phone 1-800-274-9911, fax 617-864-6286. Send check or charge to your credit card (American Express, Visa, MasterCard accepted).

U.S. ORDERS: Add $5 shipping for first book, $2 each additional for UPS surface delivery. CT residents add 8% and MA residents 5% sales tax. For each AV program that you order, add $5 for programs with 1 or 2 tapes, and $12 for programs with 3 or more tapes.

INTERNATIONAL ORDERS: Write, phone, or fax for quote and indicate shipping method desired. Pre-payment in U.S. dollars must accompany your order (checks must be drawn on U.S. banks). When quote is returned with payment, your order will be shipped promptly by the method requested.

NOTE: Prices subject to change without notice.